Writing Centers in Context

Writing Centers in Context

Twelve Case Studies

Edited by

Joyce A. Kinkead
Utah State University

Jeanette G. Harris
University of Southern Mississippi

National Council of Teachers of English
1111 W. Kenyon Road, Urbana, Illinois 61801-1096

NCTE Editorial Board: Rafael Castillo, Gail Hawisher, Charles Moran, Louise Phelps, Charles Suhor, Chair, *ex officio,* Michael Spooner, *ex officio*

Cover Design: Doug Burnett

Interior Design: Tom Kovacs for TGK Design

Production Editors: Michelle Sanden Johlas, Michael G. Ryan

Manuscript Editor: Robert A. Heister/Humanities & Sciences Associates

NCTE Stock Number: 58684-3050

Library of Congress Cataloging-in-Publication Data

Writing centers in context : twelve case studies / edited by Joyce A.
   Kinkead, Jeanette G. Harris.
      p. cm.
   Includes bibliographical references and index.
   "NCTE stock number 58684-3050"—T.p. verso.
   ISBN 0-8141-5868-4
   1. English language—Rhetoric—Study and teaching—Case studies.
2. Writing centers—Case studies. I. Kinkead, Joyce A., 1954–
II. Harris, Jeanette Gregory.
PE1404.W64447 1993
808'.042'0711—dc20
                                          93-8361
                                           CIP

Contents

Acknowledgments

Conversations about this book began in November 1987 at NCTE's Annual Convention in Los Angeles. At that time, we did not imagine that the project would consume much of our time for the next five years. We are grateful for the patience and support of the chapter authors, many of whom signed on at the start of this project and helped us reconceptualize the book as it evolved. We owe special thanks to Michael Spooner, senior editor at NCTE, and the excellent reviewers who suggested revisions. Our home institutions, likewise, have been supportive. At Utah State University, Joyce Kinkead is indebted to Andrea Peterson, Patricia Gardner, Jeffrey Smitten, Robert Hoover, Brian Pitcher, and Randy Lee. David F. Lancy gave helpful readings of the manuscript. Jeanette Harris acknowledges Jeffrey Smitten, former chair of the English department at Texas Tech University and now department head at Utah State, and David Wheeler, chair of the English department at the University of Southern Mississippi.

This book is the result of more than a decade of work and collegiality among a network of dedicated writing center professionals with whom we converse at conventions and at other times via computer networks. When we thought of whom we should acknowledge, that network of friends came immediately to mind. We wish, therefore, to dedicate this book to those writing center colleagues who have influenced our thinking about how we teach and learn. For Joyce Kinkead, the two people who have been most influential in her development as a teacher of writing are Patricia Stoddart and the late Tom Hemmens. Jeanette Harris feels a special indebtedness to Lady Falls Brown, who has been both a teacher and a friend.

Introduction

Writing centers are frequently defined in terms of an ideal or an abstraction—a vision of what should be rather than what is. Although some consensus exists as to what constitutes an effective writing center program, there is little agreement about specific political issues, administrative procedures and policies, pedagogical approaches, or even practical matters. Thus, a model writing center is difficult, if not impossible, to describe.

Rather than attempting to describe the ideal, generic writing center, this book provides case studies of twelve particular programs—detailed descriptions of how each one came into being and how it functions. The one thing all of these programs have in common, and which accounts, perhaps, for their success, is that each has responded effectively to the challenges and conditions of the school in which it exists—its context.

In *The Philosophy of Rhetoric*, I. A. Richards (1936) reminds us that words, "as they pass from context to context, change their meanings; and in many different ways." In this book, we would like to suggest that writing centers also change from context to context—that, in fact, it is their environment, academic and otherwise, that most directly shapes them, giving them form and substance and the impetus to define themselves in certain ways.

Context, in terms of writing centers, is not a simple concept. In addition to the institutions in which they are situated, writing centers often have smaller contexts—specific programs or departments of which they are a part. These smaller contexts, like the larger ones, vary widely. Some writing centers exist within departments of English, some within larger learning centers, and some have no physical "home" but serve writers across the curriculum through various outreach programs. Thus many, perhaps most, writing centers exist within multiple contexts, all of which help to define the resulting programs. Often, these different contexts exert opposing forces on a writing center program. As a result, programs must frequently compromise between the various forces that surround them, treading a sometimes tortuous path among conflicting needs and demands in order to serve each constituency fairly and effectively.

The relationship between the writing center and its context, however, is not inevitably one-sided, with the writing center merely responding to the needs of various programs and of the parent institution. Successful programs establish relationships with their host environments that are best described as interactive—the writing center shapes its context as well as being shaped by it. For example, on many campuses, writing centers have significantly influenced writing pedagogy throughout the curriculum. Peer editing, collaborative learning, and computer technology—now commonplace in most writing courses—often originate as experimental programs that were first attempted in writing centers. Writing-across-the-curriculum programs also often evolve out of successful writing center programs and indirectly influence the way in which courses in every discipline are taught.

In addition, many writing centers have modified their contexts by forging connections between theoretically and politically antithetical groups. For example, it is frequently the writing center that emphasizes the complementarity of the disparate programs that make up an English department, just as it is frequently the writing center that functions as the core of writing-across-the-curriculum programs or as the strongest link with public schools. In the all too often factious, elitist, isolated world of academe, writing centers have emphasized the value of connecting, integrating, and collaborating and, as a result, have changed academe in positive and productive ways. To understand writing centers is to understand the dynamic, interactive relationship that exists between a specific center and the environment in which it exists.

Selection of Programs

We chose the twelve programs included in this book primarily on the basis of their diversity. Even though the philosophies, practices, and histories of these programs are in some instances surprisingly similar, the programs themselves exist within very different contexts. Represented here are small private liberal arts colleges and large state universities; medium-sized land-grant colleges as well as two-year colleges and four-year institutions; schools located in urban and in rural areas and on the east and west coasts and in between. Their multiple, diverse perspectives define writing centers much more accurately than could any single definition of an abstract, model center.

In addition to diversity in size, source of funding, and location, we have attempted to include programs that also differ in their philosophical and pedagogical orientations. For example, the Writing Center at Colorado State University emphasizes writing with computers, whereas the Educational Opportunity Program Writing Center at the University of Washington focuses on the cultural diversity of its students. The Writing Center at the University of Puget Sound has been active in writing across the curriculum, while the Writing Center at Harvard is closely related to that school's expository writing program.

How This Book Can Be Used

We think this book will serve a variety of useful functions. It will provide those who are developing new writing centers with knowledge of what exists—what types of programs are already established and why they evolved as they did. It will provide new ideas and information for those who are expanding in new directions or evaluating existing programs. Also, practitioners will find solutions to common problems as well as plans that have already been implemented and tested. Scholars will be interested in the histories of the various programs—how and why they evolved as they did—as well as the glimpses these case studies provide of the roles that writing centers have assumed in shaping higher education. Finally, researchers will discover common histories, shared problems that remain to be solved, and new issues that need to be investigated.

To make this book easier to use, we have listed the major sections included within each chapter in the table of contents. The director who is interested in tutor training, for example, can easily locate specific information by consulting the contents or by consulting the comprehensive index beginning on page 253.

Overview of the Book

The main body of this book consists of twelve case studies of specific writing center programs. Each of these chapters follows a similar pattern: a discussion of the context in which the program exists, the major services offered by the center, and the programs used for selecting and training tutors. In addition, most of the chapters also include some historical background, a description of a typical day at the center, a diagram of the center's physical layout, and information about administrative matters such as recordkeeping and evaluation procedures.

Apart from this general pattern, each chapter also includes descriptions of the features which make the program unique. As a result, readers will come away, for example, with images of the cathedral ceilings and skylights of the center at Lehigh University; the idea of an electronic research notebook at the University of Southern California; an echo of the dialogue that has resulted from the collaboration between the programs at the University of Toledo and ComTech; a vision of the computer-based program at Colorado State University; and an appreciation for the decentralized model that is represented by Utah State University's Rhetoric Associates Program. Our goal was not only to make these twelve descriptions similar enough so that readers would be provided with multiple viewpoints on certain key topics, but also to allow our authors the freedom to include whatever they considered to be the defining characteristics of their respective programs. We think this book satisfies that goal.

Following the case studies is an epilogue in which we attempt to sift through the data included in the book in order to reach some conclusions. More important, that chapter suggests additional uses for the information we have collected, endeavors we hope others will pursue. The epilogue concludes with a chart that provides a summary and overview of the vital statistics of the twelve writing center programs and their institutions. The chart facilitates comparisons between the different programs and enables readers to locate specific information quickly and efficiently. The chart is followed by the names and addresses of the people one should contact if additional information about a program is desired.

Following the epilogue is a bibliographical essay, "The Scholarly Context: A Look at Themes," which includes an extensive bibliography of recommended literature on writing centers. The essay focuses on the themes and issues which have received the most critical attention in the writing center literature. Together, the essay and bibliography (as well as the literature cited by the chapter authors) provide readers with the most comprehensive overview to date of writing center research.

Although a number of complex theoretical, social, and ethical issues now confront writing centers, a lengthy treatment of those issues is not the primary thrust of this book. However, such issues cannot be divorced from the historical, pedagogical, and administrative contexts within which this book is situated; therefore, readers will find discussions of issues such as cultural and linguistic diversity, authority of tutors, and ownership of the text couched within many of the chapter essays. In addition, this book will suggest areas of future study for researchers and theorists alike. For example, the fact that all but one of our authors is female suggests a gender-related issue which has, as yet, not been fully explored.

Conclusion

Producing a book such as this one requires a long, consistent effort; writing centers, however, evolve and change quite rapidly. As a result, the descriptions in this book may not reflect with absolute accuracy the programs as they exist today. Therefore these descriptions are best viewed as "snapshots" of different writing centers, taken at certain points in time.

The programs we have included certainly do not exhaust the possibilities of what writing centers can or should become. These programs, as well as the ones still to be established, will assume new forms, use new technologies, take on new responsibilities, develop new theories, and explore new directions for the future. Therefore we offer this book, not as a definitive statement of what writing centers should become—for the future will produce its own models—but as a statement of what writing center programs most certainly can become.

Work Cited

Richards, I. A. 1936. *The Philosophy of Rhetoric.* New York: Oxford University Press.

1 A Multiservice Writing Lab in a Multiversity: The Purdue University Writing Lab

Muriel Harris
Purdue University

Diversity may not be a virtue, but for a writing lab in a large multiversity, it is a necessity. Like other huge land-grant colleges, Purdue University, with a student population of over 35,000, offers a broad spectrum of courses in which writing skills are essential. Students who seek undergraduate and graduate degrees need to write freshman composition essays, history term papers, geoscience lab reports, management case studies, doctoral dissertations in engineering, computer science proposals, child development literature reviews, audiology clinical reports, news releases for agricultural economics, co-op reports for engineering jobs, and so on. And students have a variety of other writing needs as well: to complete job application letters with accompanying résumés, to demonstrate writing proficiency for various schools and departments in the university, to write reports for student activities, to compose applications for graduate and professional schools, to complete forms for student contests and awards, etc. Students with these and other writing tasks come to the Writing Lab with equally diverse writing histories, writing needs, learning styles, and personal preferences for the kinds of help they want. Thus, because the focus of the Writing Lab is individualized instruction, we offer diverse services for a variety of students. Our goal is to offer each individual writer the particular kind of help he or she needs, in a manner in which that person will learn best. Existing within the context of a large state university with a dominant emphasis on science and technology, we must be prepared to work with students in developmental composition courses as well as with ESL students who are writing doctoral dissertations on nuclear waste containment.

Another defining characteristic of our Writing Lab is that it exists within an English department with a broad range of writing courses and a large graduate program in rhetoric and composition. Within this context we meet students in a huge freshman composition program as

1

well as in courses in business writing, professional writing, writing for the computer industry, creative writing, technical writing, English as a second language, writing for publication, and so on. As a result, the graduate students who comprise one of our three tutoring staffs have taught a variety of composition courses before they begin tutoring, and they bring to their tutorial collaboration an interest and expertise in tutoring various kinds of writing. Some of our graduate student tutors often come to the lab for their shift after an hour spent down the hall in a graduate seminar on composition theory and research. All of this means that we have tutors who can specialize in some areas and who tend in their tutoring to emphasize their particular interests or approaches to the teaching of writing. As an example of the former, business writing students will see a tutor who has taught their course, while nonnative students are directed to tutors who teach in the ESL program. As an example of the latter, one tutor who is working on a doctoral dissertation on audience tends to stress audience concerns in her tutorials, and another tutor who has been trained in an approach with complex methods of invention may introduce some of these heuristics in a tutorial. In short, there is a diversity of approaches in our tutorials, though we all work from the same basic assumptions of collaboration and individualization that define writing center tutoring.

History

In 1975, when Purdue administrators were responding to the national hue and cry about declining writing skills by calling for supplementary instruction, the English department's director of composition decided to try a writing lab for a year on an experimental basis. Several graduate students, who were willing to try their hand at tutoring, were enlisted. At the time, I was a part-time lecturer in composition (i.e., a faculty wife with advanced degrees in Renaissance literature) and unhappy with large-group instruction in writing. Because I was quite interested in trying to individualize the teaching of writing, I asked if I could help to get things organized during the summer before the lab went into operation. Since I was offering volunteer help, there were no objections.

Three graduate students and I met frequently during the summer to lay out a game plan of what we would need when the doors opened. We kept asking ourselves what a writing lab should be and how it should be structured. Solutions were debated in the abstract, but eventually we reached a consensus as to what we would be doing. With a drawer full of handouts we had made during the summer and a pad of paper to keep track of the students coming in, we opened the door. Several hundred students found their way to the lab that semester and even more the next semester.

Having proven by numbers and evaluations from students and instructors that there was a need for a writing lab on a regular basis, I found myself applying for the newly created job of lab director. I was hired and began planning in earnest to develop the lab. One problem was space, since the half of one room allotted to the lab was cramped from the start because we were asked to share facilities with a reading and study skills center. As our traffic increased (and my pleas became ever more insistent), the reading and study skills center eventually moved out, and we slowly and steadily acquired more lab instructors, added new services, wrote more materials, stepped up our publicity, and continued to grow.

In 1982, when the developmental composition course was restructured, a lab component was added, and we were given the adjoining room for this program. Since the department could not give us more graduate students as tutors for this new group, we also added a peer-tutoring program, which has flourished. We now work with about 4,500 students per semester (over 9,000 per year). Not all of those students come in for tutorial help: the figures include students who use the computers and self-instruction materials, come in for handouts, call on the grammar hotline, use the lab as a writing room, come to workshops, or are part of Traveling Teacher sessions.

The Writing Lab at Purdue is an English department service. The director is a tenured faculty member in the department; the Writing Lab instructors are graduate students in English whose tutoring assignments are the equivalent of a course assignment. The salaries of the director, the lab instructors, the undergraduate peer tutors who work with the developmental composition students, and the clerical staff are all funded by the English department. From the English department's perspective, the lab is intended primarily to serve students enrolled in various courses in the department's extensive writing program, though we welcome students from all across campus and seek out opportunities to work with a variety of courses in various disciplines where writing is emphasized. We also respond enthusiastically to faculty throughout the university's curricula who stress writing skills in their courses and want their students to work with Writing Lab tutors.

To locate the Writing Lab's place within the university structure, it is necessary to describe briefly Purdue's highly decentralized organizational structure. At the highest administrative level is the president of the university, followed by an executive vice president for Academic Affairs who oversees the various schools that comprise the university. Each school is headed by a dean who, in turn, oversees the various departments within his or her school. Thus, in terms of moving upward in the chain of command, the Writing Lab director reports to the head of the Department of English, who reports to the dean of the School of Liberal Arts (SLA), who in turn reports to the executive vice president, who reports to the president. There are other student support services, such as the Chemistry Resource Room, the Independent Study Center, the Psychological Services Center, and the SLA Learning Center, but beyond informal contacts, there is little interaction or coordination of services between various parts of the campus.

Physical Description

Our space is set up so that students who walk in first see the receptionist's desk and a smiling face staring at them, as well as the couches, the plants, and the informal arrangement of tables and chairs around the room (figure 1). To the right of the entrance is a sign-in table with recordkeeping forms, announcements, fliers, lists of workshops, drop-in hours, schedules, and other informative fliers that students might want. On the wall above the sign-in table is a bulletin board with pictures of everyone who works in the lab, so that students (and the various groups of tutors) can add names to the faces they encounter. This board is particularly helpful when a student comes in and wants to make an appointment with a particular tutor whose name she has forgotten. Along the wall, beyond the sign-in table, are bookshelves of composition journals, then cabinets of instructional materials with colored bins stacked on top of the cabinets for the various referral forms instructors want, followed by bookcases of texts that students can check out. Visually, the room is open, with no partitions anywhere, to encourage a sense of community and interaction. This also permits the receptionist to see when a tutor is winding up one session and is ready for another student. The room is also a mix of comfortable, old donated couches, tables, plants, posters, coffeepots, a recycling bin for soda cans and paper, and even a popcorn machine, all of which signal (we hope) that this mess is also a friendly, nonthreatening, nonclassroom environment where conversation and questions can fly from one

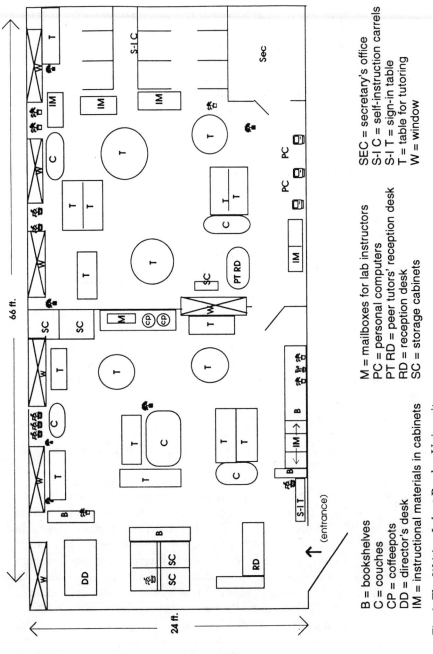

B = bookshelves
C = couches
CP = coffeepots
DD = director's desk
IM = instructional materials in cabinets

M = mailboxes for lab instructors
PC = personal computers
PT RD = peer tutors' reception desk
RD = reception desk
SC = storage cabinets

SEC = secretary's office
S-I C = self-instruction carrels
S-I T = sign-in table
T = table for tutoring
W = window

Fig. 1. The Writing Lab at Purdue University.

table to another. We want students to recognize immediately that this is a place where writers help each other and from which red pencils have been banished.

Historically, the Writing Lab began by sharing facilities with a reading and study skills center, which moved out when the lab became seriously overcrowded. Eventually, when the lab was asked to design a peer-tutoring program for the developmental composition course, the adjoining back room was added. We were never successful in getting the administration to knock down the wall between the rooms, but we did manage to get large windows put in so that the rooms are visually accessible to each other. All the computer hardware and self-instruction equipment was moved to the back room on the assumption that there would be adequate space there, but there isn't. Somehow, the peer tutors who work in the back room with the developmental students have managed to give it a clubby, hanging-out look. The sofas are even shabbier than those in the front room, the popcorn maker in there works continuously, and a graffiti wall has been created where marking pens are available for writers to write witty quips-of-the-day or to just sign their names. We are still seriously overcrowded in both rooms, but given the accompanying overcrowding in the rest of the building, there is little hope at present for further expansion. We dream of additional space for more tutoring tables and computers as well as space for more appropriate equipment for ESL students to practice speaking skills, but this is little more than wishful thinking.

Chronology of a Typical Day

On the one hand, every day in our Writing Lab is different, partly because of the ebb-and-flow traffic patterns of the semester. For example, the first few days of the semester are quiet, except for a few eager, highly motivated ESL students and some anxious résumé writers. By the end of the first week, instructors are bringing classes in for tours. Then, by the second week or so, after the first in-class diagnostic writing samples are passed back in composition courses, we have a heavy influx of students who need help in interpreting their teachers' comments about what they will need to work on for the semester. After that, the traffic continues to build so that by the fourth week, a steady stream of students flows in and out all day, every day, with a noticeable drop-off during midterm week when exams take priority over writing assignments. However, our appointment book stays filled for a week or two in advance all through the semester, and drop-in time becomes the best way for students to get quick help with papers they are working on. There is, unfortunately, a frantic rush during the last week or so of the semester, when students whom we should have seen long ago suddenly remember a teacher's referral given to them a month or two ago or a paper that has to be revised by the next day.

On the other hand, there is also continuity. Each day in the Writing Lab begins at 8 a.m., when the receptionist arrives. She uses that quiet time to get organized and ready to help the few students who come in for self-instruction or word processing. By about 9 a.m., students who want tutorial help begin to trickle in. By midmorning, both the noise level and body count are high, the coffeepots have been refilled five or six times, and the couches are filled with students waiting to see a tutor. Telephones ring, students pour into the reception area in large numbers during the ten minutes between classes each hour, tutors and students engage in animated discussion at tables all around the room, and the cabinet drawers with instructional materials regularly bang open and shut. In the adjacent room, where the peer tutors and the developmental students are working, the level of conversation and laughter is even higher, to overcome the steady hum of the computer printers that are also in the room.

If there were a magic device to freeze frame a moment during one of the busier times of the day, we would see the following. Near the entrance are several students leaning over the sign-in table, filling out record forms in preparation to see a tutor. At the reception desk is a small knot of people: one asking for a handout, another wondering if she could see a tutor soon, another holding out her identification card in trade for the word processing disk she wants in order to use one of the computers, and yet another student who is twenty minutes late for his appointment and wonders if his tutor is waiting for him. (Typically, this bunching up of students around the desk occurs during the ten minutes between classes. It is often the same time that the telephone at the reception desk is ringing off the hook.) The receptionist reaches for the telephone and nods at the students talking to her. Since the receptionist's work-study helper is not available, the director comes over to assist because she is between tutorials. The director's attention is diverted, however, because an instructor has just come in with a question about one of his students and wants a quick answer. Meanwhile, sitting on the couches are a few students, waiting to see tutors. One, a freshman composition student, looks around anxiously. He hasn't been here before and isn't sure what to expect. A senior, anxious to finish her résumé, is adding some handwritten corrections to the draft of the application letter she wants to review with a writing consultant.

In addition, two ESL students, each waiting for a different tutor, are sitting on another sofa, talking quietly in their native language. An education major, about to make another attempt at passing the writing proficiency exam in the office next door, is tapping her pencil angrily on a history text she reads while waiting for her tutor. (She plans to be an art teacher in a middle school and does not know why she has to worry about proving basic writing competency.) At one of the tutoring tables, an older student sits with a tutor, sheaves of paper spread around the table. (Eventually, it will be a lengthy research paper on whistle-blowing in industry, for a communications course; right now it is a collection of too much material she has compulsively gathered because the concept of a research paper scares her.) At another table is a student in freshman composition, explaining his assignment to the tutor so that they can begin some planning. Another tutor on the far side of the room is winding up her tutorial with a student she has been working with for several weeks. (Comfortable with each other, they have figured out what needs to be done before the next tutorial and are spending a moment rehashing the disastrous campus football game played last weekend.) At the telephone is a lab instructor who has agreed to interrupt a tutorial to answer a grammar hotline call (it's long distance) and who is thumbing furiously through dictionaries in the reference bookcase near the telephone to see if, as the caller has asked, there really is a word such as *bodacious.*

While all this is going on up front, in the back room several peer tutors are chatting at the reception desk, waiting for students from the developmental course to come in. Sitting with them is one of the students in the peer-tutor training course. He has been listening to tutoring "war stories" and wants to hear more, hoping to become experienced simply by soaking in all these tales. As they talk, the printer nearby buzzes out a paper a student has been working on, and at the back of the room in a study carrel, an ESL student, headphones clamped securely on her head, mumbles semiaudibly the English phrases she hears on the cassette tape. In this freeze-framed moment in the Writing Lab, there are also a variety of people (instructors, tutors, and students) simply "hanging out " in both rooms of the lab, stoking up on coffee, standing and talking, enjoying a break from their other activities of the day.

To return to the general passage of the day, between 3 and 3:30 p.m. the pace slows, with perhaps only one tutor and student working softly in the corner. The coffeepots are empty, the receptionist begins straightening up from the day's activities, and the director finally staggers to her desk in a vain attempt to see what people have dropped there all day while she has been tutoring, talking with instructors, answering telephone calls, troubleshooting, and attending to all the usual tasks of directing a writing lab. (Soon, the director will leave for home because she needs a quiet place where she can concentrate on work for the lab and plow into professional efforts for publication that her department expects of her.) The lab is closed from 5–7 p.m., but lab instructors regularly use the room during this interval and on weekends for their own work, so it is often a time either for quiet concentration or for shop talk among lab instructors. Twice during the week, these quiet hours are used for staff meetings for both groups of peer tutors. Three evenings per week, from 7–10 p.m., Tuesday through Thursday, the lab is open, with a few peer tutors to help the developmental students and another peer tutor to work with the students seeking help with résumés. There is also a Writing Lab instructor available for general help.

Clientele

Because Purdue University plays host to a diverse student population, the Writing Lab's client list is lengthy and reflects that diversity. We work with freshmen in the regular two-semester composition sequence as well as with the students in the developmental course and the one-semester honors course. We also tutor students enrolled in the various English-as-a-second-language courses and nonnative students who are writing graduate papers and dissertations that display general writing problems or ESL-related errors. Students enrolled in our business writing, technical writing, advanced composition, and creative writing courses come in with their more specialized writing concerns. Down the hall, in the communications department, there are a number of courses, including journalism, which require writing and use the Writing Lab as their tutorial supplement as well. Students also come in with papers from a variety of courses across campus, both at the undergraduate and graduate levels, and we have a large number of students in the lab preparing résumés, job applications, and applications to graduate or professional schools. In addition, there are nontraditional students who, particularly in a large university, need a support service where someone can talk to, as well as tutor, them.

Graduate students preparing a dissertation proposal or dissertation itself come in with large chunks of text, and though we do not act as an editing service, we can offer suggestions for improving selected segments. In addition, other graduate students come for help in order to pass a three-hour writing proficiency examination that the Graduate School requires of all graduate students who cannot otherwise demonstrate proficiency in writing. The writing exam is administered by a facility adjacent to ours, the Office of Writing Review. Here, two groups of students, undergraduates in either education or engineering, must also pass writing proficiency exams because of the writing requirements in their own schools. The Writing Lab is the tutorial facility prepared to help them pass their exams and thus complete the self-paced course in which they are enrolled. Others who come to the Writing Lab are people living and/or working in the community who have enrolled in noncredit courses through Purdue University's Department of Continuing Education. The Writing Lab offers them a self-paced course that is tailored to their individual needs. This course typically draws secretaries who want to brush up on grammar, businesspeople who want to write better business communications, and writers who work on their own projects. Still another group that uses the lab does so through our grammar hotline, which takes calls from students, staff, faculty, businesspeople in the community, local teachers, and all kinds of callers from across the country. Because we are listed with the National Grammar Hotline as well as the Rolodexes in a variety of law offices, newspaper offices, and local libraries, we regularly field calls from a number of distant cities about points of grammar or unwieldy sentences. (We even fielded a call from a budding poet in the Southwest who wanted to know how to "solicitize" her poetry. She had submitted some of her work to a journal and had gotten a rejection note which explained that they "do not accept *unsolicited* poems"—hence her need to know how to *solicitize*.)

Tutors: Selection and Training

We have three different groups of tutors: (1) Writing Lab instructors—the graduate students who handle the general traffic; (2) writing consultants—peer tutors who work with résumés, job applications, and other business writing; and (3) undergraduate teaching assistants (UTAs)—another group of peer tutors who work with students enrolled in the developmental composition program. Each of these groups is in a separate training program. The preparation for the graduate students begins at a very advanced level because applicants for these positions must have taught in the composition program at Purdue for at least one year. Since there are more applicants for lab positions than spaces available, we are free to select the best applicants, who generally tend to be experienced, talented classroom teachers.

My responsibility at our biweekly meetings, held during the lab instructors' first semester in the lab, is to acquaint them with the differences between large-group classroom instruction and tutorial interaction. We focus on the theory and practice of collaborative learning and strategies for tutoring as well as the problems and delights of giving up any authority these graduate students may have assumed in their classrooms. We have a variety of readings and topics for discussion, focusing on diagnosis, tutorial questioning, and so on. I also attempt to acquaint them with all of the lab's resources, so that they can find the right handout when they need it, and to help them master the paperwork. Although we have this formal training for one semester, the real integration into the lab goes on in informal contacts during the day as the director and tutors cross paths and discuss students with whom they are working.

Lab instructors are encouraged to develop special interests in the lab and to engage in professional activities such as writing articles or presenting conference papers about Writing Lab work. In addition, there are biweekly meetings of the entire staff throughout the year, where guest speakers discuss various topics relevant to our tutoring and where we discuss our tutoring experiences and try to learn from each other as we solve various problems that come up (see Harris 1991).

Because the graduate students who work as Writing Lab instructors will be seeking academic positions that will most likely include some composition teaching, their work as lab instructors must train them for professional roles in addition to classroom teaching. Therefore, lab instructors are given the opportunity—and are encouraged—to learn administrative skills as an assistant to the director of the Writing Lab or as a coordinator of one of the peer-tutoring groups; to gain experience as mentors for peer tutors; to attend conferences and present papers focused on writing centers; and to write articles about tutorial instruction. Because of the experience acquired in these roles and because of the opportunity to become familiar with one-to-one instruction, twenty of our Writing Lab instructors have gone on to become directors of writing labs in other institutions after finishing their doctoral studies.

Before they become paid tutors, the two groups of peer tutors must successfully complete training programs that consist of one-semester for-credit courses. The students who are training to work with business writing have successfully completed the business writing course and are chosen after interviews. Those who enroll in the course meet once a week as a group to review general tutoring principles and more specific principles for business writing. In addition, they spend an additional two hours per week in the Writing Lab assigned to a mentor, either a lab instructor or an experienced writing consultant. Initially, these students observe their mentors tutoring and then gradually ease into tutoring as each mentor feels his or her student is ready to tutor alone. Mentor and tutor-in-training meet at least once a week to discuss the student's progress and answer tutoring questions that arise. At the end of the semester, the best students in the class are asked to stay on as paid writing consultants.

The other group of students (undergraduate teaching assistants), who are training to become peer tutors and who work with developmental writers, also enroll in a semester-long course after having been selected through interviews (about one-fourth of the applicants are chosen for the course). This class also meets once a week as a group to discuss principles of tutoring, discuss reading assignments (collected in a manual), role-play various tutorial situations, do various small-group projects, hand in writing assignments (journals, reports of observations, summaries of their readings, reaction papers, tutoring tips, and so on), and discuss their experiences in the lab during the week. An additional two hours each week are spent observing the peer tutors at work and getting to know the lab. As the semester progresses, these tutors-in-training are given some opportunities to tutor and are observed as they do so. At the end of the semester, the best students in this class move on to become peer tutors. Although this means that some students enroll in the tutoring practicums with no further opportunities to tutor after the course is over, we hope that the learning experience proves valuable for them, particularly for those who go on to teach at the high school level.

Types of Services

Tutorials

The majority of our work, of course, is one-to-one interaction with writers. For students who want to work regularly with a particular tutor or who prefer to schedule the time they will spend with a tutor, we offer half-hour appointments. (We've considered hour-long appointments but have found that for a variety of pedagogical and administrative reasons, half-hour sessions are usually more productive.) In addition to the scheduled tutoring appointments, Writing Lab instructors also allot some of their time for drop-in students who walk in and get help on a first-come, first-served basis. At busy times, this can mean a student will be told that there are three people ahead of her and that she can either wait or return at a different hour. At quiet times, students walk in, ask for assistance, and sit down with a tutor within a few minutes. The rationale for drop-in help is that students cannot always predict or schedule when they will need to talk with a tutor.

Our schedule for the lab is such that throughout the day, from about 9 a.m. until about 4 p.m., there are always a few tutors in the lab, some seeing students with appointments while others handle drop-in requests. Three evenings per week, Tuesday through Thursday, we also offer drop-in and tutorial help from 7 p.m. to 10 p.m. From past experience, we have found that few students are interested in coming to the lab on weekends or during the dinner hour, but midweek evenings are very popular and heavily used by ESL students, students who have a heavy course load or long working hours, and graduate students who must spend many daytime hours in their other labs.

One way to illustrate what our tutorials are like is to listen in on a typical session. The excerpt included here has been condensed somewhat to eliminate some of the irrelevant talk that is a normal part of tutorial conversation and some portions which illustrate the same tutorial strategies at work. In this session, the tutor and student have already spent a few moments getting to know each other. The tutor is trying to determine what type of help the student wants. At first, the student does not know precisely what he wants the tutorial to focus on and indicates, in response to the tutor's questions, that he really does not know which aspects of his writing the teacher has suggested he try to improve. The two topics that are eventually elicited are the need for more clarity and for more examples, and it is evident to the tutor that the same weaknesses exist in the paper the student has with him. As the tutorial proceeds, the need for clarity becomes obvious to the writer only after hearing the tutor/reader explain her confusion in several different places. This student is somewhat passive in that he wants the tutor to do the work and to tell him how to fix the paper. The tutor repeatedly turns back the responsibility to the student.

> *Tutor:* Yeah, me too. Well, I hope you do well in that chem test....
> So ... uh, what would you like to work on in here?
>
> *Student:* Here.... Could you look over this paper? It's due in a few days.
>
> *Tutor:* Yeah, sure. What should we focus on?

Student: Uh . . . to see if . . . if it's OK. You know, if it has what's supposed to be there.

Tutor: Tell me about the assignment. What's your purpose here?

Student: It's supposed to . . . the teacher wants a solution to a problem. Like the model here in the textbook. [Opens textbook.] We're supposed to have . . . like what could be a letter to the *Exponent* [student newspaper on campus].

Tutor: OK, so you're offering a solution to a problem. What problem did you pick?

Student: The parking problem on campus.

Tutor: Well, that's certainly a problem. You'll have a lot of interested readers. Are you going to tackle the whole parking problem, both for faculty parking areas and student areas, or just one of them?

Student: Well, like what the problem is and how I can solve it.

Tutor: Ah . . . OK . . . Let's start with what you like the best about this paper. Tell me also what you like the least. Start with what really worked out well here.

Student: It's OK, I guess. I think my solution is OK. It's sort of an ideal solution, I guess. I'm not sure what the paper needs. Could you read it?

Tutor: Sure, I'll be glad to be a reader, especially with such a hot topic. Before we start, one more thing. What did your teacher say you needed to work on in previous papers?

Student: Oh . . . he's no big fan of what I turn in. I don't think he likes any of our writing. He spends a lot of time criticizing stuff that's turned in . . . sometimes shows it on a screen . . . and points out the stuff he doesn't like . . .

Tutor: What has he said on your papers?

Student: To work on . . . let's see . . . [shuffles through his folder and retrieves a graded paper]. Here . . . "Try to achieve more clarity, and use examples to illustrate your points." Yeah, he's said that a few times.

Tutor: Great, now we know some specifics for what he's looking for. Do you know what he meant by clarity?

Student: Like, complete. He wants it understandable.

Tutor: OK, so as a reader, I'll try to tell you when something isn't complete enough to be clear, and I'll look for places where examples would help. I'll read it aloud, and we'll both listen to it. [Begins reading.] That's a great opening sentence! It would certainly grab my attention in the *Exponent.*

Student: Yeah, that's maybe the third or fourth one I wrote. I worked on that. It wasn't so good at first because . . . I never know how to start.

Tutor: Your hard work really shows there. [Keeps reading.] I see where you're headed, and this is a good description of a lot of the complaints about parking. But I'm not sure whether you are talking only about C permit areas for students or also the A and B areas for faculty.

Student: I don't know much about the faculty parking areas.

Tutor: OK, so don't you think you ought to make it clear to the reader that you're talking just about the student parking problem?

Student: How would I do that?

Tutor: Do you have a particular sentence in that introductory paragraph that seems to summarize the problem?

Student: Ah ... [reads over his opening paragraph for awhile]. Here, this is like where I say what the problem is.

Tutor: Good. OK, try to pinpoint what you say so the reader knows you don't mean all the parking areas.

Student: Here ... I guess I could add the word "student" right here. [Writes.]

Tutor: That's really good. Why does that make the subject clearer?

Student: You mean because I'm being more specific?

Tutor: Suppose you were reading this letter in the *Exponent*. What do you think?

Student: Yeah, I guess it's more directed toward the students this way. I'm saying that it's student parking ... this is the problem.

[Later in the tutorial.]

Tutor: OK, so you are saying that the parking garages aren't a good solution because visitors have to pay money. That's your point here?

Student: Uh, huh.

Tutor: What do you think other students reading that part will feel about that?

Student: Well, visitors do have to pay. There are rates posted all over.

Tutor: Sure, but as a typical student, do you really care when, say, people coming to conferences or maybe businesspeople who have to see administrators have to pay to park?

Student: No, not really. But it makes me mad when my parents come and have to pay just to walk around on campus. They were pretty upset about that when they were here.

Tutor: That's a great example. How do you think other students would feel about that?

Student: I know some kids who have said the same thing. That's why I put that in here.

Tutor: So, you had a great example in your mind when you wrote that sentence. How could you remind other students reading this letter about the example of parents having to pay, too?

Student: So, I should add it in?

Tutor: Well, you made that argument come alive for me when you reminded me about parents having to pay. I wouldn't have thought about that if you hadn't said it. And, we're looking for places to add examples.

Student: So, I should add it here.

Tutor: What do you think examples add?

Student: I guess it lets you in on what was in my head and why I wrote that.

Tutor: Yeah, and it makes the point more vivid for readers, too. They can really see what you mean. Why don't you add in a sentence with that example right now, and then you can see how it sounds.

Self-Instruction

For students who prefer to work on their own, at their own pace, we have a large collection of self-instructional materials, both computer programs and booklet and cassette-tape programs in grammar, rhetorical skills, spelling, vocabulary, business writing, technical writing, and a heavily used simulation game for journalism students. For students learning English as a second language, we offer tape and booklet modules on listening comprehension, pronunciation, conversation skills, and vocabulary. Our computer-assisted instruction (CAI) materials include an extensive collection of grammar mastery programs for ESL students, plus an assortment of other CAI programs on grammar and spelling for native speakers of English. Generally, our collection of self-instruction for native speakers is lightly used, mainly by students who profess an interest in seeing what the tapes are like or who are referred by teachers. End-of-the-semester evaluations generally indicate that ESL students express great satisfaction at having materials made available that they can study on their own (particularly high-interest tapes such as those which simulate news broadcasts and offer lectures in various fields of study). The same evaluations reveal that native English-speaking students who have self-selected the tape and booklet programs appreciate the opportunity to work at their own pace. Students referred to these materials by their teachers generally view the time spent this way as less productive. Self-instruction is available during the hours that the lab is open, from 8 a.m. to 5 p.m., Monday through Friday, and on Tuesday through Thursday evenings, from 7–10 p.m.

Word Processing

Because the vast numbers of computer terminals available to students on our campus are intended for programming, there is very little opportunity for students to word process if they do not already have their own microcomputers or do not like continuously plunking small change into the coin-operated computers in the residence halls. Therefore, while we are conscious of trying to empty the ocean with a teaspoon, we have managed to get three microcomputers (an IBM PC, a Macintosh, and an Apple IIe) for students who want to word process. We supply several of the most widely used word-processing programs and ask students to bring their own disks for storing their work. (The English department also has a computer lab for classroom use, but it is not available to the general student population.) Because we want to encourage students to learn word processing, our computer consultant (a work-study student in computer science who handles our computerized recordkeeping) is available about twenty hours a week to offer technical help and to conduct regularly scheduled small-group workshops to initiate beginners into the complexities of writing with computers.

Traveling Teachers

Each semester, as a service to classroom teachers, we announce a list of presentations that we will offer, if invited to do so. In part, this is meant as a sharing of experience and materials among the composition staff. Writing Lab instructors, who must have a few years of experience before being selected to work in the Writing Lab, are considered to be "old hands," experienced in working with students on a variety of complex topics in tutorials and classrooms. As Writing Lab instructors gain tutorial experience, they begin to develop specialties (our "shtick" as we call it) that can be offered in classrooms. Typical topics for presentations include writing anxiety, basic punctuation patterns, prewriting strategies, audience awareness, documentation and formatting, sentence variety, résumés and job applications, technical writing, and so on. Composition teachers invite us to their classes for a number of reasons: they are new and unsure of how to tackle a particular topic; they think a new face and voice will add interest (a very real concern, for example, in the dark, tired days before Thanksgiving break, when even the best teachers feel overwhelmed by listlessness and student inertia); they want to see lab materials in action; they want to see a new approach to something they regularly teach; or they recognize the public relations value of having a Writing Lab instructor come to the class (i.e., students tend to be more willing to follow up on a lab referral after seeing a friendly face from the lab helping out in their classroom).

In addition to the composition teachers who make use of our Traveling Teacher service, a variety of faculty around campus ask for sessions on writing in their courses. Typically, we are asked to review technical writing format and style in engineering courses, to discuss techniques for writing résumés and application letters in courses which focus on professional preparation in various fields, or to do a session on a particular topic suggested by the faculty member. As there is not yet a coordinated writing-across-the-curriculum program on our campus, the Writing Lab is the focus for most of the outreach to faculty in other disciplines who emphasize writing in their courses and who do not have writing specialists in their own departments. In addition, I join forces with Purdue University's Center for Instructional Services and offer faculty workshops on creating effective writing assignments (or how to avoid "assignments from hell") and how to respond to student writing.

Handouts

Over the years we have developed cabinets full of homemade instructional materials—handouts on spelling, punctuation, sentence structure, usage, diction, formatting, invention, revision, proofreading, business writing, résumés and job applications, report writing, and so on. As these handouts are used and revised, they reflect our teaching strategies, our knowledge of what students need to know, and our strong awareness of the importance of visual learning. For example, we have an array of handouts with punctuation rules (the handy-dandy-everything-you-need-to-know-about-commas packet with all the comma rules as well as separate, more focused packets or sheets on particular comma rules that students frequently need to know). Typically, these handouts combine verbal explanations, examples, and visual reinforcement of important concepts. For example, for punctuation we also have a punctuation pattern sheet—a diagrammatic representation of the various patterns of sentence punctuation—for students who are inclined to be visual learners. (I would add desktop publishing to the ever-expanding list of job skills that writing lab directors need.) When working with students, we try to identify which sheets will be most effective for the particular student with whom we are working.

Students are also invited to come in and get handouts on their own, a particularly useful service, for example, for someone who wants a one-sheet summary of APA style to keep as a reference in her notebook, someone who wants a sample packet of various types of résumés, or someone (particularly an ESL student) who would like a verb tense chart to refer to while writing. These materials were originally developed (or copied out of various sources) to accompany tutorials as something that student and tutor could doodle on and personalize and that the student could then take away from the session as a reminder, but we have come to recognize that some students simply want a reference sheet for their notebook and may not, at the moment, need to see a tutor. We also find that instructors appreciate being able to come in and get supplementary materials for their classes. Moreover, as the lab staff revises these handouts and creates new ones, we are becoming increasingly aware of the skills needed for materials development. The discussions at staff meetings—as we look over the next revision—are equally useful for all of us.

Students' Resource Library

Our reference collection includes a variety of dictionaries, including the standard ones recommended for college composition courses, plus the various Longman dictionaries for students learning English as a second language. We have Fowler's book on usage, some spelling dictionaries, dictionaries of idioms, a thesaurus, a collection of recent grammar handbooks, the reference books for MLA and APA format, and an invaluable handbook for secretaries which has various esoteric rules we seem to be called on to know when responding to grammar hotline calls. For example, a lawyer's secretary in Denver called, desperate to know where to put the title "Jr." after a client's name when listing him alphabetically, last name first. (It's "Jones, Jr., John," as we found out from consulting this secretarial handbook, a fact that no standard grammar handbook on our shelves would divulge.)

In addition to the homemade instructional materials and shelves of reference books, we also have several bookcases of texts for students to check out. This collection includes handbooks, workbooks, readers, rhetorics, vocabulary builders, spelling programs, sentence skills books, and so on. Some of these are publishers' samples; others are instructors' copies that were once used in our composition program; and some were even purchased because they fill a need. Some students come in to browse through these books to find out what various textbooks say about a certain topic; other students want to see if reading another text will clarify their own textbook; other students, not presently enrolled in writing courses, are shopping for a good book for their reference shelf; and graduate students, whose time is particularly short and who want to study on their own before taking the writing proficiency exam, occasionally borrow grammar handbooks. Another bookcase contains all the ESL books that students might want to use on their own. Here are drill books on prepositions, verb practice workbooks, and so on. This bookcase sits in the back room, near all the cassette tape materials so that ESL students have all the materials they might want to use in one place.

Instructors' Resource Library

For our large composition staff (a group of over two hundred people, including faculty, graduate students, and part-timers) we offer several bookcases filled with most of the major journals in composition and a large assortment of books on the teaching of writing. Our rationale for this expenditure is that not all writing teachers subscribe to composition journals or take the time to go to the library to read journals or professional books in the field. However, on their way to pick up a handout or a cup of coffee, they are likely to take a few moments to browse. Since we encourage instructors to think of the Writing Lab as their resource place, this is a tangible example of our interest in being a place where people talk about and work on writing skills.

Writing Room

Because most of the composition classes are taught in the same building that houses the Writing Lab, we encourage students to use a quiet hour before or after a writing course to do some writing on their own in the lab. They can usually find an unoccupied chair at some table to write in an atmosphere where people all around them are busy "talking writing." If they have a quick question, a tutor can lean over and answer it, and if they need any of our references, they have easy access to the bookshelves. Some students find that the informality and the conviviality of such a setting spurs them on to better writing.

Outreach

The Writing Lab is intended primarily as a university service, but for people in the community, we do offer a grammar hotline and a non-credit course with options for grammar review or tutorial response to short writing projects. This course permits people in the community to make use of the Writing Lab on a regular basis. On an informal basis, we also make our self-instruction ESL materials available to spouses of foreign-born Purdue students. As director, I am occasionally invited to speak to local business groups about writing skills or to hold work-shops or in-service sessions with local elementary- and secondary-level teachers about a variety of writing skills topics. Helping with their new writing labs is a particularly exciting form of outreach.

Administration

Instructional Personnel

The director is a member of the English department faculty and is the only faculty person in the Writing Lab. In addition, there are fifteen Writing Lab instructors who are graduate students in the English department. These graduate students are working on advanced de-grees in literature, rhetoric and composition, linguistics, American studies, and various other doctoral programs offered through the de-partment. Because the Writing Lab is a collaborative effort and is a unique instructional setting in which we all are likely to team-teach one another's students as they return to the lab, the selection process for new lab instructors is a group process. Candidates for vacancies write letters of application that are reviewed by the whole staff and are then ranked according to the applicants' demonstrated abilities, spe-cialties, and experience. This peer review indicates, I hope, that the lab is truly a group effort.

In addition, the lab employs the two groups of undergraduate peer tutors described earlier: four to six writing consultants who work with business writing projects and résumés and about eight to ten under-graduate teaching assistants who work with students in the develop-mental composition course. There are also four or five students enrolled in the training course for business writing who do some tutoring as the semester progresses, and ten students in the training course for the other staff of peer tutors who work with the de-velopmental writers; these tutors-in-training also get some tutoring experience. Finally, a computer consultant, who is in the lab for twenty hours per week, helps students learn how to word process, runs workshops on word processing, attends to the computer equipment for student use, and manages our computerized recordkeeping system.

Service Staff

A full-time receptionist at the front desk is assisted by students who qualify for work-study clerical work. The work-study helpers are available for about twenty hours a week to help with various clerical tasks such as stocking the drawers with instructional handouts, helping out at the desk, doing routine maintenance, answering telephones, and so on. The receptionist is absolutely vital to the smooth running of the lab because without continuity and competent traffic control at the front desk, chaos would descend immediately. In addition, we have a full-time secretary to handle all the lab typing (records, schedules, handouts, announcements, etc.) as well as the typing for the *Writing Lab Newsletter*, which I edit. For the newsletter, she types manuscripts, records donations, and maintains the computerized subscription list.

Budget

We have a very meager budget for expenses provided by the English department, which must cover small amounts of office supplies and all duplicating of handouts and announcements. Since it is a constant struggle to stay within this budget, we have no means of buying additional materials or replacing worn-out equipment. There's a lot of Scotch tape, string, and rubber bands holding together most of our equipment. The major department expenditure is the salaries of the instructional and clerical staff.

Records

Records are kept of every student use of the Writing Lab to let us know how many students use the lab, what services they are using, and for which courses they are seeking help. Each time students come in for tutorial help, handouts, self-instruction, word processing, and so on, we ask them to fill out a short slip that asks for their name, their student identification number, the course for which they want help, the type of help requested, and how they heard about the lab. In addition, instructors taking handouts from the instructional files are asked to fill out slips indicating how many handouts they are taking.

To communicate with the teachers of the students who use the lab, we have a two-part noncarbon form. On that, we summarize what was worked on in the tutorial, tear off the top sheet, and mail it to the teacher. The second copy goes in the student's folder. In each student's folder there is also a one-page log sheet indicating the date, tutor's name, project worked on, and topics covered for each tutorial. That log provides a quick visual summary of what the student has been working on, but occasionally we find that the longer, more discursive notes written to the teachers are worth rereading to get a fuller sense of how the student has been progressing. Other recordkeeping has to do with evaluation, since we send out a variety of evaluation forms at the end of each semester. At the end of each academic year, I write a report to the administration detailing the ways in which the lab is used, the new programs and services, any notable accomplishments for the year, and summaries of the various evaluation statistics.

Publicity

Our primary method of publicizing the Writing Lab is through bookmarks, brochures, and one-page information sheets describing our services. These are included in about seven thousand orientation packets distributed to new freshmen by the Office of Admissions, and we repeatedly encourage all teachers of writing (particularly of freshman composition) to come into the lab and take handfuls to distribute in their classrooms at the beginning of the semester. During the first few weeks of the semester, we give fifteen-minute tours of the lab to classes whose teachers schedule tours. These tours are effective in that they bring students into the lab so that we can familiarize them with where we are and how we operate. We also show a brief videotape of the lab in order to keep from lecturing at the students who troop in. Additionally, we have tried occasional open houses for the first few days of the semester, complete with doughnuts and drinks, and I sometimes send out short "writing tips" to be placed on residence hall cafeteria tables. We also try repeatedly to get the student newspaper to run stories about our services and announcements of our workshops, but the independently owned student paper is hesitant to devote space to campus activities when it could be provided instead to paid advertisers (the paper's sole means of funding). With no budget for advertising, we obviously do not fare well with the student paper, but we do manage to get mentioned occasionally in articles or feature stories about the need for better writing skills or about getting jobs (i.e., reporters interview our writing consultants about tips for writing résumés). Periodically, we tack up fliers on building bulletin boards, but the competition for space there is so ferocious that by the next day, three other notices are tacked on top of ours. And fliers on building doors are taken down fairly quickly by building maintenance crews. We also depend a lot on word-of-mouth advertising from satisfied clients, who pass the word to roommates and friends. Still, there are occasional juniors or seniors who come in looking puzzled because they have never heard of us.

To acquaint composition instructors with the lab, I send out a flier at the beginning of each semester to all members of the English department, and at the beginning of each academic year, I meet with new teaching assistants during an orientation week held before classes begin. At the session with new departmental teaching assistants, I pass out a portfolio of materials to acquaint them with the Writing Lab, including a cover letter, sample referral forms, a reprint of an article I wrote on how to use a writing center, and so on. To provide information for students coming into the lab, there are stacks of different handouts at the sign-in desk on how to use the computers, when our drop-in hours are scheduled, when the computer consultant is available, and how to use the Writing Lab effectively (for example, a one-page sheet entitled "Tailor Your Tutorial," which reminds students that if they plan ahead for what they want to do in the tutorial, they will apply the time more profitably toward what they want to accomplish).

Evaluation and Research

Each semester we ask students to fill out evaluation forms for the tutorial help they received and for any self-instruction materials they used. Their teachers are also asked to evaluate the students' progress as a result of their work in the Writing Lab. These forms are a mixture of Likert Scale numbers to circle and open-ended questions asking for more discursive comments. As might be expected, the open-ended comments are the most useful, for it was from these comments that we realized the need to ban smoking in the lab, that we perceived how the general noise level can bother some students, and that we recognized how important a cordial greeting is at the reception desk.

We also recognize that a lot of the effusive praise is really an expression of gratitude for help received and an acknowledgment of friendships that were formed with various tutors, but we hope that some of the positive comments do reflect genuine progress made as a result of one-to-one interaction with a tutor. In addition, we send another evaluation form to all the instructors in the composition program asking for general comments and suggestions about the Writing Lab (for example, what worked well, what needs changing, why an instructor did or did not use the lab, etc.). These responses tend to vary from unreserved praise (always good material to quote in the yearly report) to complaints that the instructor's students would not go to the lab despite referrals. Included also are some very useful responses that deserve careful consideration because they offer clues to ways in which we can work more productively with some teachers or to new services which we can offer.

For two semesters we also handed out brief evaluation forms after every tutorial. We asked the students to note what they had worked on because we thought this would be a good way for students to summarize for themselves what had just been discussed as well as a means to see how closely our perceptions of the tutorial overlapped with those of the students. We asked students to rate the tutor's effectiveness.

We have, however, stopped using these forms for several reasons. We found that they either cut into tutorial time or caused the student to rush through filling out the form. And we also found that students were so overwhelmingly positive that all we were really collecting were hundreds and hundreds of thank-you notes. A few complained about feeling rushed, but that wasn't news to us, and one tutor was amused to learn that one of her few less-than-superlative ratings was from a student who wrote, "All she did was answer my questions." But the students' responses to the question about the topic of the tutorial were quite useful to me. Tallying hundreds of those responses has given me a clearer picture of students' language about writing— we may talk about "development" of a topic, but student writers talk about "getting more ideas for my paper" or "figuring out what I wanted to say"—as well as an overview of what we actually work on in our lab. Now, I have some substantiation for our claim that we collaborate with students on all their writing processes—especially planning, topic development, and organization—and that while we do help with grammar and mechanics, it is a minor part of our work.

Research in the Writing Lab goes on at many levels. On the one hand, we are an often-used resource for students doing research projects of various kinds. Students, both graduate and undergraduate, come in to gather statistics on our organizational structure for their course reports, to look for problems that need solving as the subject matter for technical writing proposals, to analyze the socialization process of new tutors, to study public relations activities, and so on.

Lab instructors conduct various projects that lead to new instructional handouts, conference presentations, journal publications, and dissertations; and as director, I often find that the subject matter for my professional articles stems from my lab work. For example, when revising our fragment handout some years ago, I did a lengthy survey of the kinds of fragments students actually write (as opposed to those artificial examples that grammar handbooks tend to use), a study that resulted in an article on fragments (Harris 1981). The results of another survey to learn more about the misinformation students bring with them to tutorials was reported (Harris 1979); a lab program to help engineering students write better lab reports resulted in a study of how Writer's Workbench, a series of computer programs for editing technical writing, assists technical writers (Harris 1985); a need to understand more about a particular tutoring strategy led to an article on modeling (Harris 1983); my questions about how to more effectively help writers cope with in-class writing and writing under test conditions were the basis of another study (Harris 1989); and so on.

These kinds of research are the result of the need to know more about how to help students and how to make tutorial teaching more effective. In that sense, research and evaluation are closely intertwined as our evaluation efforts necessarily require some research that will lead us to more helpful answers. Current evaluation/research projects include a study of how instructional materials can be more effectively written and presented; another study of students' expectations before their first tutorial and how those expectations match (from their perspective) what actually happens in the tutorial; and yet another study on the topic of audience as it comes up in tutorials.

The Future

The Purdue University Writing Lab will, I hope, continue to offer its present services, adding new ones and modifying existing ones as needed. If our new program of noncredit courses proves to tap a real need, there may be more of such courses for people in the community. And if our peer tutor training courses are seen as useful practicum experiences for English education majors, we may expand them in ways that will allow some tutoring practice in local high schools. Workshops for faculty across campus are likely to expand as I receive requests for help with other aspects of adding a writing emphasis to various courses. In addition, after consulting with a psychologist from the Psychological Services Center about test anxiety and the various coping strategies she recommends, we plan to offer more intensive help (probably in the form of workshops) to combat writing anxiety.

As our university changes and new concerns arise, the Writing Lab will change to accommodate growth in our institutional context. The need for an emphasis on retention in a time of falling enrollments will certainly have an impact on our lab, just as Purdue's expanding emphasis on interaction with the agricultural and economic conditions of Third World countries as well as with industrial concerns in Asia has meant more emphasis on assisting the rapidly escalating number of ESL students at Purdue with language proficiency requirements. More generally, I hope that the Writing Lab will continue to grow, to find new challenges, and to serve as broad a range of students as possible, but it is hard to predict the shape these challenges will take. In a tutorial, we never set the agenda without hearing what the student wants to work on. For similar reasons, it is best not to work with a five-year plan but to be receptive to whichever needs define themselves. Working within a particular context means that we must be constantly monitoring our surroundings to see that we both fit in appropriately and that we effectively support those surroundings. One of the great strengths of writing centers is that they are grounded in the theory and practice of collaboration and therefore have a built-in flexibility that naturally leads them to adapt to changing contexts.

Works Cited

Harris, Muriel. 1989. "Composing Behaviors of One- and Multi-Draft Writers." *College English* 51: 174–91.

———. 1979. "Contradictory Perceptions of Rules of Writing." *College Composition and Communication* 30: 218–20.

———. 1985. "An Interdisciplinary Program Linking Computers and Writing Instruction." *Collegiate Microcomputer* 3 (3): 213–18.

———. 1981. "Mending the Fragmented Free Modifier," *College Composition and Communication* 32: 175–82.

———. 1983. "Modeling: A Process Method of Teaching." *College English* 45: 74–84.

———. 1991. "Solutions and Trade-offs in Writing Center Administration." *The Writing Center Journal* 12 (1): 63–79.

2 The Writing Center at Medgar Evers College: Responding to the Winds of Change

Brenda M. Greene
Medgar Evers College, CUNY

Located in the central Brooklyn community, Medgar Evers College, formally classified as a community college, is one of the eighteen colleges of the City University New York (CUNY). The college, now twenty-one years old, was formed in response to the community's demand for a college which would serve the needs of the residents of central Brooklyn, an area dominated by a large number of economically and educationally disadvantaged youth.

The college is named for Medgar Wiley Evers, a civil rights leader who dedicated his life to the pursuit of the rights of minorities to economic and educational equality. The spirit of Medgar Evers is infused into the college's mission to ensure that minority students from culturally and ethnically diverse backgrounds have equal access to higher education. Approximately 58 percent of the students at MEC come from some area of African diaspora, including, but not limited to, Barbados, Trinidad, Jamaica, Grenada, Panama, Guyana, the Dominican Republic, and Haiti. In addition, at least 40 percent of the students are of African American descent. Further, over the past several years, the number of Asian students has increased.

When the college was initially formed, students were able to obtain two-year and four-year degrees; however, affected by a severe New York City budget crisis in 1975, the college lost its senior status and was reclassified as a community college. Because this was an economic crisis, a compromise was struck that enabled the college to maintain most of its four-year-degree programs. Consequently, the college is currently a hybrid, in short, a community college which offers associate and baccalaureate degree programs in the areas of business and

I consulted a number of persons in order to write this manuscript. In particular, I would like to acknowledge Louis Pogue, MEC Writing Center coordinator; Elendar Barnes-Harrison, MEC tutorial coordinator; and Sonia Greaves and Delma Simon, tutors. Their experiences, comments, and insights were valuable.

public administration, education, the humanities, the social sciences, the natural sciences, and the health sciences.

Medgar Evers College houses approximately 4,100 students, the majority of whom are female (74 percent). Forty-two percent of these students attend school full time, and 44 percent attend in the evenings and on the weekends. The average age of the students is 32 years.

The evidence of Medgar Evers College's response to its mission is apparent in the variety of courses offered in African, African American, and Caribbean history and culture; in the variety of guest lectures, colloquia, conferences, and social activities in which students, faculty, and persons in the community participate; and in services such as the Student Learning Center, the Women's Center, the Medgar Evers College Center for Law and Social Justice, the Caribbean Research Center, and the Small Business Institute. In addition, students have access to services such as counseling, athletics, career planning, veterans' affairs, and day care.

History

The Medgar Evers College Writing Center, situated in the college's Humanities Division, developed in response to the college's and the writing faculty's recognition that developmental students needed a support center where the skills which they were learning in their writing courses could be reinforced. Medgar Evers College is an open-admissions college, and approximately 90 percent of its entering students must take either a remedial writing course for zero credits and 4.5 hours, or a developmental writing course for two credits and 4.5 hours.

When the MEC Writing Center opened in 1975, students attended class for three hours per week and the center for 1.5 hours per week; therefore, students received three hours of writing instruction from their instructors and 1.5 hours of supplemental writing instruction from the MEC Writing Center. Students also used the Writing Center outside of scheduled class time or lab time; faculty in content-area and college-level courses, for example, referred students to the Writing Center to work on specific skills related to their assignments: research papers, critical essays, etc. The Writing Center thus served as a learning environment where students could seek help on an as-needed basis.

The pedagogical strategy underlying the initial model of the Writing Center was based on a skills approach to writing instruction. The students' writing instructor was responsible for introducing and teaching concepts related to rhetoric, grammar, and sentence structure, and the Writing Center (called "the lab") was the place where the concepts taught in the classroom were reinforced through skills exercises and other forms of individualized instruction. These activities were often presented in the form of modules.

Faculty were encouraged to monitor the attendance and performance of their students in the lab; however, because of the way in which student registration and participation in the lab were structured, teachers found these difficult to monitor. Students registered for the lab of their choice when they registered for a writing course. Students from one instructor's class, for example, might be registered for as many as five different laboratory classes. An instructor might even find out that two or three students had never registered for a lab.

The Writing Center was staffed by a coordinator, two instructors, and a core of tutors. The lab coordinator was supervised by the coordinator of the Humanities English Program. Because the center was staffed by instructors as well as tutors, students received individualized and/or small-group instruction. This model highlighted the benefits of peer and individualized tutoring, but it also illustrated the problems that manifest themselves when the philosophy and pedagogy of a writing center differ from the philosophy and pedagogy of a writing program.

Although one could conjecture that a possible strength of this model was that students always received individualized and/or small-group instruction because of the presence of peer tutors and writing faculty who were assigned to the center, the model's flaw was that the writing program became too fragmented. Under this model, students received one grade from their instructor and either a "P" or "R" from the Writing Center/Lab. Sometimes there were cases when a student received a passing grade as a result of his or her attendance and performance in the Writing Center and a failing grade in the course, thus creating administrative and pedagogical problems. Students, for example, attempted to enroll in inappropriate levels of a subsequent course, or attempted to negotiate to have their grades changed because they had failed one section of a course and passed another section. Problems with this model also arose when students expressed dismay, confusion, and concern over the fact that they were presented with one approach to writing in their courses and a different approach to writing in the Writing Center. In essence, the staffing of the Writing Center by a coordinator, instructor, and tutors who developed and administered their own skills approach to writing instruction created a conflicting model of instruction for students.

The impetus for solving this problem of a fragmented writing program was generated by an economic reality as well as by the writing faculty's recognition of a need to address the theoretical and philosophical problems of their writing program. By 1983, the funding expired for the grant which had been used to staff the writing center. The college was faced with developing a plan that would be informed by a sound theoretical and pedagogical basis and that would also ensure the continued operation of the Writing Center.

After a series of meetings, participation in a basic language skills institute at the college, a move to a new building, the installation of IBM microcomputers, visits to other campuses, attendance at conferences, and a great deal of dialogue concerning how best to structure the MEC Basic Language Skills Program, the writing faculty recommended that the Writing Center be staffed by a coordinator who, with the assistance of tutors drawn from the college's Learning Center, would serve as a resource person, lab technician, and coordinator. The lab coordinator would be supervised by the basic writing skills coordinator. Therefore, under the current MEC Writing Center model, writing instructors are no longer assigned to the Writing Center. All writing instructors teach writing courses for 4.5 hours, and approximately two-thirds of these instructors bring their classes to the Writing Center for at least 1.5 hours per week. (Some classes, those in the evening and on the weekend, are in the center for two hours.) Since the center must have some open lab time and since some of the faculty who teach basic writing do not wish to use microcomputers in their classrooms, there are basic writing classes which are not scheduled to come to the Writing Center.

While in the Writing Center, instructors confer with students or assign students various kinds of writing tasks. Those instructors who do not bring their students to the center may refer them for individual work or may draw upon the resources (software and skills exercises) of the center in order to supplement the instruction in their courses.

As a result, MEC's Writing Center has become one in which students' instructors present them with the tools, strategies, and resources needed to (a) understand and apply the writing process and (b) become responsible for their own improvement in writing. The MEC Writing Center is informed by a philosophy which provides students with an optimal learning environment for understanding the writing process as they develop fluency, clarity, and correctness, the concepts which underlie the philosophical basis of the writing program. In essence, the evolution of the MEC model reflects a shift in philosophy from a teacher-centered classroom to a more student-centered classroom. Instead of a center where tutors and instructors present students with a discrete set of skills, a hierarchical model, there now exists a center where students collaborate on their writing, one where instructors and tutors confer with students about how to improve and evaluate the content, organization, and mechanics of their essays. Students use the microcomputer to compose, revise, and edit their essays; they use various software programs to reinforce concepts that they have learned in class or to practice solving a variety of writing problems.

Although the philosophy underlying the MEC Writing Center is congruent with current composition theory on the writing process and with the overall philosophy of the MEC Basic Language Skills Program, it by no means reflects the philosophy of all the faculty who teach basic writing. As in many college and university environments, no one philosophy can dictate what goes on in the classroom of every instructor. Competing epistemologies thrive in academe, and Medgar Evers College is no exception. Although the college represents a minority, there exists in the Humanities Division, for example, faculty who advocate a skills-centered, top-down approach to basic writing instruction. These faculty tend either to not utilize the Writing Center or to utilize it in a narrow way; they may teach a lesson that could have easily been taught in a traditional classroom setting, or they may spend several lessons having students review tutorials on how to use a microcomputer. Hence, the MEC Writing Center, although generally based on one philosophy and approach to writing instruction, is also designed to accommodate the needs of faculty who are not necessarily proponents of its philosophy.

The MEC Writing Center, as currently constituted, is a combination of a resource center and microcomputer laboratory for students, tutors, and faculty. There is not a particular curriculum that drives the activities of the center; rather, students, tutors, and faculty determine what happens in the center, and the demands of the center change on a daily basis in order to address and accommodate the needs of the students, tutors, and faculty.

Physical Description

A writing center which addresses the diverse needs of a broad range of students, as well as the competing epistemologies of a faculty, must by its very nature be designed to be flexible enough to serve the needs of all its constituents. The MEC Writing Center is housed in a relatively modern building (built in 1988). It consists of a large room which contains twenty-five IBM PS2 microcomputer work stations, three faculty offices, and four smaller rooms where individual and small-group tutoring occur (figure 1). The twenty-five work stations are grouped in three areas: four to ten computers and a printer are located in each of these areas. Thus, there are 25 computers and four printers in the Writing Center.

The three faculty offices are reserved for the Writing Center co-ordinator, the basic language skills director, and a foreign language instructor. The foreign language lab is adjacent to the Writing Center.

Two of the small tutoring rooms are located within the Writing Center, and the other two are located within the Reading Laboratory, which is adjacent to the Writing Center. While in the Writing Center, one can move to either the Reading Lab or the Language Lab. The tutoring rooms situated in the Writing Center both contain a rectangular table encircled by three to four chairs; one of the rooms (a bit larger than the other) also contains three small tables with microcomputers on them. Each of these tutoring rooms contains a chalkboard. The tutoring rooms in the Reading Laboratory are similarly constructed. A larger tutoring room contains three microcomputers as well as a table and chairs, and the smaller room contains a rectangular table, several chairs, and a chalkboard.

As students enter the Writing Center, they first encounter two small tutoring rooms on their left. As they proceed, they find themselves in the main section of the Writing Center, where they are face-to-face with the microcomputers. Three walls sporting interesting posters, and a row of three faculty offices, constitute the boundaries of this room. Each of the microcomputers in the Writing Center is located on a rectangular table which is actually a typewriter table; there are two microcomputers on each table. The tables are grouped together to form the three computer areas. Cushioned chairs which have wheels and which adjust for a person's height accompany the tables.

During class hours, students do not have access to the core of computers located in the main section of the Writing Center; they have the option of using the computers in the tutorial rooms or requesting the instructor's permission to use computers in the main section of the room. During open lab hours, students may use the computers whenever they choose.

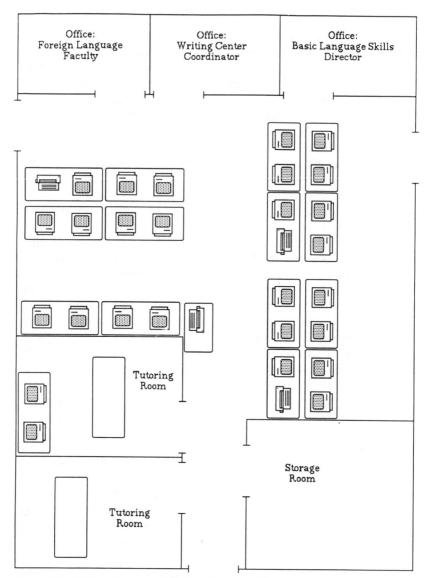

Fig. 1. The Writing Center at Medgar Evers College, CUNY.

Chronology of a Typical Day

Because the MEC Writing Center serves multiple purposes, a typical day is characterized by various kinds of activities: class instruction, walk-in referrals, tutoring, and open-access time. On most days, basic skills classes are scheduled for at least 65 percent of the day, beginning at 9 a.m. and lasting through 10 p.m. When the center is not being used for class instruction, students have "open" lab time. Many of the work stations are in use during this time. Moreover, since the structure of the center enables students to receive tutoring throughout the day, tutoring and walk-in referrals occur from morning through evening. There is usually one period throughout the day when the center is closed for at least one hour in order to provide "down time" for the computers and a transition period for the day and evening staffs.

The number of students using the center on a typical day varies because of differing class schedules; however, approximately 100 students may use the center on a typical day. This includes usage during class time, open lab time, and tutoring. The number of students using the center during finals increases by at least 40 percent. As stated previously, tutoring occurs throughout the day, and two to three students generally work with a tutor for at least one hour per day. In some cases, usually those where the student has a range of writing problems, only one student is assigned to a tutor. Throughout the day, tutors come to the coordinator to request materials and/or to discuss specific student problems. Tutors also frequently consult with one another to discuss strategies and effective tutoring techniques.

Students who wish specific help with a writing task and who may or may not have a writing tutor are referred to as "walk-ins." A walk-in may work with the center coordinator for one session, several short sessions, or sporadic sessions throughout the academic year. The walk-in generally seeks assistance with a particular paper or wants to work on a specific kind of writing task. Some walk-ins are referred by instructors in content-area courses, an occurrence most often associated with courses in the social sciences. During the day, the center coordinator works with the walk-ins, and during the evening, the part-time evening coordinator works with these students. Since most students with writing problems seek the assistance of a tutor, the number of walk-ins is small. Center coordinators may work with a group of twenty-five walk-ins over one semester.

On a typical day, the Writing Center coordinator arrives at 8:45 a.m. and prepares the lab by checking to ensure that software, tutoring materials, and hardware are available and ready for use. When the class enters, the coordinator provides the instructor with three Norton word-processing programs and three disks on sentence fragments. The instructor distributes these programs to students, and the coordinator walks around to review students' facility with the computer; he or she also assists students who have difficulty using the computer as well as those who desire help with generating ideas for their papers, organizing their papers, and determining whether certain sentences are structurally correct. Two student aides also move around the room to assist students who are having technical difficulties with the computer.

The instructor of this class session uses the center to have students work on several tasks. Some students collaborate in pairs in order to critique their introductory paragraphs for an essay; then they use the computer to revise these paragraphs. Another group of students composes, revises, or edits the first drafts of essays it has written. The instructor asks three students to work on sentence fragment tutorials. As students work on various tasks, the instructor moves around the room to review and monitor students' progress. The instructor then spends approximately thirty minutes having individual conferences with students.

At the end of this session (about 10:15 a.m.), the instructor asks students to print out their assignments and to exit the program. He or she collects the tutorials and reminds those who have not completed their assignments to come to the center during open time. The coordinator and/or student aides walk around to ensure that programs have been exited correctly, computers have been turned off, and work stations have been left neat.

Another class enters at 10:30 a.m., and the procedure is repeated. This instructor, however, has the entire class use the lab time to revise essays, and the instructors and student aides move around the classroom to assist students.

The lab is open from noon to 1:30 p.m. During this open lab time, students come to work on their papers for their writing courses as well as other courses they may be taking. The lab coordinator, meanwhile, provides students with software tutorials.

At 1:30 p.m., another class arrives at the center, and this instructor uses the lab to have students work on individual writing tasks. Several students revise drafts of essays, several work on tutorials, and several work on generating ideas for a new essay. The instructor uses this time to talk with each student about his or her paper or about a specific writing task or problem. The coordinator works with a walk-in during this class session, and the student aides assist the students with technical problems.

The center then has open time from 3 p.m. to 5 p.m. Six students come in to work on papers. One student requests a tutorial on verb tense agreement. Some students work individually and two of the students collaborate on their papers; they alternate between talking quietly and writing their papers. The center coordinator works with a walk-in.

The center closes from 5 p.m. to 6 p.m., and the day coordinator leaves. The evening coordinator arrives between 6 p.m. and 7 p.m. to reopen the center. Because of budgetary constraints, the coordinator is not always able to reopen the lab at 6 p.m. In this case, an experienced instructor opens the lab and begins her class. When the evening center coordinator arrives, she ensures that all work stations are ready for use and then distributes any materials that the student or instructor may need. There are no student aides available in the evenings, so the evening center coordinator walks around to monitor students' facility with the computers and to provide technical or tutorial assistance as needed.

A class is scheduled in the Writing Center from 6 p.m. to 8:15 p.m., so the instructor has asked the students to compose an essay. Once they have completed the essay, the students confer briefly with the instructor, who then asks the students to begin revising their essays. Not all of the students complete this assignment, so the instructor tells them that their revisions will be due within two class sessions.

At 8:05 p.m., the instructor asks students to print out their materials and clear their work stations. Another class arrives at 8:15 p.m. These students are anxious to get started, for their instructor has informed them that their revised essays are due by the end of that session, 10:15 p.m. Some students wish to confer with other students before they submit their final drafts, so their anxiety level increases.

Once the class has begun and the center coordinator has ensured that all work stations are functioning properly, she goes to her office because a walk-in has walked in asking for help with a research paper. The evening lab coordinator is fluent in two languages, so she has become a valued resource for ESL students, particularly those of Haitian descent. She assists the student in generating a thesis statement for her paper.

At 10:05 p.m., the coordinator completes her work with the student and returns to the core of the lab, where the instructor has asked students to print out their papers. There is a great amount of talking and moving about as students wait for printers, search for staplers, and proofread their papers one more time. The day has come to a close; the lab coordinator makes sure that all terminals are shut down and that the lab is left clean and orderly.

Clientele

The majority of students serviced by the MEC Writing Center (approximately 90 percent) are enrolled in basic skills writing courses. At least 25 percent of these students are also enrolled in ESL basic writing courses. When the Writing Center first reopened with microcomputers, almost all of the students who used it were enrolled in basic writing; however, as these students began to exit basic skills and to enroll in college English and other content-area courses, they continued to use the Writing Center to write their papers. At present, approximately 20 percent of the students who use the center are not enrolled in basic writing courses.

The MEC Writing Center, therefore, functions as a vital arm of the college's basic writing classes; and faculty, staff, and tutors work collectively to ensure that the needs of students in these courses are met in a way that is in accordance with the division's premise of a student-centered learning environment designed to assist students in understanding the writing process and becoming responsible for their own learning.

Tutors: Selection and Training

The writing tutors at Medgar Evers College are known CUNY-wide for their commitment to working with students. In Peggy Jolly's (1984) article on the financial responsibilities of funding developmental writing programs, she cites Donald Rippley's (1980) statement that tutorial programs reduce attrition and increase the holding power of the schools. The tutors at Medgar Evers certainly help to substantiate this view; they are known for overextending themselves to ensure that those students who have the determination and drive are offered the maximum opportunity for writing improvement.

MEC's tutors are part of the college's Learning Center, and many of them are recruited via word of mouth: they hear about the Learning Center through other tutors and at CUNY-wide tutorial meetings.

Tutors are also referred by the college English coordinator and by the humanities chair. The Learning Center coordinator is chair of the CUNY-wide tutorial program.

Most of the tutors have associate degrees, and all have an overall GPA of at least 3.5 and a minimum of 3.5 in all of their English courses. Most of them are enrolled at Medgar Evers or are graduates of the college. Since MEC does not have English majors, a tutor may have a major in liberal arts, education, psychology, etc. The range of majors among the college's English tutors attests to the fact that a good tutor need not be an English major; he or she must simply have a good command of standard written English and be willing to work with students in a supportive way.

Once tutors are chosen for the Writing Center, they are required to attend a week of training. The training is conducted through the college's Learning Center and is held every semester for prospective and continuing tutors. Seminar leaders from the areas of English, education, and counseling are invited to provide a variety of workshops for the tutors; in addition, senior tutors lead prospective workshops. Underlying the philosophy of the tutor-training program is the notion that tutors cannot tutor until they have established a relationship with their students. Tutors may find themselves in situations where students lack self-confidence, self-esteem, and motivation. They may have to spend part of their tutoring session listening to a student tell them why it is so difficult to go to school, take care of three children, and provide her family with some form of financial stability.

During the tutorial training, tutors role-play the tutor-client relationship, identify strategies for working with learning disabled students, identify strategies for using collaborative learning, and identify and share strategies for successfully working with students.

Training continues more informally during the school semester; once classes begin, tutors hold regular meetings, attend conferences and seminars, and meet with one another informally. The Writing Center coordinator, Learning Center coordinator, and instructors serve as resource persons for the tutors.

Types of Services

Tutoring

The philosophy underlying the Writing Center also forms the philosophical framework for how tutors approach the tutoring of students in writing. Tutors begin by assessing the needs of their students; they then draw upon those resources and strategies which would help them to tutor the student most effectively. The objectives of the tutoring program are derived from a philosophy which is student-centered, or in the words of John Warnock and Tilly Warnock (1984), a philosophy of liberatory learning, one which helps "students to assume authorship of their texts and their lives" (20). The tutor is thus viewed as a facilitator of learning rather than as an authority figure.

In the words of several tutors, "There is no one approach for any student." One tutor states, "When I tutor, I have all of these personalities inside of me: I have Professor A, Professor B, and Professor C. I change my techniques on a daily basis. I use trial and error, and I am always looking for new techniques. I am not afraid to tell students that I do not know the answer, and I often go and ask another tutor for suggestions." Another tutor states, "You have to reach out to the student; you spend a lot of time motivating. It's like forming a spiritual connection."

Since the budget for the Learning Center and Writing Center is really inadequate to meet the needs of the students, most tutors tutor from two to three students at a time; therefore, collaborative learning is emphasized in the tutoring session. During a typical session, tutors introduce a concept that a student has difficulty with, and then they have each student in the tutoring session discuss ways to resolve the problem. All of the students then review their own texts to resolve the problem. When a student has a special problem, such as a learning disability, or a problem with low self-esteem because he or she has failed a course several times, the tutor will request that this student receive one-to-one tutoring.

Tutors spend a great amount of time encouraging students to talk about what they want to write; they find that this is especially useful for ESL students. They show students how to brainstorm, outline, freewrite, etc., and they also find that many students know grammatical terms, but do not understand the concepts underlying these terms; as a result, tutors spend a good deal of time trying to make abstract concepts concrete. Rather than teach grammatical concepts as discrete skills, they provide students with writing tasks in which students are forced to focus on determining their own meanings and intentions. As much of the research in composition confirms, tutors find that the time spent teaching grammar is not valuable for a student who has difficulty understanding that writing is really a process that involves thinking, composing, and revising. As a result, tutors teach grammar in the context of the student's writing and set up writing situations in which students learn to identify and then take steps to resolve their own grammatical and rhetorical problems in writing.

Computers

As stated previously, the Writing Center is equipped with twenty-five IBM PS II computers. Therefore, all students who come to the Writing Center with their basic skills courses learn the *Norton Textra Word-Processing Program*. They are required to purchase the program and are told that it is a tool they can use throughout their years at the college. This program is menu driven and has an on-line student handbook; students spend at least one session reviewing the tutorials for how to use the program, and by the second class session, most are ready to begin composing short essays.

In addition to using the microcomputer for word processing, students use the microcomputer to review grammatical and rhetorical concepts such as paragraphing, developing a thesis, and organizing an essay. The Writing Center is equipped with a variety of software programs related to grammar and composition.

Testing

Writing assessment can take many forms, and this is the case in the MEC Writing Center. Instructors, for the most part, determine how students are assessed. Students are assessed at different levels as they progress through the MEC Basic Language Skills Program. Those students enrolled in basic skills writing courses are placed in these courses on the basis of their performance on the CUNY Writing Assessment Test (CUNY WAT). Once placed in these courses, students are given a diagnostic exam to validate their performance on the WAT; those whose performance on the diagnostic exam differs significantly from their performance on the WAT are referred to another level of basic skills. Since students exit basic writing courses as a result of their performance on the MEC Writing Departmental Exam, the MEC Writing Center does not play a role in assessing the performance of students enrolled in basic writing courses.

The only kind of assessment performed at the MEC Writing Center is the assessment conducted when students come in to be tutored. Students who are classified as walk-ins may be asked to write an essay, or tutors may require students to write essays in order to determine areas of weakness. Many students come to the tutoring sessions with essays that have been returned to them by their instructors; in these cases, the tutor or the center coordinator reviews the student's essay in order to determine where to begin with the student. Some students may bring a form with them that outlines the areas in which they need to work; this form is obtained from the student's instructor and enables both the tutor and student to target the areas of weakness.

Materials

Students, tutors, and faculty have access to a wide range of materials in the Writing Center. These include software materials related to grammar and composition, writing texts, and specific writing activities which reinforce grammatical and rhetorical skills. Among the software materials are a practical composition series, Quintilian analysis, and various grammatical and sentence structure tutorials. While some of these tutorials merely simulate writing activities from a textbook, they also provide students with another means of examining grammatical structures and identifying and resolving grammatical problems. The materials are located in the office of the center coordinator and in one of the tutorial rooms of the Writing Center.

Outreach

Tutors who tutor in the Writing Center have also worked or are currently working in several outreach programs, including a liberty grant program at Erasmus Hall High School and a collaborative MEC/ Thomas Jefferson High School writing-across-the-curriculum project. In these projects, tutors help high school students to improve their reading and writing skills in their subject-area courses. The Erasmus Hall High School program is located on the MEC campus; the MEC/ Thomas Jefferson project, no longer in existence because of budgetary restrictions, was located in a social studies enrichment center at Thomas Jefferson High School.

Administration

Faculty and Staff

The MEC Writing Center is staffed by two persons who function as full-time and part-time center coordinators. Both coordinators are supervised by the basic language skills director, who serves as the director of basic skills and the coordinator of basic writing. This full-time faculty person is a member of the Humanities Division. The full-time coordinator is assisted by work-study students who serve as student aides.

Budget

Since the MEC Writing Center is part of the Humanities Division, salaries for the center coordinators are paid out of this division's budget. These coordinators are appointed by the division and are reviewed annually by the division's Personnel and Budget Committee.

The supplies for the Writing Center are obtained through various college and divisional grants. There is no divisional operating budget allocated for supplies and materials.

Records

Since the majority of the students who use the lab are currently enrolled in basic writing courses, no records are kept for these students; however, tutors keep logs for their students. The center coordinator keeps records related to supplies, equipment, and hardware. Consequently, recordkeeping for the Writing Center is not extensive.

The Future

Medgar Evers College was formed in response to the identified needs of the community, and it has continually been identified as a college where struggle is a way of life. In view of the fact that this concept is infused into the mission of the college and in view of the direction that the MEC Writing Center has taken in the past two years, one might say that the center is currently involved in a struggle to maintain its existence in the midst of an economic crisis.

The center is in its infancy in one way; it has been in existence since 1975, but has had microcomputers for only two years. Faculty are still in the midst of determining how best to use the center and how to modernize it so that microcomputers can be networked and instructors can use them to individualize their responses to student papers.

Furthermore, like many other colleges, especially those within large urban environments, Medgar Evers College is in the midst of a budget crisis, one that has inevitably affected the Writing Center. As a result, the center is faced with having to justify its existence and to reaffirm its theoretical and pedagogical stance to the administration. The center's philosophy is an eclectic one, and sometimes eclectic approaches to instruction tend to symbolize weaknesses rather than strengths to college administrations. This is where the MEC Writing Center is now; it is again faced with an economic crisis; it is faced with a visit from the Middle States Accreditation Team; and it must find a strategy for evaluating what it has accomplished in a productive and constructive way. Perhaps this exemplifies a never-ending struggle in those institutions that house writing centers.

The MEC Writing Center is faced with a difficult challenge, one that involves staying alive in the throes of financial strife, political power plays, and waning morale. The faculty of the Humanities Division rose to the occasion once before; I believe they will again. The key to the center's survival is for faculty to reinforce the idea that the premise and philosophy of the center are theoretically and pedagogically sound. They must demonstrate to the administration that a student-centered writing center informed by a philosophical framework will ultimately be more effective in improving a student's attitude and performance in writing than a center without a context in which to frame its operation; moreover, this type of center will be more effective in increasing, as Donald Rippley (1980) would say, "the holding power" of the institution.

Without students, the institution will not survive; the key is to find effective ways for ensuring that students persist and that they grow as language learners. The future of the MEC Writing Center is thereby dependent on the degree to which writing faculty will help the administration to understand the necessity of having a Writing Center which is in tandem with the philosophy of the MEC Basic Language Skills Program. At MEC, so goes the way of the real world as we examine writing centers in ever-changing contexts.

Works Cited

Jolly, Peggy. 1984. "The Bottom Line: Financial Responsibility. In *Writing Centers: Theory and Administration,* edited by Gary A. Olson, 101–14. Urbana: NCTE.

Rippley, Donald. 1980. "I Never Get No Respect . . . Or Support Either." *Journal of Developmental and Remedial Education* 4: 12–13.

Warnock, Tilly, and John Warnock. 1984. "Liberatory Writing Centers: Restoring Authority to Writers." In *Writing Centers: Theory and Administration,* edited by Gary A. Olson, 16–23. Urbana: NCTE.

3 The Writing Centers at the University of Toledo: An Experiment in Collaboration

Joan A. Mullin
University of Toledo–Bancroft Campus

Luanne Momenee
University of Toledo–Scott Park Campus

One of thirteen state-supported, post-secondary institutions in Ohio, the University of Toledo has an open-admissions policy and currently enrolls close to 25,000 students on its five campuses. The original Bancroft campus sits on 255 acres at the western edge of the City of Toledo. Other campuses include the Scott Park Community and Technical College (ComTech); the Toledo Museum of Art; the R. A. Stranahan, Sr., Arboretum; and Seagate Center, a convention/university facility in downtown Toledo. Together, they comprise eight colleges and offer 140 programs of study, including eighteen doctoral programs. (These are 1990–91 statistics from the *Resource Consumption Report*, compiled by the Institutional Research Office.)

Over the past several years, the university has experienced a significant increase in student enrollment. Part of this is a response to the economic depression which has affected this formerly thriving industrial community. The newly unemployed not only find that their skills are no longer in demand but that they need more education in order to compete for available jobs. Therefore, while it is not surprising that 28 percent of the total undergraduate population in the fall of 1990 were students twenty-five years and older, new admissions also included a growing number of minorities and students with special needs. Recently, emphasis has been placed on attracting honors scholars, and this year, sixty-two National Merit finalists attended the university. While the university has always attracted students from as far

---

In the sections of this essay devoted specifically to the Bancroft Campus, the speaker is Joan Mullin; for the sections on the Scott Park Campus, Luanne Momenee. The sections on collaboration feature the collaborative voice of both authors.

away as New York and Chicago, it has nonetheless been perceived as an urban university which attracts students from only a few surrounding counties. Students now come from a broader national geographic sphere, including nearly every state and an international population drawn from all over the world.

The Bancroft and Scott Park campuses are located about a mile and a half from each other. That short but significant physical distance has long determined the state of the collegial and professional distance maintained by those on each campus. When both of us began our jobs, Joan at the Bancroft campus and Luanne at the Scott Park campus, we were not aware of each other's existence. Yet within a year, we saw the necessity of working together with others toward providing a comprehensive support system for our students. In the four years we have both been here, we have seen the changes brought about by a substantial increase in student population and complicated by significant administrative changes, state budget crises, and the voting in of a faculty union. Fortunately, the chaos which accompanies such changes bred opportunities for positive change, and the Learning Assistance Center at Scott Park and the Writing Center on the Bancroft campus have flourished. We see this growth as a result not only of our own staffs' hard work, continued administrative backing, and growing support from faculty, but also of our working relationship together. What follows are our individual stories and our collaborative narrative.

History

Bancroft Campus

When I was hired as the first Writing Center director for the Bancroft campus, it was with the intention that before a writing-across-the-curriculum program could be established, a support service must be in place. However, it was later explained to me that, because of overcrowded conditions and a tight budget, I would have no clerical staff, no typewriter, no furniture, and, in fact, no office (though I could share one with an emeritus professor in the Honors Program suite). My contract stated that, because of these constraints, it should be understood that I would spend my first year "as a presence on campus." Since the idea of walking around campus wearing a sandwich board declaring I was the new Writing Center director did not appeal to me, and since I had a vigorously supportive dean in the College of Arts and Sciences, with which I was affiliated, I soon found a typewriter, desk, supplies, and chair in my shared office—and promises of more.

Indeed, though I arrived at the end of June, by the start of school at the end of September, I had a half-time secretary, permission to teach a writing theory and collaboration course as an independent study through the English department, most of the rest of the Honors Program suite (two small rooms plus a reception area), and the promise of more furniture plus all the tutors I could hire in order to start a writing center that January. Along the way, the chair of the secondary education department—a Ph.D. in English—managed to get some of the last funds tagged for special graduate assistantships. I now had, through the English department, a graduate assistant. I had also spent the summer meeting all the arts and sciences chairs and any university administrator I could think of, as well as trying to find the learning disabilities resource person whom everyone thought we had, but no one could name. In exploring campus perceptions about writing and the student population, I learned that tutorial services were suspect. It was generally believed that tutors of subject areas completed their students' work for them. In addition, tutorial services, as a whole, were viewed as remedial, and in some cases, as services for people "who shouldn't be here in the first place." Because of these obvious barriers to the idea of a writing center, I was careful to explain the nondirective philosophy which guided writing center work. As understanding increased with visits, so, too, did support. By the time January came and the Writing Center opened, some faculty requested class presentations in which services would be introduced to students.

Meanwhile, the soon-to-be-tutors were getting a crash course in collaborative, nondirective tutoring. The students in the writing theory and collaboration course had the first three weeks of winter quarter to learn all they could before the center opened. The initial clientele came largely from the international community, but because of the excellent work of those first tutors, the center soon attracted students more representative of the campus population.

By the third year, the work load was too heavy, and the administration agreed that I could hire an assistant director; but by the fourth year, the center also had two graduate assistants, cooperative tutor exchanges with those trained in special education, fourteen part-time tutors, six computers, three printers (including two lasers), and ample furniture to fill the entire suite plus a temporary annex we are allowed to use when we have an overflow of students. Other efforts that year stimulated support from faculty: faculty now receive copies of daily tutor reports, if their students request that these be sent; class visits can be requested via a form sent out at the beginning of each quarter; brochures, posters, and bookmarks are highly visible around campus;

faculty are asked for their syllabi, assignments, and writing instructions. In addition, the staff's participation on campus committees (Retention Council, Strategic Planning, faculty search committees, and the like) introduces faculty to our services and philosophy.

What gave impetus to the Writing Center this fourth year was its connection with, as well as the growth of, the Writing-Across-the-Curriculum Program. With the adoption of this program in the College of Arts and Sciences, the creation of a WAC implementation committee (for which I serve as chair), and the inclusion of a campus-wide Writing-Across-the-Curriculum Program in the university's new five-year strategic plan, both WAC and the Writing Center seem well supported. This is evidenced by the University of Toledo Foundation grants totaling $20,000 for tutors and writing workshops over the past two years. Application for this money is competitive and is granted in addition to our regular university line budget.

Scott Park Campus

Enrollment at ComTech numbers about 4,600 students who, for the most part, plan to receive an associate's degree in one of the forty-five technical programs offered. A significant number of students who apply to the university's baccalaureate programs are counseled to enroll at ComTech, take developmental education courses, and bring up their grade-point averages. Hence, the college has become an unofficial port of entry for these "conferenced" students. However, over 45 percent of our graduates continue their education at a four-year institution.

Application for admission to ComTech mandates that all students take placement tests to determine whether they will be required to register for prerequisite math, reading, or writing courses. If students have to take two or more of these courses, an additional introductory course orienting them to university studies is required. The Learning Assistance Center (LAC) completes this support system, offering students opportunities for enhancing their chances for success while enrolled at the college.

Before I was employed as the LAC's first manager, I had taught developmental writing classes at the college and tutored in the Writing Lab. The college administration and the director of Developmental Education had determined that in order to make the center more viable, a full-time coordinator was needed for the LAC. Entering the college that first day as the LAC manager, I had the notion that somehow the position would be a temporary one, since it would not require too much time to set up a workable system for providing services to the few students who came to the center seeking help. Looking at the piles of work today, more than four years later, I have to laugh as I think back on that time when we tutored a total of 400 students during a school year. In the time that I have been at the college, we have tutored over 15,000 students. During the past year alone, more than 5,000 tutorials took place in the LAC.

Prior to my appointment, services were provided by a skeleton staff of peer tutors; several math and accounting faculty members, who volunteered their office-hour time to meet with students in the lab; and a part-time basic writing instructor, who worked approximately ten to twelve hours each week tutoring in the Writing Lab. If it had not been for the meticulous recordkeeping of this writing tutor, ComTech administrators would never have realized the necessity of hiring a manager for the LAC.

The fact that I had taught at the college and had made concerted efforts to meet and network with faculty members during that time enhanced their acceptance of me and my nonfaculty position as manager. Because I had taught with them and knew current pedagogy, they trusted that I would promote a nondirective approach to tutoring students. I continued to talk with faculty and administrators to determine their perceptions of the LAC and the services we should offer.

Because the Scott Park campus is physically isolated from the Bancroft campus by nearly two miles, I decided to concentrate public relations efforts on the faculty and administration at this college. Visits with the deans and members of the faculty, follow-up letters, memos detailing plans, requests for suggestions for implementing programs and for tutors poured out of the office. Frequently, I felt that I was running a one-woman show. While verbal support was prolific and encouraging from administrators and faculty, funding was limited, and I found myself alone in my office sharing secretarial services with eighteen faculty members from the general studies department. Undaunted, I initiated a campaign to raise the salaries of the student tutors from the minimum-wage level they had been receiving to a salary more commensurate with the professional standards they were expected to maintain. Furthermore, instructor/tutors would be compensated through the college budget, a practice which continues and has proven to be a great benefit to the LAC.

Since I believe every student should become acquainted with the center, I took my "dog and pony" show on the road and visited as many classes as would have me during the first week of each quarter that year. While the visits are less frequent now, I still make an effort each quarter to let the students know where we are located and to tell them about the many services we offer in the Learning Assistance Center.

With the network tapped and some groundwork laid, I began the task of developing a centralized records management system, employing a user-friendly database that had been recommended by a consultant from the university computer center. My prior experience as a tutor had made me aware that records in all tutorial situations other than in the writing area were, at best, haphazard and, in some cases, nonexistent. The database has proven a valuable tool in generating statistical information for report writing, tracking progress of the students using the center, and providing a comprehensive picture of the increasing numbers of programs we are integrating into the LAC.

An outside grant (Carl Perkins) provides funds for improving the delivery of our services to academically and economically disadvantaged students enrolled in a two-year program. As a result, we now have a full-time secretary and student clerical help, a part-time supervisor of the Supplemental Instruction program, and approximately twenty tutors each quarter. Still, our student evaluations indicate that we should provide more tutors each day for longer hours.

Our Collaboration

One of the first memos that came across Luanne's desk from the director of Developmental Education suggested that she contact Joan to explore possible areas for collaboration. We met soon after and exchanged ideas about how we planned to proceed with our individual programs. Both of us believed that this meeting was fundamental to the events that have followed; it was an open door through which we could explore academic support programs.

We also found that when we exchanged ideas, our combined perspectives gave us a more complete picture of students' needs. Then, too, because we each operated out of different colleges as well as campuses, our joint perspectives gave us a broader view of the politics at the university. We began to coordinate our experiences and our services with the directors of Retention Services and Student Support Services. When we realized that one of our offices had a particularly well-developed service, we would transfer funds to that office and eliminate our duplicated efforts. Therefore, instead of continuing to train their own writing tutors, Student Services funded LAC and Writing Center tutors.

Similarly, Luanne and the director of the Center for the Physically and Mentally Challenged (CPMC) talked extensively about collaborative efforts to provide services to his clients through the LAC, and the CPMC initiated a client referral system with the Writing Center. The director of the CPMC also called during spring quarter of that first year to tell Luanne he knew of a grant which would help employ a part-time specialist for ComTech. The Writing Center took advantage of this specialist and worked with her when tutoring students with special needs.

As we became more familiar with the capabilities of each other's offices, we made frequent referrals and, when appropriate, mentioned each other's services and accomplishments at university committee meetings. We decided to formally organize ourselves into a Committee on Learning Enhancement (COLE). One of the COLE meetings targeted a need to network with services in other institutions; from that need evolved the successful first Tutoring Colloquium on Learning Enhancement, in 1990. This colloquium, which drew participants from Ohio's and Michigan's community colleges, four-year colleges, and universities, was followed by an even more popular conference attended by over 200 people, in 1991, featuring keynote speaker Uri Treisman. This time, more faculty and administrators attended, and participants came from as far away as New York and South Dakota.

But the primary goal of COLE has always been to improve our range of services and their delivery to students. To that end, COLE members coordinate academic student services on campus to develop a network of referrals, avoid duplication of services, and share research and staff when appropriate; we hope to deliver quality assistance to students with a minimum of bureaucratic inconvenience. In so doing, we act in the best interests of the students by providing immediate support and in the best fiscal interests of the university. We believe that those of us who are directly responsible for the students can most appropriately distribute funds for those services if we coordinate our efforts.

Physical Description

Bancroft Campus

Our campus, serving over 20,000 students, has a woefully small center due to severe space shortages. However, our location carries its own charm. The Writing Center occupies a suite of offices near the northwestern end of the campus. While not a well-known structure—one student who followed directions from her teacher ended up in a broom closet in another building—Tucker Hall's charm and comfort recall the days when it originally served as faculty apartments, before it housed offices. The three-story, English Tudor row houses contain the history, political science, and philosophy departments. The Writing Center occupies one "apartment" on the first floor. This does give the physically handicapped access to us, but our 619 square feet of usable space—minus closets and bathroom— leaves little room for tutor meetings and privacy. We are to be moved to larger, permanent quarters "soon" (figure 1).

Scott Park Campus

The Learning Assistance Center (LAC) is located on the second floor of the Learning Resource Center (LRC) at ComTech. For the most part, sharing space with the LRC has worked out well. Students may move from a tutoring situation to using some of the audiovisual materials and software available at the circulation desk. Occasionally, we have found ourselves in a territorial skirmish, but generally, the marriage has been a good one. The LAC is housed in a spacious open area, encompassing approximately half of the 7,500-square-foot room. Alcoves and tables are allocated for specific tutorial services (figure 2).

Also located on this floor are the Reading Lab and the Computer-Assisted Instruction Lab, where basic writing is taught. A circulation desk and book stacks divide the room physically through the center. On the far side of the LRC, one will find the Center for the Physically and Mentally Challenged and Student Services, where students receive specialized help, as well as the DEAL Center, which provides resources for parents who are receiving aid to dependent children.

Chronology of a Typical Day

Bancroft Campus

Any typical day is hectic. The secretary—still a three-quarter-time position—arrives by eight in the morning to start the coffee pot, straighten up the tutorial areas, and pull files on students who have scheduled appointments. She leaves the files out for the tutors before she begins entering data from the previous day's tutorials. By 8:30 a.m., the assistant director and director have either checked in (before going off to various committee meetings, class presentations, or classes they may be teaching) or have met briefly with the secretary to discuss anything which "must be done today."

Depending on their schedules, the assistant director and/or the director will read the previous day's tutor reports before they are sent to instructors in the morning mail. These reports are read for content, accuracy, and appropriate wording—even our well-trained tutors may give in to a moment of frustration and indicate that the assignment was ambiguous or lacked clear direction. If there is some question about the tutorial report, a note is attached, and the tutor will discuss with the director or assistant director whether any changes are necessary. This morning reading is a good time for both administrators to find out what has happened during other tutorials: What issues are repeated? What resources are lacking in the center? What recurring or unusual sessions could be discussed at this week's in-service?

By 9 a.m., the tutors have wandered in, poured their coffee or tea, chatted briefly with the staff, met with the secretary, greeted the first students, and settled in for their four-hour shift. From 9 a.m. to 1 p.m., they will tutor, write their reports, and tutor some more. If there is a break in the day—something which is never predictable—they will help answer telephones, schedule appointments, take walk-in students, or read and discuss strategies for improving their tutoring. The assistant director, director, and tutors will also discuss the tutor reports, our own writing projects, research material recently read, or ideas for the next in-service meeting. We also may take advantage of a break by listening to one another's tutorials; we often develop our own best strategies that way. All of us exchange stories to continue improving our nondirective collaborations with students.

On alternate Fridays, the Writing Center closes its doors from 1–2 p.m. for our tutor meeting (this day happens to coincide with payday). We usually begin with daily business ("Keep writing legibly on those tutor reports, please"), proceed to a special topic reinforced by some brainstorming and freewriting (as when we collaboratively constructed our mission statement and tutor evaluation procedures), or have a special guest. While this last category often includes an instructor who explains his or her area of expertise (cultural differences in Asian populations, learning modalities, business report writing), our last guest this year was the president of the university.

We had asked the president to learn who we are and what we do by attending our meeting. As usually happens with all guests, he became involved in a theoretical/pedagogical discussion centering on an instructor who penalized a student for writing an excellent argument which, unfortunately, did not support that instructor's view. "What is

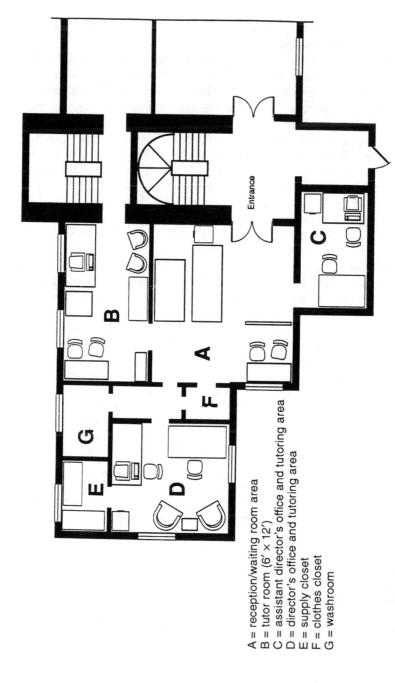

A = reception/waiting room area
B = tutor room (6' × 12')
C = assistant director's office and tutoring area
D = director's office and tutoring area
E = supply closet
F = clothes closet
G = washroom

Fig. 1. The Writing Center at the University of Toledo, Bancroft Campus.

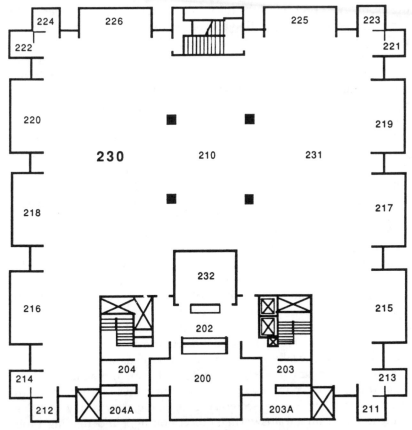

210 = book stacks
211 = manager
213 = advisor
215 = staff workroom
217 = writing lab
219 = supplemental instruction
221 = computer programmer
223 = faculty resource room
225/231 = reading lab
226/230 = computer-assisted instruction lab
Open area near 211 and 213 = math and accounting labs
Open area near 217 = reading/study strategies lab
212–224 (even numbers) = Office for Special Services, Center for
    Physically and Mentally Challenged, the DEAL Center.

Fig. 2. The Learning Assistance Center at the University of Toledo, Scott Park Campus.

the best way to proceed?" the tutor asked. The president immediately sympathized with our position and began to explore ways of working with both the student and the faculty member.

We moved into a discussion of our mission statement and its relation to the university's mission, exchanging ideas about the misconceptions faculty and students have about the Writing Center. All of this, while part of a normal agenda, also served to educate our special guest. After taking our mission statement for dissemination to the faculty in the fall (under his signature), the president wrote a thank-you which included how wonderful "it was to be a part of an academic discussion again." As with most administrators on campus, the president has theoretically and verbally supported the Writing Center, but this opportunity to experience who we are proved invaluable for us—and, we would like to think, for the president.

After a meeting, while the tutors concentrate on the writers, the director and assistant director proceed with paperwork, tutor students as scheduled or as needed, work on PR materials, meet with faculty who are planning writing-intensive courses or who want a class presentation, gather materials for the Writing Center resource files, teach, attend meetings, answer tutors' questions, answer faculty telephone calls about their own research, and sometimes get lunch before 3 p.m. With luck, the director and assistant director may even leave before 6 p.m., though technically, the day runs from 8:15 a.m. to 5 p.m.

The tutors, meanwhile, change shifts at 1 p.m. and again at 5 p.m. At 4:30 p.m. (or 2 p.m. or 3 p.m., depending on how her hours are arranged that week), the secretary goes home after a day of filing, photocopying, phone answering, "receptioning," and fielding problems (students upset by instructor's comments, a graduate student who wants a tutor "now," an instructor calling to clarify an assignment). This means that the evening tutors either take calls or turn on the answering machine until their day ends at 9 p.m., when the coffee and teapots are unplugged, the lights turned out, and the door locked—finally—unless, of course, the director or assistant director either returns or is still there, filling out the last report, writing conference or research papers, trying to find a strategy which will answer that last student's "assignment from hell."

Scott Park Campus

My first inclination in describing a typical day in the LAC is to say (and I believe most tutorial administrators will agree) that every day is atypical. Yet the thread of continuity and day-to-day management unfailingly weaves its way through the fabric of the daily routine.

A day in the LAC begins at 7:30 a.m., when our computer "expert" arrives. Her first duty is to update records from the previous day's visits. I used the word *expert* in quotes because she has, with very little formal training, mastered the use of the computer so that her role has expanded from that of an assistant in the reading lab to that of the person responsible for our three computer databases and for tracking student persistence through the developmental courses. She enjoys the hour she has before the secretary and I arrive, since it is the only time of the day totally free from distractions.

At 8:30 a.m. the secretary comes in, takes care of filing for the day, tidies up the reception area, and photocopies the list of appointments and meetings for the manager and the academic advisor for developmental education, whose office is also located in the LAC. Also, the secretary is responsible for managing our testing service, so she arranges the tests for the day.

By 8:45, the manager and advisor have arrived, checked their schedules for the day, and addressed any urgent questions or problems. A brief meeting with the secretary usually clears the agenda. My day is consumed by meetings, public relations efforts, and advising of students.

Since the labs are handled on a drop-in basis and lab schedules depend on tutors' commitments to teaching and school, the hours vary for each lab; however, labs are usually open 25–30 hours each week. I will focus for the rest of this typical day on the Writing Lab.

One writing tutor comes in at 9:30, puts out her welcome sign, pulls reference books out of the cabinet, readies pens, papers, etc., and waits for business. A student writer arrives for the first time this quarter, registers at the reception desk for this free service, receives a tutor's "activity" sheet, and comes to the writing table, usually with all his anxiety intact. The student is followed closely by three more writers, who pick up their activity sheets at the reception desk, come to the writing area, and settle into working on their assignments while waiting for the tutor to see each of them.

One may question the advisability of open labs, but we believe they provide a nonthreatening atmosphere for the less-assured writer. While we do accept appointments for tutoring, we have found that many students feel less intimidated when they can simply walk in and ask for help. Moreover, many students discuss their writing progress or problems with one another as they wait, and we find that such a discussion is an excellent opportunity for unstructured collaboration.

A second writing tutor comes in from 10 a.m. until 2 p.m. and works with students during this busy time of the day. At times, each tutor may be working with as many as four students. The writing tutors work with the students, helping them to understand that writing is a process, and create a dialogue through which the student writers are able to discern their needs. For example, after they hear a few introductory comments and several open-ended questions about the purpose of the writing assignment, student writers are able to focus more clearly on the approach they will take in their writing.

Sometimes, however, student writers require a more directive approach from the tutor. Consequently, tutors will spend time demonstrating a method, follow it with guided practice, and finally get the student to practice writing independently. For instance, verbalizing thought processes as they proceed, the tutors may demonstrate how the student can combine short, choppy sentences into complex or compound ones. When the student understands the principle, the tutor guides the student through the practice of writing complex and compound sentences. Then, the student is ready to practice the sentence-writing techniques independently. The entire process may be repeated several times until the writer feels more confident about writing. The flexibility of the open lab concept supports this method, since the tutor is able to spend as much time as necessary with the writer.

The tutors continue to meet with students throughout the day, assisting with their individual writing problems. The tutorial activity sheet is filled out and returned to the reception desk, where the information is entered into the computer. Then the sheet is placed in the student's file to be picked up the next time the student visits the Writing Lab. This activity sheet often acts as an icebreaker, giving the writer and the tutor a starting point for subsequent tutorials.

The Writing Lab closes from 2:30 until 4:30 p.m., when another tutor arrives to work with student writers during the evening hours, usually until 8:30 p.m., when the lab closes for the day.

This scene in the writing area is repeated at all the tutoring stations. An average of 1,700 tutorials, of which approximately 700 are writing tutorials, takes place in the LAC each quarter.

The secretary and student aides are in the office until 5 p.m. They are busy answering telephones, making appointments, meeting students, helping them register for services, proctoring tests, and handling general office business.

Clientele

Bancroft Campus

The Writing Center staff works with everyone. Although initially beset by images of remediation, we have gained a staunch following of faculty and students who know that good writers bounce their ideas off others. This group continues to tell others; so while some prejudice against any tutorial service still exists on our campus, a growing number of writers from across the university community who use our services helps dispel the bias. For example, I just took a call from a business professor who was referred to the Writing Center by another colleague. Since he is a new convert to the Writing Center, I tried to explain that we should go over the paper together. "Oh," he said, "you want to teach me how to write. Well, I need that!" That positive attitude typifies the response from faculty who hear about our work from others.

The diversity of the university's student population is well represented in the Writing Center. A majority of our undergraduate writers come from the English or composition classes because approximately 6,000 freshmen take these courses each year; the bulk of the writing on campus is still assigned in these classes. About 15 percent of our students come from the history department, across the hall, and another 15 percent come from the College of Engineering. The remaining students have assignments from across the disciplines, though there are also special populations that we serve. Sophomore education students must pass a fifteen-minute essay exam, which determines whether they will be allowed to pursue their major; students who fail that exam often come in for essay strategies—and encouragement. A business professor has his students tour the local Jeep plant and write a report, which at some stage, must be worked on in the Writing Center.

In all cases, our ability to work with students is limited by our lack of space. Even though we are open 49 hours per week, we can only serve—working at full capacity—1,000 students per quarter in the center itself. However, in addition to assisting those students who come into the center, we also link tutors to writing-intensive classes. In a given quarter, this new project allows us to work with about 300 additional students in history, geography, sociology, educational philosophy, English, philosophy, and political science. Seldom, however, is there an extra conference room or corner for tutorial meetings in any department. About 80–88 percent of our student tutoring is with undergraduates. Though the College of Arts and Sciences is the home base for the Writing Center, we generally attract majors in equal numbers from arts and sciences, business, and engineering, with education majors representing the majority of the other students. The remaining 12 percent of the students are masters and doctoral candidates from various fields. No one field dominates the graduate area, though English majors do not show up and engineering students consider us their best friend. Since we began a writing-across-the-curriculum program in pharmacy, our population from that group is beginning to increase; the same is true for nursing. Any of our hours prove inconvenient for those students who work and attend school through University College, but we still work with a small percentage of those students as well as a few students from ComTech. This latter group shows up because we have longer hours than the LAC on the Scott Park campus. Because of the Law School's constitution, we may not work with any of the law students; that school considers collaboration of any kind to be plagiarism.

Consistently, around 60 percent of our writers are what we term "self-referred"; the remaining 40 percent are referred by an instructor or advisor. Interestingly, despite all of our publicity, the vast majority of students initially hear about the Writing Center from their friends. That percentage has shifted in such a way that students now report that 55 percent of them first heard about the center from their teachers (or through our class presentations), 20 percent from friends, 15 percent from advisors, and the remaining percentage from other offices on campus.

Seventy-five to 80 percent of our writers consider English their first language, while the remaining group reports that its primary language originates in either the Middle East, Asia, Southeast Asia, or South America. The international students have other resources they can use—such as the American Language Institute on campus—but they also tend to work with and help one another, in addition to using the Writing Center. This situation will change significantly in the future because the new Writing-Across-the-Curriculum Program went into effect this year. As a result, international students will find more writing required of them than in the past.

Scott Park Campus

On the whole, the student population at ComTech is different from that at the Bancroft campus. Many students who apply for admission are underprepared for college course work and are placed in developmental courses. Many are displaced workers who are exploring the possibility of a college education as an avenue to career changes. Many plan to transfer to a baccalaureate program, either after they complete their associate degree or after they improve their grade-point average. Add to this picture the students who plan to work either full- or part-time and raise a family while attending school full-time, and one has a fairly good idea of the student population.

The LAC is open to all students at the university. But because of the campus' location, most students who use the LAC are enrolled at ComTech. Though the LAC is part of the Developmental Education Program, we see ourselves as serving the entire student population and often working with skilled writers as well as the underprepared.

Our Collaboration

One of the problems evident in the Writing Center is our inability to work effectively with students who have special needs. Limited space and staff prevent the Bancroft campus from having the kind of resource already available to students at ComTech's LAC: a learning disabilities specialist. Writing Center staff now refer students to the LAC specialist for assessment, tutoring, and advising. In return, the LAC specialist's advice has increased our staff's knowledge about special students and tutoring practices that support them. But because of our offices' continual exchange about this group of students, the two of us have been able to help students who were on the Bancroft campus find much-needed courses in study skills and time management at ComTech. It is also not unusual for us to discover students who drift between the two campuses, dropping and failing courses and accumulating negative self-images because their special needs have never been assessed. Between the two of us, we can muster enough contacts, guidance, and advice to steer these students toward successful academic experiences. This collaboration benefits not only the student but both of our offices, introducing each of us to the other's unique campus resources at the same time that each campus sees our collaborative efforts.

Tutors

Bancroft Campus

Over the past few years, we have worked toward the following tutor requirements: a course in current writing theory and pedagogy taught through the English or secondary education departments, demonstrated knowledge of the writing process and competency in grammar, and an understanding of nondirective tutoring. Experience can substitute for some of these, but we seldom schedule new tutors for more than one shift the first quarter they work.

Prospective tutors fill out an application form that provides background and references. They come in with writing samples for an interview, during which they are asked to read a sample student paper, analyze its strengths and weaknesses, and explain how they would work with the student. Despite the drift of conversation during the interview, it is this latter request which often tells us a great deal about the tutor. One student with excellent grades, training, and references looked at the student paper, reached across my desk, grabbed a pen and started marking all the errors, smiling as she did so. Her subsequent analysis and procedure assured us that her directive approach would be a real barrier to collaborative work.

At the beginning of fall quarter we have three evenings of workshops for new and veteran tutors. We provide food, topics (usually decided upon by the veteran tutors), and guest speakers from campus and from among our own staff. During this time, we talk about new questions and research on writing theory, encouraging tutors to pursue their own questions. Of course, we outline standard office procedures, but we also create new ones from the group's suggestions. We point out that recent articles will be available in a tutor folder or put in mailboxes for discussion at a tutor meeting, and we talk about keeping a tutor journal and sharing our own writing. The tone set during this initial meeting carries us into our daily Writing Center life, the bi-monthly meetings and the three-day workshops for winter and spring quarters.

Our tutors reflect the diversity of the university population. They range in age from about nineteen to sixty and include independent journalists; reading teachers; composition instructors; graduate students in English and history; and undergraduate peer tutors in English, philosophy, chemistry, pharmacy, sociology, or education. The center has two graduate assistants from the English department, but as more departments expand their writing-intensive courses, additional graduate students from other disciplines will be trained in writing theory and practice. These graduate students from other disciplines take a writing theory course during fall quarter, apprentice in the center during winter quarter, and then work in both their department and the Writing Center during spring quarter.

Scott Park Campus

Many of our student tutors are referred by instructors from both campuses; some regularly send memos recommending students. Frequently, one of the tutors will mention a friend or classmate who would be a good tutor. Some of our tutors have been tutored themselves and have a respect and appreciation for the position. All candidates fill out an application form and are interviewed by me. During the interview, we address the philosophy and ethics of tutoring in a college setting and discuss their perceptions about tutoring adult students. Additionally, candidates write a brief commentary on their perceptions of tutoring and what they believe they can contribute as tutors. Once they are employed in the center, student tutors work ten to twelve hours each week.

Part-time instructors are often happy to have the opportunity to tutor in the labs. Usually, they are referred by a curriculum coordinator, answer advertisements that have been placed in our local paper, or contact me personally. Traditionally, it has been the policy in the LAC to employ only instructors for the Writing and Reading/Study Strategies Labs because they have demonstrated an ability to meet the needs of our student population, which represents radically diverse cultural and educational backgrounds. One instructor/tutor works in each of the other labs and serves as a mentor for the student tutors in those disciplines.

Tutor training covers myriad subjects, from opening a tutoring session so the student feels comfortable to filling out timecards. During training sessions, tutors become conscious of students' learning modalities and collaborate to work out methods to help students adapt their assignments to their strengths. Role-playing is incorporated into these sessions, with one tutor playing the part of the student writer and another acting as the tutor. Since the tutor often becomes a friend, a confidant, to the student, it is important that the tutor knows how to affirm students' feelings of frustration without encouraging those emotions. We also incorporate into the sessions information regarding ancillary services available at the university. In discussing the philosophy and ethics of tutoring, we remind tutors that we are continually trying to empower students to gain the self-confidence they need to succeed; a tutorial should never merely provide a Band-Aid for the situation.

At least three times throughout the quarter, meetings are scheduled to give tutors the opportunity to share ideas and experiences.

Our Collaboration

When Luanne began the Supplemental Instruction Program, Joan helped with the training of student leaders; Luanne, in turn, presented an in-service to writing center tutors. In the past, our two staffs have joined for an in-service, and we intend to continue that collaboration. By getting to know one another we can often recommend to a student a tutor with a particular expertise who works on the other campus. This is important for students who decide to move from a program on one campus to one on the other. The fact that we support each other and work together gives students the sense of continuity and support they need for a successful transition.

We further encourage tutor collaboration by fostering their participation in state conferences and at the COLE tutoring colloquium each year. This latter event offers opportunities for tutors to work together on organizing the conference and to share presentations and ideas.

Types of Services

Bancroft Campus

Tutoring, especially one-on-one tutoring, remains our priority in the center. However, tutor-linked courses introduce more students to the idea of collaboration, and more faculty are using the center for their writing assignments (though the number of faculty who do so may be as small as a dozen per quarter). This tutoring activity coincides with our general goal of expanding writing and collaborative practices.

Faculty development definitely forms a growing activity of the Writing Center. In addition to conducting WAC workshops and teaching individual faculty about their own writing while we work on their articles, we have developed other ways of initiating faculty into composition vocabulary and theory. The recent revision of our tutor report includes a split report form (figure 3). On the left side is a checklist and on the right is a section for written comments. Since faculty often do not think about writing as process or know the terminology we use in our reports, they can use the report form as a teaching tool. From it, faculty learn that writing takes time and involves drafts, that the center stresses ideas over the fine-tuning of grammar, and that international students may have difficulty with writing because they do not understand the academic conventions we take for granted.

Class presentations originally were fifteen-minute talks about why writing is difficult, how center staff act as an audience, who the staff are and how they work with students, when the center is open, etc. However, the assistant director began structuring presentations around a particular class's writing projects, and that idea has become our standard. The instructor provides the presenter with a sample paper from a previous class. Students read and analyze the paper collaboratively, noting its strengths and weaknesses, and then devise strategies for writing their own papers.

Presentations change the class, since students definitely benefit from the analysis taught by the procedures. But before the presentation and during the class, it is often instructors who learn most about their assignments and expectations; they also learn about the real difficulties students have with the assignments.

Tutor-linked classes involve tutors who have demonstrated exceptional facility with students and faculty. Since the university has not yet established a budget line for the Writing-Across-the-Curriculum Program, linking a tutor to a writing-intensive (WI) class provides faculty with an incentive to teach such a course. The 1990 freshman class was subject to WAC requirements (Composition I and II were to be completed by sophomore year, along with two other WIs before senior year—one in the student's major). As a result, WIs have only begun to be offered, even though the tutor-linked program has been in a pilot stage for two years.

Prior to the beginning of the quarter, the tutor, instructor, and I talk about the course, syllabus, and assignments. Together, we also define the tutor's responsibilities (attending class, keeping set office hours, etc.) and explain the nondirective methodology under which we operate. Through the discussion of both the class and assignments, the instructor learns the application of writing-across-the-curriculum theories.

Over the past two years, faculty word-of-mouth has created a demand for these tutors who, besides tutoring students, serve as teaching mirrors and mentors for instructors. This program has contributed toward breaking down institutional barriers to the Writing-Across-the-Curriculum Program and the Writing Center because faculty see our practice in action and learn about the theoretical grounds on which it is based.

Computer acquisition is limited by space (and some state budget constraints regarding computer purchases). Nonetheless, we have recently managed to put a computer on every tutorial desk and to link them to a laser printer. In our offices, that comes to six computers: five

Writing Center Tutor Report

Name of Student: _____

Tutor: _____

Instructor and Dept.: _____

Type of Writing Assignment: _____

Intended Audience: _____ unspecified   _____

_____ Student HAD   _____ DIDN'T HAVE actual assignment sheet

COMMENTS

Writer is at what stage of the
writing process?

_____ prewriting:

    _____ reading/thinking/
          talking about topic

    _____ researching

    _____ exploratory writing

    _____ outlining

_____ rough draft

_____ revising

_____ editing

_____ final draft

_____ rewriting previously
    turned-in paper

Writer needed assistance with
content:

_____ understanding the
    subject matter

_____ determining a main idea
    (thesis) for the paper

_____ using logic

_____ developing ideas
    through explanations
    and examples

_____ adopting appropriate tone
    and diction for situation,
    purpose, audience

Fig. 3. Writing Center tutor report.

	COMMENTS
Writer needed assistance with *organization* or *format:*	
_____ organizing information in a way that is easy to follow and makes sense	
_____ arranging information into introduction, body, and conclusion	
_____ following specific format required	
Writer needed assistance with *grammar* or *mechanics:*	
_____ using correct punctuation	
_____ understanding subject-verb agreement	
_____ eliminating fragments, run-on sentences	
_____ using correct spelling	
This *international student* needed assistance:	
_____ finding adequate vocabulary to express ideas	
_____ using appropriate articles, prepositions, verb endings	
_____ understanding American cultural conventions	

Fig. 3. *Continued.*

IBM compatibles and one new Macintosh. The computers will also be connected to the university's mainframe, and we will be looking at software and discussing CAI during tutor meetings.

Materials consist mainly of various grammar and composition dittos, but we find that our most valuable materials for tutoring are paper and pencil. Each tutoring area has a large desk pad with paper on it.

We have found this much more convenient for drawing pictures of ideas, cognitive maps, and organizational images. Once students leave the center, they also tend not to lose the large sheets among their other papers.

We keep a stock of resource materials for students and tutors. I take advantage of conference discounts to load up on recent theoretical and practical books for our tutor library. Since the Writing-Across-the-Curriculum Program also operates out of the Writing Center, we continue to develop a library of resources— books, journals, and articles—for faculty. There is also a drawer in which faculty syllabi, course guidelines, assignments, and discipline-specific style sheets are kept.

In addition to these materials, we have the usual pieces devoted to publicity: fliers, bookmarks, requests for class presentations, and information sheets, which go out each quarter to faculty and staff. We keep a stack of these in our reception area, along with information on counseling, subject tutoring, and services available at the Community Technical College.

The Writing-Across-the-Curriculum Program cannot be separated from the Writing Center since I direct both. This union has been advantageous to each program because faculty contact with one familiarizes them with the other. Though the College of Arts and Sciences is the only college that has a formal Writing-Across-the-Curriculum Program, inroads have been made with other colleges: the American Association of Colleges of Pharmacy funded the Pharmacy College and Writing Center to develop a writing-across-the-curriculum program; the education college has participated in the tutor-linked program and has begun to look at a writing-intensive curriculum; the business college has its plan on paper while it restructures its curriculum and funding; engineering, along with the ComTech faculty, enthusiastically attended the most recent writing workshop on campus, which featured Toby Fulwiler.

The WAC workshops for faculty cover a variety of areas in writing topics and serve different groups of people on campus (experienced and inexperienced WAC faculty, discipline-specific groups, etc.). Fulwiler has been here three years in a row, and each year a series of workshops is given by someone from the Writing-Across-the-Curriculum Program central committee (usually me) or another outside speaker.

Outreach cannot be organized formally with our current paucity of staff and budget. Some community residents find us, and we have worked with those who are "loosely tied" to campus (maybe they walk their dog across the mall every day). With the help of an individual from the community, we recently created a $20,000 grant proposal for a project aimed at educating the public about elderly abuse and providing shelter for abused victims. This person had never written a grant before and was thrilled when it was funded. So were we.

But limitations (space, staff, and budget constraints) do not allow a lot of community outreach. The Writing Center participates in admissions programs and university open houses; we work on the occasional community grant; and I have worked with the local public school system by participating in the National Writing Project, which is located in the College of Education. Likewise, we have a grant application pending which would create a collaborative portfolio project among targeted public high schools, the Writing Center, College of Education, and two English department composition instructors.

Scott Park Campus

Tutoring is the most significant aspect of the services offered through the LAC. Although certain students may be referred to our labs by their instructors and some may prefer to make an appointment, generally, tutorial services are conducted on a drop-in basis and are open to all students at the university. Students learn of our services through classroom visits, bookmarks, table tents in the cafeteria, composites of schedules at the student information desk, closed-circuit television, and their instructors.

Supplemental Instruction (SI) is structured after the University of Missouri–Kansas City model, where student leaders who have successfully completed targeted high-risk courses are hired to attend class, complete all reading assignments, and conduct two to three study sessions each week for the students enrolled in that section. The purpose of these study sessions is to provide a student-centered opportunity for academic enhancement. Workshops covering topics such as note taking, textbook study, test taking, time management, and test anxiety are offered each quarter. Computer banks are available for student use in the LAC, and technicians are employed through the computer center to assist students who may be having difficulty using a particular program.

The athletic department and the LAC have developed a study strategies curriculum for student athletes and offer the course each quarter. The program has some unique features: students are mentored by the instructional team; former athletes who are college graduates are invited to speak about the importance of a college education; writing across the curriculum is integrated into the course.

A Faculty Resource Center, located in the LAC, has recently evolved into a center for faculty and staff. The LAC plans to work with faculty and staff to provide resources for professional development. Although still in its early stages, it is the first center of its kind at the university.

Computer banks are located in the LAC. One, a group of eight IBM and IBM-compatible computers, is available for student use from 8 a.m. to 10 p.m. The other, a bank of twenty-four networked IBM computers, reserved for basic writing classes several hours during the day and evening, is open for student use at other times.

Testing services were initiated two years ago so that a student, with the professor's approval, may make an appointment to take a test in the center. This situation occurs for a number of reasons: students may have been absent at the appointed test time; they may suffer from test anxiety and require extra time; the professor may allow students to retest in certain areas. More than 2,000 tests were administered in the center during the past school year.

Materials consist of word-processing and tutorial software as well as audiovisual materials. They are available for student use in the center through the circulation desk. Additionally, one writing tutor who has worked in the center for ten years has developed a bank of resources, including handouts, reference materials, sample résumés, and writing texts. Currently, she is putting together a booklet on how to write a research paper using the resources available in the three libraries at the university. We continue to look for excellent materials for students; however, we find that the majority of our students prefer the personal contact of a tutorial situation.

Outreach efforts to the community have been spearheaded through a project establishing a conversation table for ESL students. A retired professor volunteered to donate eight hours a week to work with international students on their speaking and writing skills. This service has been well received by our students, who are thrilled when the professor, a student of languages, greets them in their native tongue. Additionally, in January, a gentleman telephoned the LAC, identified himself as a retired teacher, and asked if we could use a tutor. I replied that we would love to have another tutor, but that, unfortunately, there was no additional money in the budget to pay him. He informed me that he was interested in volunteering his time, and I invited him to come in for a visit. Since that time, he has volunteered over 200 hours of his time and helped countless students.

Reviewing these two success stories and realizing that many professional people in our area are opting for early retirements, we were prompted to submit an internal grant proposal for program excellence to fund a pilot project which would recruit retired citizens from the Toledo community to serve as tutors in the center. This small grant ($5,000) will provide funding for a part-time coordinator who will act as a liaison with the community, plan special interest programs at the college for this select population, and encourage qualified people to volunteer several hours to assist our students. We anticipate that the benefits of this program will be twofold, enhancing our delivery of support services and providing an opportunity for retirees to share their expertise.

Our Collaboration

This past year, Joan invited interested faculty from the Community and Technical College to participate in a WAC workshop with Toby Fulwiler. While this may not seem a monumental venture, such common opportunities for faculty on the two campuses is unusual. However, as a result, not only were new collegial contacts made, but the ComTech staff enthusiastically began planning their own WAC program. Since students transfer between the two campuses, this project will be another on which the two campuses can collaborate. To continue the collaboration this past term, Luanne invited Joan to facilitate a faculty roundtable discussion on writing across the curriculum. This was well received by those who attended, and we plan to hold more of these sessions next year.

Administration, Staff, and Budget

Bancroft Campus

Staff consists of one director, a part-time secretary, and in the last two of those four years, an assistant director. Our tutoring staff is composed of two graduate assistants and about twelve part-time peer and professional tutors, who are largely responsible for what we have been able to accomplish. However, those accomplishments have also been facilitated by our administrative structure.

At the time the university hired me, it was most politic not to associate the Writing Center director's position with its counterpart in the English department. Otherwise, resistance to a writing center and writing-across-the-curriculum program would have been even greater because, in a hard budget year when everyone was fighting for space,

money given to a center located in a department would be perceived
as a bid by the department for staff, money, and room. Since then, I
have maintained my distance for philosophical reasons: If I joined the
English department, faculty in other disciplines would resist "being
made into English department faculty"; they would claim they were
being asked to "perform obligations that belong to the English department." My independence from department politics, despite my Ph.D.
in English, has continued to assure faculty that writing is everyone's
business.

As a result of my independent situation, I have been in an advantageous position concerning funding and decision making on campus.
Since I report to the dean of the College of Arts and Sciences, my
budget is on the same level as a departmental budget. I also sit in on
the college's monthly governance meetings and therefore have greater
access to the dean and other administrators. My presence at these
meetings allows me to announce new plans, survey the state of the
departments, and give small workshops to chairs and others who
direct and work with faculty.

The budget for the Writing Center, despite state cutbacks, remains
healthy. The former dean's insistence that we have a university line
budget has enabled us to plan from year to year. In addition, the
Graduate School has assisted with funding for graduate assistants by
providing money, or by allowing assistants to include time spent in the
Writing Center as part of their obligations. Departments such as history or sociology, for example, will "give" a graduate student to the
center for two quarters. During this time, the graduate students learn
composition theory and collaborative techniques and serve appren-
ticeships as tutors. These graduate assistants eventually collaborate
with their instructors in the tutor-linked project. All of this costs the
center nothing, and I have been able to use the money saved from the
cooperative project with departments; that is how the new computers
were purchased. The university budget-oversight committees have
generously (and surprisingly) supported my bids to switch funds
originally targeted for tutors to our computer account.

Scott Park Campus

The staff is coordinated by the manager of the LAC, and as manager, I
report directly to the director of Developmental Education. She is
responsible, in turn, to the dean of Instruction. I, therefore, take charge
of all operations in the center, including hiring tutors, scheduling labs,
publicizing services, preparing budgets, and submitting an annual

report to the administration and the Developmental Skills Education Advisory Committee.

The budget for the LAC has changed dramatically in recent years. When I started as manager, I was told that I had less than $1,500 to hire student tutors. Today, the LAC operates with a budget well over $100,000. The greatest share of this money comes from the college's general funds; however, a small amount is set aside in the DSE budget to pay for student tutors. Carl Perkins Grant money earmarked for students enrolled in two-year technical programs has permitted the center to broaden its scope and initiate new programs. Moreover, this year, provisions for renewing the grant included a provision that the institution commit to meeting standards set by the State Department of Education. The Operations Council has approved this college-wide fiscal support of the LAC.

Our Collaboration

Our collaboration in terms of staff consists mainly of sharing tutor training, but occasionally, one of us will recommend a tutor for the other's office. We do pool our budgets, however, when it comes to the COLE conference. Each one of us picks up the cost of whatever we can during the planning of the conference. While it is understood that monies spent on printing or mailing will be reimbursed from conference funds, we commit time and staff resources as much as we can.

Records, Research, and Evaluation

Bancroft Campus

Besides the records kept on budget and the reams of administrative directives, we have records of tutors and students, past and present. Past records of tutors serve as information when we discuss the growth and history of the center, and they also come in handy when I am asked to write references.

Student records include a questionnaire students fill out each quarter that they come to the center. The information given includes name, telephone number, address, program, ethnic origin (optional), primary language, level (graduate or undergraduate), class(es) for which they are coming to the center, instructor, whether they were referred, whether their instructor should be notified of their attendance at the center, and perceived weaknesses and strengths of their writing. The responses are entered into a PCFile database, along with a daily record of the dates students attended the center, their tutor, and the amount of time each tutorial took. The questionnaire is filed in a student folder, along with a carbon copy of the tutor report.

Each day, the Writing Center also sends out with the tutor reports a short form, which instructors can return. We encourage faculty to read the reports, to let us know whether they have any suggestions about their students' work, and to pass along any assessment of their students' writing since they started using the center. The daily feedback creates a painless collaboration between faculty and Writing Center that always benefits the student.

In addition to these records, we also send questionnaires to students at the end of each quarter, asking them about their Writing Center experiences; included is a self-addressed, stamped, return envelope. Our return rate is 35–40 percent, and student praise, complaints, and suggestions have helped us improve our services and supported us in our bids for increased facilities and monies. Similarly, the questionnaire we send to faculty at the end of each quarter asks for a short assessment of each of their students who came to the center (and who gave permission to send reports to their instructors). Again, our response rate averages around 35 percent, and faculty's positive comments have been used on our quarterly reports to the dean, the vice president for Academic Affairs, and the president.

Besides the quarterly administrative reports based on our data, separate reports on WI classes, including the student and faculty evaluations, are sent forward to the administration. (I notice I'm lapsing into administrativese even as I type.) I encourage the president and vice presidents of Academic Affairs and University Relations to use these figures for their own public relations purposes and assure them that we can duplicate materials or pull together specific information when needed. Our recordkeeping provides the kind of qualitative and quantitative assessments that seem to keep everyone happy.

The center has provided a source for some research in our academic community, but only recently have faculty understood what a rich resource it really is. While the assistant director and I have used our experiences and data for many conference presentations and publications, our tutors have also presented at the National Peer Tutoring Conference on subjects such as their tutor-linked experiences, tutoring the underprepared student, and tutoring students from different cultures. However, I continue to point out that faculty need to investigate the possibilities for research in the center (without turning us into a guinea pig lab). As a result, an English graduate student is evaluating the results of a survey distributed to students before and after their work in the Writing Center, special education faculty have used the center as a resource for studying tutor interactions, and the sociology department is investigating the perceived differences in sociological styles of writing. Many of the faculty who teach writing-across-the-curriculum courses are now designing research projects involving writing in their disciplines; in some cases, the tutors contribute to these investigations.

Scott Park Campus

Recordkeeping is extremely important to the credibility of any academic support program, and we have concluded that centralizing the system and maintaining the computerized database have worked well for our situation. Students are required to register each quarter that they request services, therefore allowing us to update the files and keep information current. For purposes of reporting, the data collected includes such information as gender, ethnicity, and major. Using this database with the computer mainframe, we are able to determine whether students passed the course for which they requested help and if they are persisting in school. Additionally, supplemental instruction data is also collected and entered into a separate program, which provides information on the academic status of the students for whom this voluntary service was offered. Finally, a third database is used which lists placement test scores and course recommendations for premajor students.

Student evaluations of all the services in the LAC are distributed each quarter. Moreover, programs are evaluated by tutors, faculty, and administrators. Along with the college administration, we are looking at outcomes assessment instruments that might be adapted for our use.

Current research dictates that we continue to strive to discover new methods for meeting the cultural and educational diversity of our growing student population. Because we feel such a sense of commitment to our students, we attempt to remain on the cutting edge of current practice.

The Future

Bancroft Campus

The Writing Center will move into a new and larger space within the next three years, enabling us to work with more students, expand our services to include more CAI, provide group tutoring in particular areas (concentrating on essay exams, the thesis proposal, state licensing tests), and develop closer connections with offices serving students with special needs.

Because writing across the curriculum is part of the Strategic Plan for the university, there will be a need to train more tutors for WI classes, to offer more faculty workshops, and to arrange more exchange sessions for participating faculty and tutors. Coordination of all the colleges' writing-across-the-curriculum goals and programs will be a priority.

Scott Park Campus

The future of the Learning Assistance Center at ComTech looks exciting. Physically, space will be better defined with the placement of soundproof dividers around the computer lab, the reading area, and the supplemental instruction alcove. With the integration into our services of the volunteer program, we see an opportunity for community outreach which has not existed in the past. Additional grant funding will be needed to provide money for expanded access to computers for the increasing numbers of students with physical disabilities. Basically, more tutors, more hours, and more money will be necessary to meet our goals for the future.

Our Collaboration

As with most institutions today, our future is driven by our budget. Nonetheless, our penchant for "making deals," bartering services, and looking for other ways to work together serves as a means of expanding, and introduces faculty and students to what we do. Since the majority of students report on our questionnaires that they heard about the center through friends or faculty, we believe that increasing class presentations, faculty workshops, involvement on university committees, and participation in open houses seems most productive. But there are several areas in which we will grow, both by choice and because of institutional change:

- The Community and Technical College offers subject tutoring as well as tutoring in writing; Writing Center tutors will continue referring students to these subject-area tutors, and the Learning Assistance Center tutors can refer students who need services during the hours when only the Center is open.

- The Community and Technical College's interest in writing across the curriculum indicates that a collaboration of services and staff will continue to develop in this area.

- Both the Learning Assistance Center and the Writing Center will continue sharing resources (like space and staff) and training sessions. A former Writing Center tutor will now be working as the Learning Assistance Center's supplemental instruction supervisor, and we will lead sections of each other's tutor-training sessions in the future.

- The Learning Assistance Center has much to teach the Writing Center about collection of data regarding retention; there is even potential for tracking students who use both the ComTech Center and the Writing Center.

- The LAC grant, which includes expanding a conversation table for international students, will be a welcome resource for Bancroft campus students. The Writing Center will work with the LAC to develop this idea.

- Future COLE colloquiums will include preconference workshops for faculty development on both campuses, giving each faculty an opportunity to meet and work with the other.

Education continues to be a goal for both centers. Writing Center staff are often our best advertisements and therefore our best educators; they can dispel the myths we all hold about writing, thinking, and learning. So, too, the staff at the Learning Assistance Center works against the myths associated with community college populations. We know that our work together on building writing and learning communities has already dispelled some of the misconceptions held by students, faculty, and administrators on our campuses. We will continue to seek creative ways to bring the academic community into our collaboration.

4 The Lehigh University Writing Center: Creating a Community of Writers

Edward Lotto
Lehigh University

Lehigh University has something of an identity problem. In as far as it is known in the world at large, it is considered an engineering school. And its history marks it so. Founded soon after the Civil War by Asa Packer, a railroad tycoon, in the industrial Lehigh Valley of eastern Pennsylvania, it was supposed to provide the sturdy young men of America with a practical education that would help our country find its proper place in the world of industry and business. And this it has done admirably well, with alumni finding remarkable success as engineers and executives in the wide world, the most famous example being Lee Iacocca. On the other hand, Lehigh's president of the past nine years wants to make the school a "complete university," by which he means a university in which the arts and humanities have a strong place. As part of his plan to achieve this end, he has turned his attention to the various arts and humanities departments and has done everything from trying to increase the number of students in the humanities to speaking to the incoming freshmen about the importance of writing in their lives.

Thus, Lehigh students have been getting something of a mixed message. Traditionally, Lehigh has been an engineering school, and many come here for that reason, a large number following in the footsteps of their parents and siblings and arriving with expectations about the university which they learned at home. But once they get to school, they find that the administration and many members of the faculty stress the importance of the arts and humanities.

Of course, this split is also reflected in the atmosphere at the university itself. Even though there is a new emphasis on the arts, the president and provost are engineers, and the dean of Arts and Science is a physicist. Although the 4,000 undergraduates are divided fairly evenly among engineering, business, and arts and science, most of the 2,000 graduate students are in engineering and science. The faculty members perpetuate this engineering ethos since many of the older faculty members in engineering and the sciences see themselves as the power in the university, while many of the older members in the arts and humanities see themselves as powerless in the university structure. In addition, a strong fraternity system reinforces the power of the male-dominated College of Engineering.

The attitude of these various power centers toward writing is in itself mixed. The university as a whole has a two-semester English requirement, most of which is devoted to writing. Members of the English department have given a series of workshops in writing across the disciplines for faculty members from the entire university. The College of Arts and Science has a junior-year writing-intensive requirement, the College of Business has just implemented a similar requirement, and there is speculation that the College of Engineering will follow suit.

In addition, many of the faculty members in engineering and science realize the value of writing and try to stress its importance to their students. Only a few, however, put this emphasis into practice by spending time in their classes dealing with writing in any way. Too often the plea is heard that there just isn't time for dealing with writing in the busy syllabus. The students have to learn so much about the subject of the course that they will have to learn about writing on their own.

The students add to this denigration of writing. Many come here to be engineers, having little idea of what engineers do. In fact, they often are students who do well at science and mathematics and have tried to avoid writing as much as possible. Until just recently the application to Lehigh had no essay question, an important consideration for some of the students who apply. These students do not realize the importance that writing will have for their careers, even if they are told about it by their engineering professors. They certainly do not believe what their English professors have to say on the subject. I have even heard engineering students fall back on the old cliché that they will never have to write because their secretaries will take care of all that, although this illusion is perhaps more common among the students in the College of Business.

This is the institutional context in which the writing center at Lehigh University must do its work. It is not the atmosphere most conducive to teaching writing, but it does offer footholds for a writing center that is willing to adapt to the world in which it must live, if live it will. To find these footholds, the center must be willing to think of writing in ways somewhat different from those common in departments of English elsewhere. On the other hand, I believe that the center must not forget the basic assumptions about writing that make it valued in English departments: writing functions to help human beings think and learn, and to do so it must, to some extent, exert a force for change on the minds of students. Only by finding a balance between these two forces, the force that emanates from the engineering and business ethos and the force from inside the English department, will a writing center be able to create a community of writers that draws on all the strengths to be found in a school like Lehigh University.

Definition of the Writing Center

Within an institutional framework like that at Lehigh, defining the writing center becomes an important task. Without a clear definition from the center itself, the other forces within the university will define it within their own context of needs and desires, thus creating a bewildering array of definitions of the center which will in turn create an impossible mixture of demands upon its limited resources. These problems can exist, of course, at other types of universities, but the changing and confusing identity of Lehigh makes this confusion particularly powerful there.

Fortunately, we have a powerful statement of the definition of a writing center in Stephen North's "The Idea of a Writing Center" (1984). In this essay North defines a writing center as a place that writers use to talk about writing. As North puts it, "This new writing center, then, defines its province not in terms of some curriculum, but in terms of the writers it serves. . . . In a writing center the object is to make sure that writers, and not necessarily their texts, are what get changed by instruction" (438). To help define the purpose of all this talk, North falls back on an analogy. He claims that the heritage of the writing center goes "back, in fact to Athens, where in a busy marketplace a tutor called Socrates set up the same kind of shop: open to all comers, no fees charged, offering, on whatever subject a visitor might propose, a continuous dialectic that is, finally, its own end" (446).

But I would argue further that the purpose of any dialectic is, finally, change, learning defined as the bringing together and interacting of different points of view. It is change of a particular kind, change enacted within a community of readers and writers, but it is change nonetheless, and in this interaction both the tutor and the client, the writing center and the students, find themselves changing. Within this dialectic, two different perspectives find the place where they can coexist. Creating a community of writers out of this dialectic, then, is what I take as the defining characteristic of writing centers in general.

One place to see this dialectic at work at a slightly different level is in the history of the writing center at Lehigh. The center itself is the product of the interplay among the forces within the university and the forces from the wider world of the discipline of composition, each of which has had to learn to listen to the other and change in order to produce an institution that has meaning and value for both.

History

Organized tutoring in writing at Lehigh had its start in 1978 with the founding of the Learning Assistance Center. This center grew out of the work of two faculty members in the English department who saw a need to help students meet the rigorous academic standards at Lehigh. This perceived need, in turn, grew out of a sense that there would be fewer students applying to college over the next ten to twenty years, and thus Lehigh would be forced to accept students with relatively poor academic preparation.

In its initial conception, the center was designed to work with study skills and writing. The first director of the center had a background in education and ESL. He emphasized the importance of study skills and left the tutoring of writing essentially to the graduate students from the English department who worked as tutors. In addition to these tutors, there were also graduate students from the School of Education to work on study skills. After the first few years, graduate students from the mathematics department were added to tutor in calculus, and the center changed its name to the Learning Center.

The first director left his position after two years, and the university had to decide how to fill the directorship. Like many engineering schools, Lehigh found itself at that time with a lot of graduate students for whom English was a second language. It was decided that an increased emphasis on ESL was appropriate, and a director with a specialization in that area was hired. He expanded the ESL program greatly and even taught the graduate students in English how to teach ESL, but he did not do much with tutoring the writing of native-born students.

This director quit his position after three years, and a series of interim directors ran the Learning Center while the university decided what to do about the directorship. In the end, it ran an advertisement for someone with two areas of expertise out of a list of five areas including ESL, basic writing, and education. After two "permanent" directors and several temporary ones in five years, the university did not really know what it wanted to do with the Learning Center. There was a sense, however, that too much work had been done in ESL, and perhaps it was time to return to more traditional work in writing.

I applied for the position, and with work in composition, experience working in a writing center, and experience running a basic writing program that had close ties to a writing center, I was chosen. In my interviews with the department and administrators, I made it clear that I was interested in running a writing center that dealt with writing all across the campus and that I did not have any experience in ESL. I also stressed that I felt a writing center was a place where people talked about writing and that I would emphasize tutorial work as opposed to programmed instruction. All this seemed to satisfy the people who were concerned with the Learning Center.

Since becoming director of the Learning Center, I have worked hard to convince students of the value of the service offered there for writers. The number of freshman appointments has tripled, and the center is working increasingly with upperclassmen. The writing part of the center has become its biggest part, followed closely by mathematics and then study skills. In my talks to the freshman writing classes, I emphasize both the practical benefits and the more subtle values of writing. In dealing with the practical side, I use statements from engineers, businesspeople, and various administrators at Lehigh about the importance of writing in engineering and business, but it is more difficult to convince Lehigh students of the place writing and language have in creating their world. To do so, I stress the motivating power of language and thus play on the pragmatic desire of many students at Lehigh to get things done. If students can come to see that motivation is a complex and difficult process, they then can be convinced of the value of dialectic as North defined it in his germinal article. I hope that I do not distort my understanding of language too much in talking about writing in this way, but of such compromises is communication made.

Even though I am the administrator for the mathematics and study skills programs, I rely on faculty members from mathematics and education to monitor the real work of the tutors there. In essence, there are three centers in the Learning Center. Although pedagogically this may not be an ideal situation, it does make sense financially. There are savings to be made in consolidating everything from recordkeeping to appointment making. One other benefit is that students who come to the center to work on one subject often stay to work on another. And finally, at a school like Lehigh, it helps the prestige of a writing center to be aligned with a mathematics tutoring service. Surely something serious and important is going on in such a place.

Physical Description

The Learning Center is located on the top floor of Coppee Hall, one of the historical buildings on campus, near the University Center, with its student center and snack bar, and thus in the middle of the students' daily activities. Most of the dorms are just up the hill, with the fraternities just above them, and most of the classroom buildings and the library are down the hill. The only other department in the building is modern foreign languages; the English department is near the foot of the hill at the edge of campus. Although it is difficult being so far from the English department, it is better for the Learning Center not to move down to the English department since that would take us away from the center of student activity. In an ideal world, the English department would move up to a building near the Learning Center, but I'm afraid this is not to be.

The space the Learning Center occupies is light and airy. It has a cathedral ceiling twenty-five feet high and skylights as well as small windows on the side. The main area is a large rectangle divided into two rooms by a wall ten feet high (figure 1). Thus, the wall does not go all the way to the ceiling and allows noise to travel back and forth between the two rooms. The receptionist's desk is at the front of the first room and has all the records for the center as well as a computer for keeping the records up to date. To the side of the receptionist's desk is a waiting area with a comfortable couch and chairs. Behind the receptionist's desk, and separated by a movable partition, is a table for the staff to use for eating. Behind the waiting area, and once more behind a movable partition, is a computer area with several microcomputers and a laser printer. The rest of the front room is divided into tutoring carrels with round tables and chairs. There is a small area near the back for the photocopying machine.

The back room has a large area in the front with desks for small classes and several more carrels partitioned off. In the back corner is a small office for the director of ESL. The director of the Learning Center has an office off the front room. The director's computer, that of the receptionist, and one of the microcomputers are connected to the

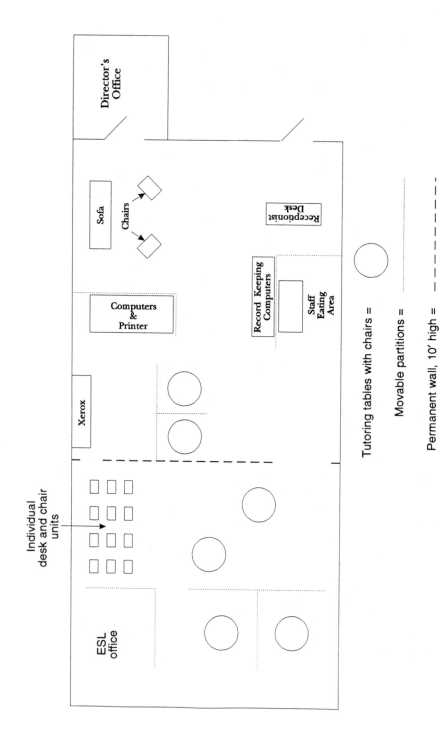

Fig. 1. The Learning Center at Lehigh University.

Tutoring tables with chairs =

Movable partitions =

Permanent wall, 10' high =

university's network. This network has jacks in every dorm room, classroom, and office on campus.

At the back of the front room is a collection of reference books and dictionaries. There is also a small collection of books pertaining to ESL. In the director's office is a small library of books on composition theory and writing centers, which is available to the staff. Since plants thrive in the light of the center, the director and staff have collected everything from common fig trees to an angel-winged begonia.

The plants, as well as the high ceiling and comfortable furniture, help create a welcoming atmosphere. One drawback of being on the third floor is that the room becomes quite hot in the summertime, and since the ceilings are too high to make air conditioning practical, the center cannot be used in the summer. In addition, at the beginning of the school year, which is at the end of August at Lehigh, the center can be very uncomfortable. Another problem is that, because the center is in a historical building, there are no elevators. This causes some inconvenience, but since Lehigh's campus climbs a mountain, the students and faculty are used to exercise. These hardships are, in part, softened in the winter when the center is full of light on clear, cold days.

Chronology of a Typical Day

A typical day in the Learning Center starts at 8:30 a.m., when the secretary arrives to open up and the director gets to work. For an hour or so things are quiet as the secretary enters records from the previous day into the computer, and the director prepares for a freshman English class and a staff meeting later that day. In addition, the secretary answers the telephone and makes several appointments for students to see a tutor.

The first tutor arrives around 9:30 a.m. and starts to work with a student who has been waiting for her. The director leaves to teach his writing class, and the secretary is busy making appointments and greeting students. Two more tutors arrive at 10 a.m. and meet their students. The director returns at 11 a.m. and gives an orientation session for a writing class a teacher has brought to the center. At 1 p.m. there is a staff meeting, and the director and tutors talk over any problems they have had during the week. They also discuss a recent article from the *Writing Center Journal*.

After the meeting, the tutors stay awhile to chat informally about their work, and one meets a student who is having trouble getting started on a paper. The last tutor leaves around 4 p.m., and the secretary gathers the tutors' comments to enter into the computer the next day. The telephone rings a few more times with students making appointments, and the director stays on awhile to grade some papers. The center closes at 4:30 p.m., and then at 7 p.m. it opens again for drop-in time. Two tutors deal with twenty students over the next three hours in a hectic atmosphere and finally manage to close the center at 10:15 p.m.

Clientele

The students at Lehigh tend to come from the urban centers on the East Coast and to have better math than verbal skills. The SAT scores for the middle 50 percent of the class range from 600 to 700 on the math section and from 510 to 620 on the verbal. Lehigh students tend to have a curious mixture of sophistication and naiveté, of intelligence and ignorance. They tend to know a great deal about math, technical subjects, good cars, and even something about wine, but very little about the realities of politics and human interaction. Many conceive of writing as a skill that will have little importance for them.

The students who come for work on writing are a skewed sample from the whole. For the most part they are self-selected; I do not encourage teachers to require students to come to the Learning Center. A typical student, if there is such a thing, is enrolled in freshman English and is doing pretty well, perhaps earning a high C or low B, but wants to do better since she is used to doing well. She has some trouble understanding why she is not doing better because she was rewarded with an A in high school for the kind of writing that now receives a C.

The problem the tutor faces is turning this concern for a grade into a concern for better writing. Although it will probably be impossible to forget the concern for a grade at a school where students compare their GPAs to the hundredth place, we try to follow North's maxim of improving the writer, not the writing. Doing so entails a series of trade-offs between the tutor and the student.

The crisis point in these trade-offs often comes when a student has worked hard at invention and revision under the guidance of the tutor and produces a potentially excellent paper that is flawed because the student has not quite gotten all of its parts under control yet. When the paper receives a grade that is no better, and sometimes worse, than previous ones, she is often discouraged and wants to give up working on writing. All the tutor can do is be encouraging and stress that improvement in writing takes time and does not proceed linearly. Some students will persevere and usually make a breakthrough both in the quality of their writing and in their grade, while others will just give up and disappear from the writing center. With these latter students, all we can do is hope that we have planted the seeds for later writing improvement.

These "typical" students make up perhaps a third of the students who come to the Learning Center. The rest vary from the very good writer who responds to the slightest suggestion with originality and insight to the writer who is struggling to pass a course. Both these kinds of writers are easier to work with than the "typical" one. Working with the good writer is more like working with a colleague on a paper. The writer who is struggling usually has relatively straightforward problems and knows he has to work on them.

Although most of the students who come to the Learning Center come from English classes, some also come from other courses ranging from government to biology. The number of students who come from these other courses depends to a large degree on the emphasis their teachers put on writing. In addition, we get students who are working on applications of various kinds. And some of these clients are graduate students.

Tutors: Selection and Training

All the writing tutors are graduate students in the English department. For their assistantship, they work fifteen hours a week, which includes an hour a week for a staff meeting. The chair of English and I consult about possible tutors, and we choose them from among the graduate students who have expressed an interest in tutoring. Since I team-teach the writing pedagogy course for new teaching assistants, I know all the prospective tutors quite well. I look for ones who are good classroom teachers and enjoy using group work and individual conferences. I also like to choose tutors who have the ability to listen to what the students have to say. Finally, I look for graduate students who have an interest in teaching composition, both practical and theoretical. Tutoring is an opportunity to see firsthand what goes into a piece of writing, and I would hate to waste the opportunity on someone who does not want to learn from this experience.

I train the tutors for six weeks during weekly seminars. Since all the tutors have taken a pedagogy course that introduces them to the theory and practice of composition and have taught freshman English,

I spend the time in the seminar stressing what does and should go on in a writing center. We read a series of articles, including North's "The Idea of a Writing Center," analyze videotapes of tutoring sessions, role-play tutoring sessions using our own writing, discuss the place of grammar in the writing process, and go over the practical problems every tutor faces, from recordkeeping to dealing with the student who wants to enlist the tutor in a battle against a teacher.

After the seminar is over, I hold weekly staff meetings which may just provide an opportunity to discuss the problems and successes of the week or may have a more formal agenda. People sometimes report on professional conferences they have attended, and a few times during the semester I try to get outside speakers ranging from the director of the minority student program to a visiting Woodrow Wilson Fellow on campus. These weekly meetings are important to make sure that all the tutors keep in touch with what the others are doing. They help to reinforce the community of tutors, even if much of the time is spent on seemingly insignificant matters.

Types of Services

Tutoring

Like most writing centers, the one at Lehigh offers, as its basic service, individual tutoring on whatever writing project the student brings to the tutoring session. In the session, the tutor first tries to put the client at ease and then explores the rhetorical situation in which the writer is working, which includes everything from the assignment, if there is one, to the teacher's comments on previous papers. Once this starting point has been established, the tutor begins with whatever problems are most pressing. In this sense, the session always starts from where the student is and takes as its agenda the problems the student is facing.

One common type of session takes place when the student has no clear idea of what to write about. This session will often start with a discussion of the topic at hand and follow the student's interests and understanding. At times, the session will develop into a discussion of a reading assignment that the student has not understood, and at other times, the session will range among the student's interests and feelings about the topic. Whatever the case, it is important to allow the student time to explore a variety of topics and points of view.

One problem the tutor faces is that students often try to "short-circuit" the process. They hate to "waste" time on areas that will not appear directly in the paper and thus want to give up on topics that do not produce immediate results, that do not produce a focused thesis they can develop without too much other thought. Although it is always dangerous to make generalizations about students, my sense is that this kind of problem is more common among our engineering students than others. These students are used to straightforward tests and problems. Most of their exams are such that there is only one right answer, and most of their projects either work or don't. The computer program will either work or it won't, and the bridge will either hold up or it will fall down. In addition, the engineering students have tremendous demands placed on their time and a schedule that offers no choices. They are used to getting things done efficiently and often work according to a strict timetable.

Because these students bring their engineering context to the tutoring session, it is important to work within the world they understand. Here the perspective provided in Linda Flower's *A Problem-Solving Approach to Writing* (1989) can be useful. The students are used to the idea of problems and finding solutions to them. They even are used to the idea of multiple solutions to the same problem, with some solutions being better than others. All we need to do as tutors is to provide the framework of a rhetorical situation, thus providing an analogy with which such students are comfortable. With an audience, a topic, and a situation, they can manipulate their writing to solve the problem as effectively as possible.

In using this approach with engineering students, and others with the same perspective, we need to be careful, however, to avoid the problems that Flower's book demonstrates. She undervalues the degree to which writing is the creation of meaning. In writing, in creating meaning, the writer is finding a place within a network of texts and voices. If we stress the problem-solving and rhetorical nature of writing too much, we tend to treat meaning as a thing that we simply transfer from one person to another and tend to lose the strength of writing as learning, writing as a tool for change.

To counterbalance the tendency at a school like Lehigh to treat writing as a transparent medium through which the world is observed, I like to use a technique I call the "dramatized reader." This is a simple technique in which the tutor simply dramatizes the responses of a reader. If a particular section of the paper seems confusing, the tutor simply puzzles out loud about the possible meanings the section might have. If there is a break in the logic of a section, the tutor can talk about how abrupt the change in topic seems to be and what the tutor expected to follow as opposed to what did follow. If the paper wanders from its topic, the tutor can muse about what seems to be going on. Whatever the case, the tutor should make an effort to present what is going on in the mind of the reader as forcefully as possible.

The point of this dramatized reading is to let the client hear the other voices that go into deciphering meaning from a text. Certainly some of the things the tutor says will be idiosyncratic, but most will not. Instead, they will be the connections the tutor sees between the paper and other works the tutor has read, along with the reading strategies implied in those works. Dramatizing reading in this way helps the clients see that meaning is not some object that is simply transferred from one person to another. It helps to embed the writer within the web of language in which meaning takes shape.

Computers

Lehigh University is committed to making the greatest possible use of computers. Five years ago, the president had a campuswide network installed that links every classroom, dorm room, and office on campus. Anyone with an IBM-compatible computer can plug into the network and communicate with all the other computers on campus, as well as gain access to Bitnet. Every faculty member has been given a computer, and there are numerous computer labs on campus.

The Learning Center has tried to find a reasonable position among all these computers—one that does not become enamored of technology for its own sake yet does take advantage of the computers available. We use the computers for our recordkeeping and to gain access electronically to the latest budget figures. We have sponsored a bulletin board called *Grammar-Net*, which answers grammar questions from around the campus. We have several computers as well as a laser printer available in the Learning Center for students to use when working on their papers. By far, we find simple word processing the most useful function a computer serves in teaching writing. Students bring their writing assignments on a disk and tutors work with them on a screen. Or a student may talk with a tutor for a while and then work on an assignment to bring back to the tutor at the end of the day.

Testing and Materials

The Learning Center has a full supply of exercises and modules, but we do not find them very useful. Sometimes a student will need help on a specific problem and an exercise can help, but for the most part exercises do not address the needs of writers. The Center does not do any formal testing, but we do consult informally with teachers on the placement and skills of students. Sometimes we channel students to the ESL director. Other times we consult about learning disabilities. Although no one on the staff is an expert in this area, at least our attitude is enlightened.

Writing Across the Curriculum

The Learning Center does quite a bit of work with students in the writing-across-the-curriculum program at Lehigh. Every junior in the College of Arts and Science and the College of Business must take a writing-intensive course in his or her major. I speak about the services offered at the Learning Center at all the workshops for the teachers of these courses, and most of them at least mention our services to their students. In addition, I work to bring together the WAC classes and the Learning Center, consulting with teachers about their assignments and grading and sending tutors to WAC classes on a regular basis to help with the writing instruction.

Administration

Faculty and Staff

The Learning Center staff is made up of the director and two half-time secretaries. As the director, I am a recently tenured member of the English department, which has been supportive of the Learning Center from my first days at Lehigh. In particular, the two members of the department who founded the center in 1978 and who are now full professors have been helpful in negotiating a way through the power struggles that are a part of any university. Originally, as director of the center I reported to the dean of Arts and Science, but four years ago the structure was changed, at my instigation, so that now I report to the vice-provost. I have found that it is helpful to be closer to the top of the organization in matters of budget and resources. In fact, this change in organizational structure grew out of a situation in which I found myself helpless to stop a decrease in staff size because the layers of bureaucracy above me hid the source of the decrease. Now, at least, I know where decisions are made.

Because of my administrative duties, I teach only half-time in the English department. Until recently, the department taught a 3–3 schedule, so I had a load of three courses per year. Often, however, I have found myself teaching more than that simply because it is hard to teach a range of courses when there are only three a year from which to choose. In addition, I have always team-taught the course for new teaching assistants on how to teach writing, and I teach a section of freshman English in order to be able to speak with authority in the course for teaching assistants. This schedule leaves me only one other course to teach each year. I have alternated between teaching a course for undergraduates, called Theory and Practice of Writing, and a graduate seminar, the most recent one being Modern Rhetoric and Literary Theory. Recently the department's teaching load has been decreased to 3–2, so I will teach even fewer courses. This problem will be alleviated by the hiring of a new faculty member in writing who can help me teach the writing courses we need. Until now, I have been the only writing specialist on the faculty.

In general, the university and the department have been supportive of my work both as director of the center and as a teacher of writing, an immensely important advantage for any director of a writing center. This support grows, in part, out of the general feeling among the administration and faculty at an engineering school that writing is important. In addition, the administration and faculty have been open-minded about how to teach writing and have given me the freedom I need to develop my own program. In part, this open-mindedness can be traced to a belief among engineers that there are several solutions to any problem, and the choice should be left up to the experts. Finally, the administration has been generous with resources since they are used to spending lots of money on faculty and projects. There is a trickle-down effect in an engineering school which actually seems to work, as opposed to the situation for our nation as a whole during the last ten years.

The two half-time secretaries split the day, so one comes in during the morning and the other during the afternoon. They overlap by an hour so that they can talk about common concerns. Their main tasks are scheduling students, keeping track of the tutors, and keeping the records and budget. Although having two secretaries may not be the ideal situation, it has worked out well for us. The situation grew out of a time when the center had only one part-time secretary. When we needed more secretarial time, the secretary we had did not want to increase her hours, so we hired another. The original secretary is still with us and helps us tremendously with her store of knowledge about the workings of the center and the university. In this case, as in most, a consideration for historical context is more important than a desire for an abstract ideal.

Budget

Since I report directly to the vice-provost, the Learning Center's budget comes out of the provost's office. This direct connection helps keep the needs of the center above the fray at the budget table every fall. When the center's budget came from the dean's office, it tended to get lost among all the departmental concerns the dean had to worry about. The budget itself covers equipment, supplies, and the secretaries; my salary and that of the tutors comes out of the English department budget.

Records

Each time a tutor sees a student, she fills out a form that includes general information about the student, the date of the session, and the content of the tutorial. At the end of the day, the secretaries enter this information into a database. At the end of the semester I can use the database to learn the number of students who have used the Learning Center, what courses they came from, what year they are in, the number of students who came to the center a certain number of times, and a variety of other information limited only by our cleverness in creating the database and manipulating it. Right now we are using *Reflex* for our database, but I would like to move to a more powerful one, *dBASE III PLUS*, in the future.

Evaluation

At the end of every year I send an evaluation form to every student who has used the Learning Center. In truth, the information I get on these forms is not very useful. Not many students return them, and those that do tend to say simply that they found the center very helpful. This kind of evaluation can be useful in dealing with administrators, but it does not help much in improving the quality of our services. More important is the ability to listen and respond to what tutors, teachers, and students have to say.

One important source of evaluation is the weekly staff meeting. The tutors know what is going on in the trenches, and it is vital to listen to what they have to say. Their perspective is the one that really dominates what actually goes on in the center. During the staff meetings, I encourage the tutors to discuss what is on their minds, and I act on their concerns in everything from the scheduling procedure to the need for a water fountain in the center. My job is to make their work as easy and effective as possible.

Another source of evaluation is discussion with the students. When I talk with the freshman classes, I stress that I am the person they should go to with any concerns about the center, and students do come to see me frequently. Although I have to make sure I put everything they say into the whole educational context, it is important to hear their views. No center can survive long without the confidence of the students it serves.

Finally, teachers are another source of evaluation. With them it is important to be approachable and nonjudgmental. It is difficult for any teacher, especially a new one, to talk about a class objectively. In the end, the teacher is part of the rhetorical context that the students must deal with, and the center has a duty to understand that context. Changing it, if need be, is a much more difficult problem and probably is not part of the center's duties; the director of writing is responsible for that. But the center can at least be a force for change as long as it is not too dogmatic about its beliefs.

Research

I have taken advantage of the opportunities offered by a writing center for several research projects. The tutorial session itself offers a chance to see the writing process at work, and with careful notes and copies of a student's papers and drafts, it is possible to gain an insight into the writing process. I used this technique to gather the data for "The Writer's Subject Is Sometimes a Fiction" (1985), an article I published in *The Writing Center Journal.* I also used much the same technique to learn the effect of using Burke's pentad when tutoring and reported on the results at the 1989 Conference on College Composition and Communication Annual Convention, in a paper entitled, "The Dramatized Reader: The Flowering of Burke in the Writing Center."

Working with students from other disciplines also offers the chance for gathering data. Two tutors, Richard Gaughran and Lucy Bednar, and I worked with government, history, and computer science classes to discover the differences in writing in those disciplines. We wrote a practical article about our results for the *PCTE Bulletin* (Lotto, Bednar, and Gaughran 1987), and I wrote a more theoretical analysis for the *Writing Center Journal* (Lotto 1988). All this work demonstrates the wealth of knowledge generated in a writing center if we are careful enough to keep track of what is going on. Writing centers are where much of the writing process comes out into the open, and we need to analyze this information both practically and theoretically for the sake of both writing centers themselves and our understanding of composition in general.

The Future

The future of a writing center is never easy since there are always new problems and situations that must be negotiated, but I feel we have a solid base from which to negotiate in the university. One major problem we will have to face is a growing lack of funds in the university. The university has overextended itself to a degree with the expense of the computer network and the purchase of the mountaintop, with its research facilities from Bethlehem Steel, so money will be tight for quite a while. With the Learning Center's position under the vice-provost and my own tenure, we are in about as strong a position as we could hope for. I also feel we benefit from a great deal of goodwill among the students and faculty.

On the positive side, the university is paying attention to its writing program and sees the center as an important part of that program. We will have a review of the program by the Council of Writing Program Administrators in the fall, and their policy statement indicates that they believe all programs need a writing center. I have every hope that their recommendation will strengthen our position.

In terms of our work, we have a solid reputation among the undergraduates, although we continually have to fight against the negative attitude toward writing among many of them. Another problem is that, with a change in the teaching load of teaching assistants, fewer of them will work in the center. In the past, I have tried to make sure that all of the graduate students tutor for at least a semester, both for their own experience and to make sure the connections between writing instruction and the center are as tight as possible. With this change, I will have to work harder to make sure the teaching assistants know what is going on in the center.

The opportunities for the center to improve the quality of writing instruction in the university remain open. I hope to do more with the WAC courses and perhaps to reach out to the area high schools and colleges. As always in teaching writing, I often feel overwhelmed by the difficulty and complexity of the task. But whenever I feel this way,

I can usually find refuge in working on a single piece of writing, a single project. Doing so helps to make sense of the world. In writing, in making sense of the world, I negotiate a place that satisfies my needs and those of the people I deal with, at least for a while. This is, perhaps, the most we can hope for.

Works Cited

Flower, Linda. 1989. *A Problem-Solving Approach to Writing.* 3rd ed. San Diego: Harcourt Brace.

Lotto, Edward. 1989. "The Dramatized Reader: The Flowering of Burke in the Writing Center." Paper presented at Conference on College Composition and Communication. Seattle, Washington. March 16.

———. 1988. "The Texts and Contexts of Writing." *The Writing Center Journal* 9: 13–20.

———. 1985. "The Writer's Subject Is Sometimes a Fiction." *The Writing Center Journal* 6: 15–20.

Lotto, Edward, Lucy Bednar, and Richard Gaughran. 1987. "Moving Away from the Text: Tutoring Writing in Government, History, and Computer Science." *The Pennsylvania Council of Teachers of English Bulletin* 55: 13–21.

North, Stephen. 1984. "The Idea of a Writing Center." *College English* 46: 433–46.

5 The Writing Center at the University of Southern California: Couches, Carrels, Computers, and Conversation

Irene L. Clark
University of Southern California

The University of Southern California is a large university located in downtown Los Angeles, an area that is not usually regarded as one of the city's prime tourist attractions, unlike Disneyland, Beverly Hills, or Hollywood. The surrounding neighborhood, with its low-income housing, car dealerships, and start-up ethnic enterprises, presents a curious contrast to the USC marching band, cheerleaders, and general affluence of the students. Enthusiasm for sports runs high at USC, and the victories and defeats of the USC Trojans are shouted throughout halls and across tree-lined campus promenades. The movie industry is also a tangible presence at USC—every few weeks large vans of film equipment and impressive-looking film types, complete with sunglasses, megaphones, and directors' chairs, arrive on campus to film a scene. Yet in the surrounding area, real-life dramas are enacted daily, most of them without happy "Hollywood" endings.

Despite the problems indigenous to its urban setting, USC is a university on the rise. It boasts many prestigious schools—the film and business schools are particularly well known—and it also has respected law, medical, and engineering schools as well as many excellent academic departments. It prides itself on concern for its students, exemplified by smaller classes than one might expect at such a large institution, and by a serious concern with teaching. The Writing Center reflects this concern.

The Historical Context

The Freshman Writing Program was created in the fall of 1978, and at that time, the Writing Lab, as it was then called, was conceived of simply as a place for students to work on grammatical problems such

97

as sentence fragments, comma faults, and surface errors of all kinds. The theory behind this model was that "editing and composing, essentially different skills, are best learned in different 'scenes'" (Bamberg 1982, 181). Composing skills such as prewriting and revision were regarded as best learned in a classroom "workshop," whereas editing skills were regarded as best learned in a laboratory, where rules could be isolated and taught systematically and sequentially. As might be expected, such a lab functioned with a great many materials, modules, cassettes, slide programs, and workbooks, but relatively few tutors.

After one year, however, in accord with an increasingly integrated approach to composition advocated by the program, this concept of separating composing and editing and of using the Writing Center primarily for basic skills was discarded in favor of a more comprehensive, collaborative approach, substantiated by the work of Krashen (1982) and the early work of Bruffee (1973), and after two years, the name was changed to Writing "Center." This new emphasis on conversation rather than on drill and practice created the need for additional tutors, and accordingly, the number of tutors was increased each year, until it now totals approximately one hundred. Communication, not exercises, is now considered the essence of the Writing Center, and students are urged to assume an active role in conferences, discovering ideas for themselves through discussion. Tutors, now called "consultants," encourage students to explore their own ideas and to generate their own suggestions for revision. Although surface error is regarded as an important concern, one that must ultimately be addressed, conferences in the Writing Center usually focus on global areas of discourse—thesis, focus, organization, and audience.

The Departmental Context

In accordance with its interest in quality undergraduate education, USC requires all undergraduate students to demonstrate the ability to write acceptable college-level expository prose to fulfill the university's general education skills requirement. This responsibility is assumed by the Freshman Writing Program, of which the Writing Center is a significant component. The program consists of four permanent members: the director of the program, the director of the Writing Center, the director in charge of evaluation and testing, and a director concerned with special populations, such as nonnative speakers or athletes. These four members work closely together, creating the

101–102 composition course curriculum (111–112 for nonnative speakers) and determining policy that affects both the program and the Writing Center.

Thus, because of this administrative structure and the collaborative working relationships among these four members, the Writing Center significantly reflects the pedagogical approach of the Freshman Writing Program.

Tutors: Selection and Training

The other part of the program consists of about 120 graduate students from several academic departments on campus. These students teach the freshman writing course sequence and also tutor in the Writing Center, where they are known as "writing consultants." The largest group of graduate students in the Freshman Writing Program usually comes from the English department, but some are from cinema, religion, law, anthropology, psychology, linguistics, or professional writing. Varying considerably in age and experience, these graduate students apply to the Freshman Writing Program after they are admitted to a degree-granting department. They are selected on the basis of academic excellence and, in some cases, teaching experience; if chosen, they receive free tuition (a considerable savings) and a salary in exchange for teaching in the program and working in the Writing Center. New Freshman Writing Program instructors work three hours a week in the Writing Center during the fall semester and four hours a week during the spring. Experienced instructors work five hours a week in the Writing Center during the fall semester and four hours a week during the spring.

Approach to Writing

Because the same graduate students who work in the Writing Center also teach the course sequence, the Writing Center and the Freshman Writing Program adhere to a consistent composition pedagogy, an approach which views writing as an "exceptionally complex human activity—one that is conditioned both by the individuality of the writer and by the social, cultural, and linguistic forces which situate any instance of discourse" (*Freshman Writing Program Assistant Lecturer Handbook*, 1990–1991). Theoretically, the program conceives of writing as a process that must remain sensitive both to the needs of the reader and to the conceptual and stylistic expectations of an appropriate discourse community. Pedagogically, the program stresses dialogue as the basis for the instructional relationship. Classroom meetings are usually conducted as discussion sessions or workshops rather than as lecture periods, and a substantial proportion of instructional activity is carried out in small groups or one-to-one conferences. The Writing Center thus provides a significant forum for dialogic pedagogy.

Tutor Training

Training for both teaching and tutoring occurs during the last two weeks of August, immediately before the fall semester begins. Training consists of a wide variety of approaches: role-playing, discussion, paper diagnosis, modeling, and exposure to composition and learning theory. First-year graduate students in the Freshman Writing Program also attend a composition teaching course given during their first semester in the program, as well as continuing staff development sessions, which are also a requirement for more experienced teacher-tutors in the department.

The Student Context

Although Writing Center policy is conceived of as a component of Freshman Writing Program policy, program policy issues are also influenced significantly by the pragmatic concerns of the varied students who visit the Writing Center. Most students who visit the Writing Center are freshmen, although the center is available for all students at the university and is, indeed, utilized by writers at a variety of levels. Writing Center policy focuses on helping students develop a more effective writing process and on encouraging students to use the Writing Center for all facets of the writing process throughout their academic careers. The goal is for students to view the Writing Center as a valuable resource which they will continue to use on their own, even when they are no longer enrolled in freshman writing.

To ensure that students know about the Writing Center before they complete their composition sequence, instructors in the Freshman Writing Program who are teaching the first-semester course (Composition 101) are required to create one individualized Writing Center assignment for each student in the class, staggering these assignments throughout the semester. This first Writing Center assignment is a required component of the 101 course, since it is recognized that students with busy schedules are unlikely to perform any extra nonrequired tasks (Clark 1985). Some students may be required to complete several Writing Center assignments throughout the semester for specific purposes at specific times. Other students may not be required to come to the center more than once, but may choose to do so on their own. Since there are approximately 2,500 in the incoming freshman class, this requirement that all students in the Freshman Writing Program visit the Writing Center at least once means that the center is rarely quiet.

International Students

As may be expected at a sizable university in a large, multinational city, many of the students at USC are from other countries and/or do not speak English as a first language; about ten percent of the freshman class are nonnative speakers. Some of these students may be carrying visas from foreign countries; others might be second-generation U.S. citizens or permanent residents of the United States. Many of these students are under pressure from other academic departments to learn to write "error-free" English, an unrealistic expectation that creates tremendous student anxiety and a disproportionate concern with surface-level editing.

These students haunt the Writing Center, requesting additional help with what they refer to as "grammar"; however, the pedagogical approach of the Freshman Writing Program, based on current composition theory, suggests that students should focus on global areas of writing before addressing surface concerns. This tension between students' concern with surface editing and the pedagogy of the Freshman Writing Program creates a dilemma for Writing Center consultants who are often undecided about how much and what kind of assistance they can or should provide. Students usually want to optimize a given text in order to obtain a satisfactory grade, while consultants urge students to develop an effective writing process beyond the constraints of the specific text, to take responsibility for their own writing, and to use the center as a resource for continual writing improvement. Sometimes these goals are curiously incompatible, as when students want a "quick fix," while consultants wish to address long-term writing improvement as well.

Types of Services

The services provided by the Writing Center have evolved in response to the academic needs and professional goals of the students. Thus, the tutoring service, the materials, and the computer labs aim to assist students both in their freshman writing courses and in other academic classes as well as to prepare them for the world they will encounter beyond the university.

Tutoring

In the fall of 1990, the word "tutor" was changed to that of "consultant," a term which connotes a professional image appropriate to the professional aspirations of many of the students. Consultants are considered the most important resource of the Writing Center at USC; friendly and helpful, they create a nonthreatening environment for student learning. Most consulting consists of one-on-one conferences, although group consultations are now being experimented with for designated nonnative speakers.

Some students are required to come to the Writing Center on a weekly basis for a standing appointment. Many of these appointments are mandated by the program on the basis of a composition proficiency exam; others are initiated by individual instructors or requested by the students themselves. Many nonnative speakers have standing appointments.

The system of standing appointments has been extremely successful as a means of facilitating communication between the Writing Center and the classroom and as a useful strategy for working with nonnative speakers. Moreover, since the consultants work with students in an ongoing relationship, they are able to address both global and surface issues of text.

Despite the success of the system of standing appointments, some Writing Center consultants feel that seeing students only once a week is not enough, particularly if the students are nonnative speakers. These instructors point out that when students come for their standing appointments, they have usually already written a first draft which, too frequently, does not address the assignment satisfactorily because they did not really understand what was expected of them. As a result of this misunderstanding, the entire paper sometimes needs to be reconceptualized; yet at that point, students do not have the time to revise adequately and may resist discarding work which had involved considerable effort. To address this issue, the Writing Center is currently attempting a twice-weekly requirement for designated students, the first appointment for small-group discussion about the assignment and the second for an individual conference once the student has written an initial draft. This new system is based on the idea that if instructors and students engage in purposeful conversation about the assignment and the topic, students will have a better understanding of the requirements of their assignment, develop the necessary topic-specific vocabulary, and ultimately write a more suitable first draft. This draft could then be more easily revised during the second appointment.

Materials

The Writing Center has shelves of textbooks (rhetorics, workbooks, grammars, etc.) which both students and instructors can use, although only instructors are allowed to borrow them. A number of handouts for students are also available which focus on particular topics and genres useful in both academic and professional contexts. Examples of these handouts are "Writing about Film," "Writing Applications for Professional Schools," "Writing a Book Review," or "Using the Comma." Copies of the *Writing Lab Newsletter, Writing Center Journal, The Writing Instructor,* and *MacWorld* are available to instructors for professional development. The Writing Center also has several tape recorders available for both students and tutors. Sometimes students are assigned to read their papers into these tape recorders and then listen to the reading, a process that enables them to hear as well as see when their papers might be awkward or incoherent.

Macintosh Computers

Included in the Writing Center are two rooms of Macintosh computers, one functioning both as a classroom and as a drop-in lab, and the other functioning only as a drop-in lab, mainly for word processing. Because computer literacy has become so important in a variety of fields, and because word processing so easily facilitates revision, many instructors require their students to word process their papers, either on their own or in the Macintosh labs. Both classroom instructors and Writing Center consultants occasionally work with students directly at the computer to demonstrate both brainstorming and revision strategies. All of the computers were obtained through grants; they are supported through the Humanities Division or by a separate entity called the Center for Scholarly Technology.

Maintaining and upgrading the computer labs poses a problem for the Writing Center and the Writing Program, as computers require not only serious examination of their role in teaching composition but also the allocation of sometimes considerable funds. The two computer labs were obtained through outside grants; however, daily maintenance, staffing, and expansion of both hardware and software requires additional resources, which the university is always reluctant to appropriate. Despite tightening budgets, however, the Writing Center will continue to press for additional funds for its labs so that it can participate in the growing use of technology at the university.

The Researcher's Electronic Notebook

One of the most important functions of the computer labs is to serve as a development site for the *Researcher's Electronic Notebook,* originally called *Project Jefferson* (Clark 1988; 1991), a set of computer programs designed to implement the concept of the "researched paper" developed by the Freshman Writing Program. The researched paper, which is an adaptation of the traditional research paper, is a relatively short paper (5 to 8 pages) which includes the use of secondary sources but which is not intended to be either extensive or exhaustive. The researched paper is conceived of as an argument concerned with a complex topic, its support derived, at least in part, from secondary sources. In writing the researched paper, which is an important component of the 102 course, students develop skills through a process of "staged acquisition," meaning that before they are expected to grapple with and locate sources, they first complete preliminary activities and assignments that are essential for any research task. Such activities may include locating information, evaluating sources, summarizing and paraphrasing texts, note taking, writing preliminary exploratory drafts, comparing points of view, and engaging in debate.

These concepts of the researched paper and staged acquisition have been implemented through the *Researcher's Electronic Notebook,* a topic-specific on-line information retrieval system located in the Macintosh labs and also in the college library. The *Researcher's Electronic Notebook* serves as an important first step in preparing students to incorporate sources into their papers in freshman writing and ultimately to use the full range of library resources, skills they will need in other university classes.

The *Researcher's Electronic Notebook* enables students to access key terms, background information, and secondary sources for their writing assignments. Using the concept of hypertext, the computer allows students to establish links between chunks of information, thus simulating the associative cross-referencing characteristic of the research process. It also enables students to write responses to prewriting questions associated with their assignment, take notes, outline, and word process their papers. The interface created for the *Researcher's Electronic Notebook* also serves as a model for the new teaching library, which is in the process of being constructed. Thus, the computer programs designed by the Freshman Writing Program have had a significant influence on how research skills will be addressed by the university.

The main components of the *Researcher's Electronic Notebook* are the Notebook, the Encyclopedia, and Citations. The Notebook is on the student's own disk, and students take notes there or download and store information there, much as they did in notebooks in the past. Within the notebook are the assignments, prewriting questions, a notepad, and an outliner. The Encyclopedia, as its name implies, contains background information and definitions for key terms and concepts associated with the assignments and topics listed in the Notebook. The Encyclopedia enables students to access one chunk of information from another; information is structured either associatively, hierarchically, or alphabetically. If students wish to copy information from the Encyclopedia into their Notebook, they do so with a camera icon. Citations consist of bibliographic information concerned with the articles in the database, including abstracts. As students browse the citations, they can also photograph relevant ones using the camera. If students decide that they would like to read the entire article, they can read it in paper copy in the Mac lab, photocopy it in the college library, or purchase it at a nearby copying center.

Once students have gathered sufficient information for their assignment, they can then convert it to a *Microsoft Word* file, enabling them to print, cut and paste, and work with it using the word processor. Thus, they will have accumulated a substantial resource file that will ultimately be incorporated into their papers.

The *Researcher's Electronic Notebook* has enabled the Writing Center to become involved in helping students to acquire an effective "research" process as well as a writing process. Unlike the educational cassettes which were once a staple of writing center instruction, the *Researcher's Electronic Notebook* fosters, rather than inhibits, collaboration, and because the computer labs are located in the Writing Center, students and consultants can work together in accessing and compiling information through all stages of the writing process. Moreover, since it is expected that the computer lab will soon provide access to university library databases, consultants will then be able to assist students in locating and evaluating information beyond that contained in the *Researcher's Electronic Notebook*.

Physical Description

"Manifest Destiny" is the principle underlying the physical layout of the Writing Center at USC. Like many writing centers, the original Writing Lab was located in a windowless basement room and consisted only of a few tables and chairs. However, as the number of students and computers has increased, the center has pressed for correspondingly larger quarters, and it now occupies a space encompassing the size of six classrooms (figure 1). Two of these rooms are computer labs which may be accessed either through the Writing Center or through their own doors.

The remainder of the Writing Center, aside from the reception area and the director's office, consists of two large tutoring areas used for working with students in a variety of arrangements at sofas, carrels, or tables. Looking across the main room from the reception area, one will immediately hear a buzz of talk and catch a glimpse of plants, pictures, and posters. In a corner of the room is a blue-and-white sofa/loveseat combination for those who prefer a relaxed informal tutoring style; on a nearby coffee table is a plant, a dictionary, and a few haphazardly placed, brightly colored textbooks. This main area, which is often the scene of great activity, has several tables of different sizes and a few study carrels, where students and consultants can work either one-on-one or in small groups. It also has bookcases containing grammars, rhetorics, and readers for both consultant and student use, and a variety of handouts helpful for particular writing tasks and genres. In the adjacent smaller room are two screened-off areas where consultants can work with small groups. Both rooms are carpeted, so students and consultants sometimes sit on the floor.

The Writing Center and the computer labs are open Monday, Tuesday, and Thursday from 9 a.m. to 4:30 p.m., Wednesday from 9 a.m. to 6 p.m., and Friday from 9 a.m. to 3 p.m. At all times, the computer labs are staffed by a consultant, and usually six to eight, but often as many as ten, consultants in the main areas.

A Typical Day

A typical day in the Writing Center at USC is not easy to describe sequentially, as so many activities occur simultaneously, a bit like a three-ring circus. The hub of the Writing Center is the reception area—it is here that students make appointments (either in person or by telephone), that instructors reserve the computer rooms, that people

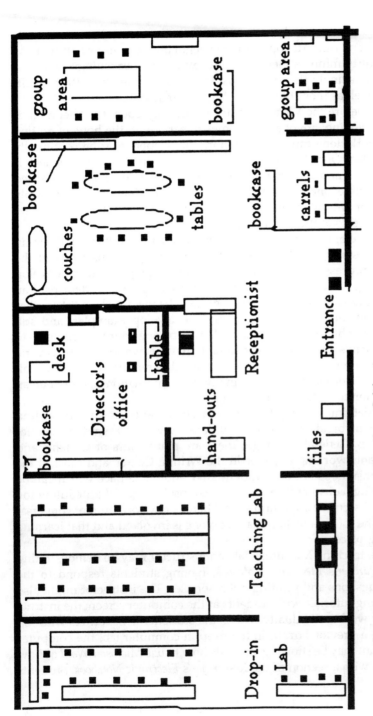

Fig. 1. The Writing Center at the University of Southern California.

call with grammatical questions, and that consultants and students check in and out. All appointments begin on the hour or half-hour, so every thirty minutes there is a new exchange of consultants and students. Amazingly, the receptionist knows the names of all the consultants as well as those of most of the regular students.

Long before the Writing Center is officially open, the telephone is already ringing; anyone who comes in early with the hope of getting some work done must either ignore the telephone or be continually interrupted. Once the Writing Center opens, the receptionist's desk is rarely quiet, and at busy times in the semester, two people are needed to work there, one to match students with consultants, another simply to answer the telephone and deal with the students trying to get appointments at the last minute.

As the telephone rings in the reception area, consultants at the main tables or study carrels work with students on various facets of the writing process. One consultant may be helping a student develop prewriting strategies; another may be listening to a student read an introduction aloud, trying to determine if the focus is clear. Yet another consultant might be helping a student develop examples; and still another might be acting as the audience, posing counterarguments to the student's position. A consultant may be working with several students from the same class, comparing different positions on a similar topic. Another may be working with an international student on an application to USC's business school.

At quiet times during the semester, consultants can sometimes find a half-hour break if appointments are slow or if a student has not shown up. Generally, though, there are many pairs of students and consultants working together in the Writing Center, and most of the time, consultants see one student after another, a pace which can be exhausting (consultants are usually counseled against scheduling too many consecutive appointments). There is always a hum of conversation in the room, a feeling that everyone is involved and that learning is taking place.

In the teaching Macintosh lab, an instructor may be demonstrating the *Researcher's Electronic Notebook*, having students respond to the focus questions and printing out responses. The instructor might also be holding tutorials with students at the computer screen; the instructor may work individually with some students while others work on revising a previous draft. In the drop-in computer lab, the computer consultant may be showing students how to use *Microsoft Word* or how to work with a section of the *Researcher's Electronic Notebook*. Students already adept at using the system may be printing out background material or adding source material to a paper in progress. The computer labs are not usually as noisy as the main consulting area, but they are not silent rooms either. Students will often confer with one another about parts of the system; the computer usually generates a collaborative spirit, particularly since some of the software is just being developed and is therefore a mystery to everyone.

Amid all this activity, the director usually moves between her office, the consulting area, the computer labs, and the main office of the program. (An appropriate costume for the director would be a track outfit and a pair of running shoes!) In her office, the director may be holding small-group training sessions for new instructors or retraining sessions for those with more experience. Such sessions might be focused on working with international students or on maintaining the balance between authoritative and facilitative collaboration. The director might also be consulting with students in the main area of the Writing Center, holding conferences with students from her own writing class, or teaching either a writing class or a session in the teacher-preparation class required of all teachers in the program. She might be meeting with computer consultants about their schedules or discussing demonstration lessons or assignments for the *Researcher's Electronic Notebook*. She might be helping the consultant in one of the labs, particularly when there is a software or hardware snag (in which case she might be under the table looking for a disconnected cable), meeting with the other members of the Freshman Writing Program, developing curriculum, writing requests for additional resources, evaluating possible new software, or meeting with consultants in crisis. Sometimes the director works on an academic paper or book; occasionally, she goes to the library to do some research. The days pass quickly—they are interesting and rewarding, but somewhat hectic!

The University Context

Writing Across the Curriculum

The director of the Writing Center is often consulted by other departments about specific assignments or student writing problems. Sometimes a particular instructor in an academic department will apprise the director of a specific assignment and request that consultants with expertise in that discipline work with students from the class. The interdisciplinary nature of the tutorial staff makes such requests easy to implement.

Outreach

The Writing Center has often been included as part of the USC Writing Project and in workshops for advanced placement teachers in the high schools. High school teachers sometimes tour the center, visit the computer labs, and talk with the director about implementing writing center pedagogy in other settings. The *Researcher's Electronic Notebook* and the concept of the researched paper are frequently demonstrated to visiting teachers as well as at national conferences; at the present time, they are being adapted in an interdisciplinary context for the Maricopa Community College district in Phoenix, Arizona.

Administration

The administration of the Writing Center consists of a director and a receptionist/secretary. The director reports to the director of the Freshman Writing Program, and the budget is administered through the program. The Writing Center director works with other members of the program to ensure that the program philosophy is implemented in the Writing Center; the director is also responsible for consultant training and maintaining communication between the two facets of the program, the classroom, and the Writing Center. The director also teaches a writing class, participates in the orientation and ongoing training of teachers and consultants, and is in charge of the computer labs.

Records

For each student who comes to the Writing Center, a permanent record of visits is kept in a file folder bearing the classroom instructor's name. The record indicates the date of the visit, the name of the consultant, and the nature of the work, and feedback is provided to each instructor on a weekly basis. For standing appointments, students complete a form aimed not only at recording their presence and the nature of the work, but also at generating awareness of their own writing process and of how that process can be implemented in the Writing Center. After each appointment, students are asked to answer the following questions: "What did this appointment show you about how to improve your writing?" and "What skills would you like to concentrate on in the future?"

Evaluation

The Writing Center is evaluated at the end of each semester as part of the overall evaluation of the program. Discussion at staff meetings is concerned with ongoing evaluation also, and the Writing Center director and other members of the Freshman Writing Program are always seeking new methods of maintaining pedagogical standards and meaningful communication in such a large program.

Portfolio Grading: A New Challenge

When the Writing Center is so closely linked with a composition program, any policy changes in the program are likely to have a profound effect on the Writing Center. This has indeed been the case during the past year, when portfolio grading was instituted as a program-wide method of composition assessment, replacing a holistically scored final exam. According to a recent survey, both students and instructors are enthusiastic about the new system; however, what has become increasingly apparent is that portfolio grading has significant pedagogical, ethical, and administrative implications for the Writing Center.

Pedagogically, the extensive use students make of the Writing Center when they revise papers for their portfolios raises questions concerning the relationship between extensive revision and the acquisition of writing skills. Because students use the Writing Center for revising and polishing prospective portfolio papers, the focus of Writing Center conferences has, at least during the weeks preceding portfolio grading, shifted somewhat toward optimizing a given text, rather than toward helping students to develop a more effective writing process, the established rationale of the Freshman Writing Program. In addition to influencing Writing Center pedagogy, portfolio grading also raises the ethical issue of the extent to which repeated Writing Center visits influence the quality of the portfolio. The question then arises as to the number of preportfolio Writing Center visits students should be permitted before collaboration becomes collusion.

Portfolio grading also has significant administrative implications, since it causes extreme overcrowding during the weeks preceding portfolio grading (at the peak of the rush during the fall semester, the Writing Center was turning away 100 students per day). This situation called attention to the necessity of planning ahead for peak center use and also raised important questions concerning the distribution of appointments, staffing, and budgeting. Finally, portfolio grading called into relief a number of ongoing Writing Center issues, in particular, the problem of how to address poor assignments, the question of legitimate and illegitimate collaboration, and the extent to which Writing Center consultants should sensitize students to the concerns of prospective evaluators.

The Writing Center and Its Context

As a large writing center visited by a large number of students at a large university in a large urban setting, USC's Writing Center is faced with the ongoing concern of how best to fulfill the needs of its diverse populations. As the Writing Center has expanded over the past nine years and has become well known throughout the university, the question of what constitutes effective tutoring and of determining which population of students should receive such assistance has become correspondingly problematic, because no matter how many consultants work in the Writing Center, they constitute a finite resource that must be utilized purposefully. How best to assist nonnative speakers is another continuing problem, which is likely to increase as Los Angeles becomes increasingly diverse in its ethnic composition. Finally, because the Freshman Writing Program is also quite large (with approximately 140 graduate student-instructors), facilitating communication between the program and the Writing Center presents another challenge.

Despite the issues of determining resource allocation, working with an increasingly diverse student population, fostering effective communication within the program and the university, implementing portfolio grading, and obtaining funds for upgrading the computer labs, the Writing Center at the University of Southern California is a cheerful energetic facility where important learning takes place. The ringing of the telephone, the clicking of the computers, and most important, the perpetual hum of conversation are indicative of a great vitality that contributes to its increasingly important role, not only within the Freshman Writing Program, but throughout the university.

Works Cited

Bamberg, Betty. 1982. "The Writing Lab and the Composition Class: A Fruitful Collaboration." In *Tutoring Writing: A Sourcebook for Writing Labs*, edited by Muriel Harris, 179–86. Glenview, IL: Scott, Foresman.

Bruffee, Kenneth A. 1984. "Collaborative Learning and the Conversation of Mankind." *College English* 46: 635–52.

———. 1973. "Collaborative Learning: Some Practical Models." *College English* 34: 635–43.

———. 1986. "Social Construction and the Authority of Knowledge: A Bibliographical Essay." *College English* 48: 73–90.

Clark, Irene Lurkis. 1985. "Leading the Horse: The Writing Center and Required Visits." *The Writing Center Journal* 5 (2)/6 (1): 31–35.

———. 1988. "Project Jefferson: A Hypertext Application for Teaching Students Research Skills." *Research in Word Processing Newsletter*, 6 (9): 2–7.

———. 1991. "The Writing Center and the Research Paper." In *The Writing Center: New Directions*, edited by Ray Wallace and Jeanne Simpson, 205–215. New York: Garland.

Krashen, Stephen. 1982. *Principles and Practice in Second Language Acquisition*. New York: Pergamon.

6 The Writing Center at Harvard University: A Student-Centered Resource

Linda Simon
Harvard University

Visitors to Harvard, which is located just outside of Boston in Cambridge, Massachusetts, are sometimes struck by the lack of a bucolic and secluded campus. Harvard has no rolling hills or acres of landscaped lawn. Instead, the university sprawls throughout Cambridge, extends along the Charles River, and has some of its professional schools in Boston. Old Harvard is evoked in its famous quad, surrounded by freshman dormitories and some ivy-covered classroom and administrative buildings.

The area of Cambridge that surrounds Harvard certainly has responded to the university's population. There are many bookstores, stationery shops, funky clothing shops, coffeehouses, and enough movie theatres and pizza shops to satisfy the student population on Saturday nights.

Harvard's undergraduates live on campus. Many have jobs and also engage in a wide range of extra-curricular activities. A large group of students participates in social service activities in the greater Boston community. Harvard has no sororities or fraternities, but students have ample opportunities to socialize with their peers. Despite their admirable academic achievements, Harvard students are not unrelentingly immersed in their studies. They are, of course, an impressive gathering of young men and women, a richly diverse group from all over the world. Most of them are well prepared to do college-level work in all areas. We rarely see basic writing problems, although, as in many other schools, we increasingly must find ways to support students who are nonnative speakers of English.

Harvard's Writing Center is part of its Expository Writing Program, which offers a required course in composition to all freshmen. Expository writing is the only required course that Harvard students take, and their initial response is not always enthusiastic. Nevertheless, by the end of the semester, the vast majority of freshmen are thoroughly convinced of the course's value. The Writing Center shares the underlying philosophy described in the booklet about course offerings in Expository Writing: "That writing and thinking are inseparably related and that good thinking requires good writing if we are to avoid the vagueness, the contradictions, and the inaccuracies of minds unable to arrange their ideas." All Harvard and Radcliffe students take this half-year course in the writing of literature, history, or social and ethical issues; they may also choose The Essay, an interdisciplinary section, or Writer's Craft, where students write fiction as well as critical essays.

The Expository Writing Program is not affiliated with any department; it is overseen by an interdisciplinary committee, run by a director and an associate director, and staffed by preceptors. These preceptors come from a wide variety of backgrounds. Some are professional journalists with no advanced degree in rhetoric or in any academic field; some are poets, literary critics, novelists, or essayists. Many have doctorates in English or a related field, and some have M.F.A. degrees. All are working writers, and many have years of experience in teaching composition before they come to Harvard.

Although Harvard students may enroll in creative writing courses in the English department and in one advanced composition course offered through the Expository Writing Program, there are no other courses available for them beyond the freshman level. The Writing Center, therefore, serves as an important resource for writing across the curriculum and across the university.

While we do not have some of the basic writing problems that instructors see in other universities, we do see students who have many of the same problems that undergraduates have elsewhere: inability to focus an essay, timidity in stating a thesis, trouble organizing ideas, strange conceptions about what is expected of them stylistically, inexperience in thinking critically. Freshmen come from a wide variety of academic backgrounds. Some have had experience in research and writing long essays; others have rarely used a library. Upperclassmen, even those who do well in their expository writing course, sometimes confront new problems when they need to write in their field of concentration. They lack knowledge of the conventions of writing in their field, or they are overwhelmed by the material they unearth as they do their research. The Writing Center responds to all of these needs.

It is a significant resource for instructors, too, many of whom are graduate students with no experience in teaching writing and considerable responsibility in evaluating students' work.

History

The Writing Center began as an experiment in 1981, at the suggestion
of a preceptor in the Expository Writing Program. From the beginning,
the Writing Center saw itself as a student-centered resource: no one
could be sent to the Writing Center, all conferences would be confiden-
tial, and the center would be staffed by peer tutors.

The instructor who developed the initial model for the Writing
Center defined the center as a counseling service and placed great
emphasis on the student-tutor relationship. Students were called clients; tutors were called consultants, and much of their training focused
on establishing a supportive, nurturing, and even therapeutic environment in which to discuss writing. Although the Writing Center was
well-used during that period, it was not generally seen as a resource
by the instructional staff, and its credibility in the Harvard community
was shaky.

In 1986, a new director decided to work toward giving the Writing
Center a more professional image. Whereas previously most material
emanating from the Writing Center served the tutor-consultant, now a
growing list of handouts addressing writing concerns was made available to the entire Harvard community; currently, these handouts are
used extensively within the Expository Writing Program itself. In addition, training material was published as *The Harvard University Writing Center Training Manual* for use within the center itself and for sale
to colleges and universities throughout the country and abroad. In
1989, the Writing Center published *Improving Student Writing: A Guide
for Teaching Fellows*, also for use within and outside the university. This
publication was a direct response to the needs of graduate students
teaching throughout the university.

Workshops, which previously operated as support groups for trou-
bled writers, now focused on particular concerns: one workshop addressed the needs of students in one large lecture course that assigned
an especially challenging paper; one workshop addressed research
paper writing; another addressed the writing of fellowship and grant
applications.

In addition, the Writing Center, which originally had served only
undergraduates, now began to respond to an increasing need among
graduate students. Special tutors were hired to serve these students,
and staff meetings were devoted to addressing the concerns that they
brought to us. Within a short time, the Writing Center had a reputation
among both students and faculty as an energetic and intellectually

sound academic service for students. Faculty members endorsed us, and student use of the center increased.

Physical Description

Visitors are often surprised that Harvard's Writing Center is not a model of high technology. Although we do have one computer, it is used by the director for administrative purposes rather than as a writing center tool. Most Harvard students have access to computers in their rooms, dormitories, or at the computer center in Harvard's Science Center, and we decided that they would not view computers in the Writing Center as a needed service.

We are housed in the Freshman Union on the same floor as the Expository Writing Program, sharing space with writing faculty. We have a wing of that floor: a reception area and three offices—one large enough for staff conferences, one for the director, and an additional small office for conferences (figure 1). The Writing Center is open from 9 a.m. to 5 p.m. daily, with two or three tutors available at every hour.

Conferences are made by appointment. There is an appointment book near the telephone, and students may call or drop by to sign in. During high-use periods, students often need to make an appointment several days in advance in order to be seen.

One wall of the reception area is covered with "hot files" containing multiple copies of our handouts. These handouts are available free to any student or faculty member and may be duplicated for classroom use. Handout topics include "The Mysterious Comma," "What Is a Thesis," "Analyzing a Text," and "Peer Review." (A current list is included later in this essay.) The list of handouts grows constantly, responding to the needs of both students and staff.

In addition, all of the offices within the Writing Center have floor-to-ceiling bookshelves containing copies of handbooks, rhetorics, essay collections, and selected journals on writing. This material is available to students and staff. File cabinets contain model papers from those departments that care to submit them, administrative material for the Writing Center, and student files. When a student has a conference at the Writing Center, the tutor writes a conference note summarizing the hour's work. This note helps the director to oversee the tutors' work, serves as an ongoing record of each student's progress, and helps the tutors to focus on particular concerns during staff meetings.

Our furniture is comfortable and inviting, with two couches and several chairs in the reception area, rugs in all offices, and attractive posters on the walls. Each fall, we have a photograph of the current staff blown up and hung in the reception area. At high-stress times, we offer trays of cookies or fruit to those who visit us.

In addition to the main Writing Center in the Freshman Union, we have two evening drop-in centers at two undergraduate libraries and in several undergraduate houses (Harvard's dormitories). These are staffed by one tutor for a two-hour period one or more days each week at each location (tutors sign up for days convenient to them). The conferences are held in quiet offices in the library or house, and publicity posters and advertisements alert students to this service each semester.

Chronology of a Typical Day

At 9 a.m. the first tutor comes to the Writing Center, turns on the lights, listens to messages on the answering machine, and, if there is no student signed up for a conference, returns any calls necessary. Tutors are not required to stay for the full hour if no one has signed up; instead, they may cancel that hour and sign up for another time at their convenience. Or they may choose to stay, catch up on writing conference notes, or do their own work. Whatever they do, they are paid for the hour.

Each hour, new tutors come, check the appointment book, and either hold a conference or do other work. The tutors are responsible for answering the telephone, making appointments, and taking messages for each other or the director. The last appointment for the day is at 4 p.m., ending at 5 p.m., when the answering machine is switched on, the lights are switched off, and the Writing Center is closed for the day.

On a typical day, tutors may see freshmen from expository writing classes, each with a draft of an essay, and upperclassmen from a variety of courses (except the sciences; we rarely see these) who may have drafts, but just as likely may have assignments, notes, outlines, or a jumble of ideas. Some of these students will be good writers who lack the confidence or skill to edit their own work; some will be less able writers, who still have not mastered the formulation of a strong thesis statement.

Since there are frequently two or three tutors at the Writing Center at each hour, the tutors themselves come to know one another very well and see the Writing Center as a social center. Since we are located

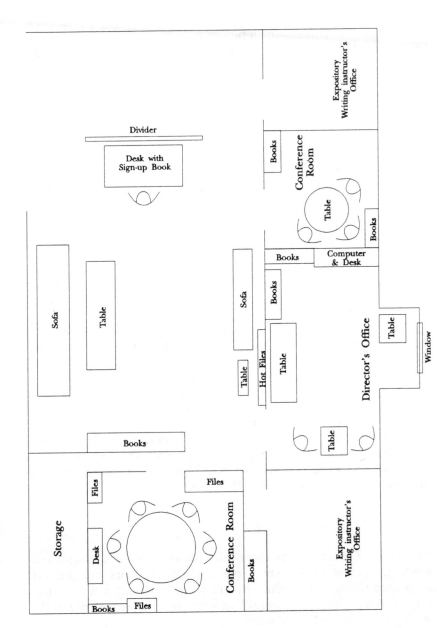

Fig. 1. The Writing Center at Harvard University.

in the Freshman Union, which houses a dining hall, they often bring breakfast or lunch up to the Writing Center and spend time informally together when they are not assigned to work. There is a close and warm community among the tutors.

Clientele

Harvard's Writing Center is available to all students throughout the university, and we are used by all students. Half of our clientele comes from expository writing courses, but the other half comes from upper-classmen in all areas and from graduate students, for whom English is often a second language.

Students learn about the center from publicity brochures that are distributed in all expository writing courses each semester, from advertisements in the student newspapers, from posters, teacher referrals, and word of mouth. Because students are never sent here, but come of their own free will, there is a positive and energetic atmosphere at the Writing Center.

Most Harvard students know that they do not need remedial help for their writing, so they come instead for the kind of editorial response that most professional writers seek from their colleagues or editors. Sometimes, students come in and tell us that they just want someone to look over a paper to tell them if it is "correct," but after a few minutes of discussion, we find out that they have some real concerns about coherence, about whether they conveyed their ideas clearly and strongly, or about whether they have supported their argument well. Because Harvard students are often writing interesting essays about a wide range of topics, Writing Center tutors find that they truly enjoy their sessions with clients.

Tutors: Selection and Training

The Writing Center is staffed by twelve undergraduate tutors, several graduate student tutors who serve graduate students, one adjunct tutor specializing in ESL concerns, one former expository writing faculty member who serves senior thesis writers and works only in the spring semester, and one director.

For the undergraduates we hire, working at the Writing Center is a prestigious job that affords considerable status and autonomy. Students are paid student-aide wages (in 1991, $8/hr.) and work ten hours per week. Our graduate student tutors are teaching fellows who get a larger stipend.

Students are alerted to our staff search through advertisements, posters, and announcements in expository writing classes. We read applications from freshmen (they are hired as freshmen in the spring and begin working as sophomores), sophomores, and juniors. We prefer to hire freshmen and sophomores, since they will be with us longer and benefit from ongoing training. But often juniors impress us with their maturity and achievements, and we are willing, then, to hire them just for their senior year.

Tutors are hired through a long and rigorous process each spring. Applicants must fill out a multipaged application, giving us grades, previous work experience, references, and a writing sample. We ask applicants to comment on two pages from typical problem papers and to respond to two typical scenarios that might come up in the Writing Center.

We all read these applications and comment upon them on a cover sheet, recommending whether to interview. Each application gets three readings. Two "yes" votes indicate that we will interview; two "no" votes, that we will not. Typically, we interview about four applicants for every position available. Positions open up when tutors graduate. Usually, tutors continue to work for us from year to year as long as they are enrolled here.

The director and two tutors sit in on each interview. We ask the applicant to engage in role-play with each tutor, and we talk generally about the applicant's own process of writing. What are we looking for? Warmth and responsiveness, to be sure. Good grades, because we believe that a student will feel more confident knowing that her tutor received an A in the course she is taking. And finally, the ability to talk about writing concretely and helpfully.

We have some applicants who are obviously successful at their own work, but who cannot seem to convey to others how they achieve that success. We look for applicants who are able to think quickly on their feet, to see alternatives in solving writing problems, to identify priorities in responding to a student's paper, and to smile easily.

We do not look for tutors from any particular concentration. We have had tutors from English, social studies, history of science, European history, mathematics, chemistry, history and literature, comparative literature, government, economics, and political science. We are concerned less with background than with breadth of interest. Potential tutors need to be confident, warm, and friendly people; they need to believe, even before they are hired and trained, that good writing transcends any particular discipline and that the concerns one has about writing usually are not discipline-specific or paper-specific. They need to be good listeners, thoughtful, helpful, and caring. They are, one might guess, a delightful group of undergraduates.

By the end of the spring semester, a new staff has been hired to replace those tutors who graduate. As soon as school begins in the fall, these new tutors bring in their schedules so that training can begin. New staff have twenty hours of training (two weeks, at ten hours per week) before they begin to give conferences. Then, they give five hours of conferences for the next two weeks, meeting with experienced tutors or the director to get feedback on any concerns they might have. By the time the first month is over, they are ready for anything.

During the first twenty hours, training consists of role-playing and reading student papers. New staff members meet individually with experienced tutors and the director, participate in small-group discussions, and attend general staff meetings. We have a large file of "problem papers" donated by expository writing teachers, and we read these together, focusing not on how to "correct" the paper but on how to intervene in the student's writing process at a place that will be most helpful to the student. Our overriding question is: How did this paper get this way? What skills does the student lack? How can we best use one hour of conference time to help this student improve not only this paper, but his writing in general?

Training continues for the entire staff in weekly meetings during which we discuss particular kinds of students (the procrastinator, for example, or the perfectionist), plan workshops, and discuss possibilities for outreach, as keeping the Writing Center visible to students and faculty is an ongoing concern.

Services

Tutoring

The main service of Harvard's Writing Center is one-on-one conferences. Students are urged to return as often as they wish, and more than half of our clients make multiple visits to the Writing Center during each semester. Some set up individual tutorials with the same staff member. If we see that a student is flitting from tutor to tutor, we usually recommend instead that the student see the same person, if possible, in order to have some continuity in his or her work on writing.

Conferences are scheduled hourly by appointment. Drop-in conferences, during evening hours, usually last about twenty minutes. Many students who come during drop-in hours follow up with an hour's conference the next day.

Workshops

In the fall semester, the Writing Center offers three workshops, one correlating with a large lecture course that many undergraduates take in the fall; another on the research paper; a third on a selected topic each semester that the tutors believe is important to undergraduates. In addition, the Writing Center co-sponsors, with the Office of Career Services, a workshop on writing grant and fellowship applications.

These one-hour workshops help to introduce undergraduates to the range of services that we can offer them. We distribute relevant handouts, give general advice on the workshop topic, and invite students to come by with their specific concerns. Many new clients are attracted through these workshops.

The Writing Center has also offered workshops focusing on designing assignments and evaluating student writing to new teachers in the Expository Writing Program.

Publications

The Writing Center sees itself as a writing-across-the-curriculum resource for the university. Besides the training manual and teaching fellows' guide, we offer more than two dozen handouts on a variety of writing concerns. These include:

"What Is a Thesis?"

"Introductions"

"Quotations"

"Macroediting and Microediting"

"The Mysterious Comma"

"The Mysterious Semicolon"

"The Book Review"

"Documentation"

"Bibliographic Form"

"What to Footnote"

Style manuals for the humanities, social sciences, and sciences

"Ten Red Flags" (copy editing)

"Weak Sentences"

"The Summary"

"The Experimental Psychology Paper"

"Conclusions"

"Early Intervention" (revising)

"Grant Applications"	"The Research Paper"
"The Experimental Research Report"	"How to Read an Assignment"
	"What Is an Argument?"
"Taking Notes"	"Peer Review"
"What Is Revision?"	"Analyzing a Text"

The handouts, with a few exceptions, are written by the director. Each semester, a list is circulated to the expository writing faculty, and they are invited to use the handouts in their classes. The handouts are distributed to interested departments for the use of their teaching assistants and faculty members; they are free to all students and faculty. The Writing Center plans to collate these handouts in booklet form for distribution within the university and for sale elsewhere.

Our current project is a booklet for undergraduates, "Writing at Harvard," which will help students understand the expectations of their instructors and will offer them suggestions to make the writing process more successful and satisfying.

Writing Across the Curriculum

There is no mechanism within the university whereby the Writing Center can require departments to send teaching assistants to us for instruction on dealing with student writing. Nevertheless, through a "perc" effect (the opposite of "trickle down"), we have become increasingly well known and well regarded in the university as students speak positively about us to their section leaders (graduate student teaching assistants). As a result, teaching assistants bring our work to the attention of tenured faculty. Several departments come regularly for advice on integrating writing into their courses; many teaching assistants come for consultations with the director on particular writing concerns.

The Bok Center for Teaching and Learning cooperates with us fully in disseminating information about writing on campus. The director of the Writing Center and selected tutors have participated in their programs for teaching assistants and teaching fellows.

Administration

The Writing Center is administered by one director, who reports to the director of the Expository Writing Program. The Writing Center has its own budget covering tutor and staff salaries, equipment, photocopying and printing, meetings and conferences, travel for the director, books, postage, telephone, office supplies, etc. This budget is planned for and administered by the director of the Writing Center.

The director of the Writing Center is also a member of the Expository Writing Program, participating in policy decisions of the program, hiring and training of new staff, and changing curriculum. The position of director is a full-time, twelve-month administrative position.

Within the Writing Center, the director's duties vary throughout the year. In the early fall, her primary responsibility is in training tutors and setting up a new schedule for the semester. She also is involved in planning publicity, distributing materials to expository writing faculty, placing advertisements, and securing rooms in libraries for evening hours. Before the semester begins, the director participates in many orientation programs throughout the university, including sessions for new teaching fellows, for international students, and for graduate students.

Once the fall schedule is set up, she works to oversee the efficient working of the center, while at the same time planning outreach programs and writing, editing, and publishing new material for the center. She is responsible for supervising tutors, reading and filing conference notes, planning weekly staff meetings, and troubleshooting any problems that may arise. The director is available for consultation by faculty members and often tutors individual students. She is responsible for all Writing Center correspondence and recordkeeping. There are no separate secretarial services, except for tutor payroll, for the Writing Center.

In the spring, the director plans for and executes the hiring of new staff, which includes advertising for applicants, reading applications, interviewing, and final hiring. She also writes recommendations for graduating tutors, most of whom highlight their work at the Writing Center in applying for jobs, grants, and fellowships.

Records

Conference notes indicate the name of the student and the tutor, the student's classification, and the course for which the paper is being written. Tutors also indicate the main focus of the conference: thesis, organization, style, ideas, ESL concerns. The tutor then records a paragraph or two summarizing the conference and indicating any problems she may have encountered while talking with the student. The conference note, in addition to being a record of the student's visit, is a letter to the director, bringing up tutoring concerns that may well be discussed at a staff meeting.

These conference notes are filed under the student's name and are available for tutors to read at any time. Tutors are encouraged to consult these conference notes if they are working with a student who has come in for multiple visits with different tutors. The conference notes are also used for statistical purposes at the end of each semester.

The appointment book is another record we have of the use of the center. In this schedule book, the tutor's name is written above an empty block for each hour. Students telephone or come in to sign the book. The pages are removed weekly and kept on file so that we can determine how well the center has been used.

The Future

Meeting the needs of graduate and undergraduate ESL students is of increasing concern to us. Undergraduate tutors do not have the training or patience necessary to address the needs of ESL students; our graduate tutors are able to work with only a small portion of the graduate students who need our help.

Harvard's Writing Center has gained steadily increasing prestige in the past several years, earning the confidence of both faculty and students. We are seen as a serious academic support organization rather than as a student advocacy group, and we are invited to participate in writing-related discussions throughout the campus.

Harvard's students enter as freshmen with writing skills that students at some other colleges may lack. Still, when they face the demands of different disciplines and the challenging material to which they must respond, they see the value of peer response and critique. We present ourselves as serious writers able to discuss the issues that confront all writers, in and out of the academy. One of our publicity fliers states: "Every writer needs a reader." All of us who write know the value of a sensitive, responsive, and helpful reader, and we know that sharing our work-in-progress enriches us and results in stronger writing. Through the Writing Center, students at Harvard are able to participate in this experience.

7 The Writing Center at the University of Puget Sound: The Center of Academic Life

Julie Neff
University of Puget Sound

A small liberal arts college is in many ways an ideal place for a writing center. Writing center values—writing as process and product, active learning, the worth of the individual—are also the values of the institution. With an enrollment of 2,800 undergraduates and an emphasis on excellent teaching, the University of Puget Sound provides just such an ideal environment for a writing center.

Even though writing is a part of the ethos of the University of Puget Sound, the director of the Center for Writing Across the Curriculum has had to work to ensure its success. And the center has been successful. Every year since it opened in 1985, the center has increased the number of individual conferences its writing advisors have conducted from fewer than 100 in 1985–86 to more than 1,300 in 1990–91. The center has moved from an alcove in another department to its own large classroom. It opened with two writing advisors; in 1990–91 it had nine. In 1985, faculty and students barely knew what it was; in 1991, it was pictured in the Admission department's *View Book.*

What has happened that can account for the growth of the center and its increased prominence on campus? Skeptics may argue that writing centers flourish because of the need to serve underprepared students. But at Puget Sound, declining student scores cannot account for the change. In fact, SAT scores are on the average 100 points higher than they were a decade ago. And by all measures, the school has become more selective. Still, the center has flourished. Essentially, the growth can be attributed to three factors: the design of the center; a clear, unwavering sense of the center's purpose; and strategic alliances within the university community.

A Design for All Students

The original design of the center has contributed greatly to its growth. Hans Ostrom, associate professor of English, designed and proposed the center to the deans in 1984. According to the original design, the center was established as an independent department with its own budget and with a director who reported directly to one of the two associate deans. The deans accepted the plan and the center came into being during the next budget year. Ostrom saw the center as a way to improve the writing climate at the university and to introduce faculty to a process-model of writing that could improve teaching and learning across the disciplines. More practically, with the public and the press scrutinizing the reading and writing ability of all college graduates, the center was a way to assure everyone that Puget Sound was addressing the issue.

The center's name, the Center for Writing Across the Curriculum, was important because it took the emphasis off "skills" and made it possible for the center to establish itself as a center for all students, at every level. It was not a fix-it shop for weak writers or for those struggling with the Freshman Writing Seminar. The name also helped the center differentiate itself from the Learning Skills Center, which had a penchant for product and a reputation for being remedial. Although the Learning Skills Center had been fixing problem papers for years, The Center for Writing Across the Curriculum took a process approach, dealing first with the cognitive issues of focus, tone, organization, and development.

With a budget of its own, the center was not dependent on the goodwill of the English department or its chairperson. Historically, the director of the center has been a faculty member in the English department and has maintained close ties to that department. Having a director with faculty status and with departmental affiliation has been tremendously helpful to the center. With faculty status, the director has access to other faculty through departmental and university committees. Having a faculty member in charge of the center gives the program credibility with students and with other faculty, while putting the center's director in the classroom at least once or twice a year keeps him or her in the mainstream of the university. Faculty status also gives the director access to faculty enrichment and travel funds, both of which are in short supply for staff members.

Because the center's director controls the budget, the director can allocate that budget to the good of the center. Thus, it is able to sponsor various writing-related events, such as the hosting of a visiting poet, journalist, or composition expert, without the blessing of the English department. The Center for Writing Across the Curriculum often collaborates with a number of departments to co-sponsor writing-related activities like the bring-your-best-writing-assignment wine and cheese party.

The center's budget allows it to have equal status with other departments on campus. Line items include:

professional travel	books
public relations	subscriptions
professional memberships	supplies
printing	telephone
mileage	copying
speakers	publications

Most important, other departments on campus have equal and direct access to the Center for Writing Across the Curriculum and its services. The director can assist and work directly with any and all departments on campus, a situation that has allowed the director to build those important connections and strategic alliances that are so important to a cross-curricular writing center at a small institution.

Mission

As a way to clarify its purpose and to position itself within the mission of the university, the center has articulated its goals: "The Center for Writing Across the Curriculum at Puget Sound promotes writing as a tool for teaching and learning in every discipline."

This mission statement gives the center staff a consistent voice when they communicate with colleagues who may not be familiar with writing center theory and pedagogy. The programs and services it offers grow out of that statement of purpose, and every activity the center undertakes in some way fits into its goals. The mission statement also tells the center director what the center should not be doing. Because grammar workshops and grammar hotlines put emphasis on the product rather than the process, the center does not conduct them. Because testing puts emphasis on evaluation, not growth, the center does not do that, either. Center faculty and peer advisors are committed to helping every student become a better writer and to helping every faculty member become a better teacher of writing.

Consistent with the center's mission, the director helps faculty members incorporate writing into their courses and into departmental curricula. In 1990, the university curriculum committee asked each department to provide a significant writing experience for its majors. As a result, the director has worked with departments as well as individuals to develop writing assignments and to incorporate them into the departmental curricula. To help faculty with the writing they are assigning and evaluating, the center's director has organized one day-long writing workshop and one two-day workshop on revision, as well as informal lunches and coffees. All of these activities have the same goal: to promote writing as a tool for teaching and learning.

With its mission clearly in mind, the center engages in a number of writing-related activities. The most important is the one-to-one conference. Although the length of conferences varies, most last forty-five to sixty minutes, and though students from every department on campus use the center, the majority of conferences are with students enrolled in humanities courses. Students come in at all stages of the writing process: some, with only an assignment sheet, who need help getting started; others with notes or outlines, but no draft; some with a draft who need advice on focus, development, or organization; others who have graded papers, but who want help interpreting the professor's comments. In still other conferences, advisors answer questions about grammar or style.

The faculty in the center often talk to students about writing that is not done for a particular class: a short story or poem, a news story for publication, a medical or law school personal statement, or a major scholarship application, like a Fulbright, Marshall, or Mellon.

Working with all kinds of writers has helped assure faculty and students that the center is not a place for remediation. As one faculty member said, "Every writer needs a reader."

A typical day in the life of the Center for Writing Across the Curriculum reflects how these writing conferences actually work on a day-to-day basis.

Chronology of a Typical Day

The day begins when Maria opens the door at 8:55 a.m. The room is bright, even on a foggy Northwestern morning. The paned windows run the whole length of the room and look out onto the tree-lined lawn, which runs between the dorms on the east side of campus. On the left side of the room, four MacIntosh computers, 2 IBM compatibles, and two printers sit quietly for the moment. In the far corner, separated from computers by a noise-absorbing partition, one of the faculty members from the English department has a desk and a typewriter that is also available for student use. (This is one of the last typewriters on campus, and students use it to complete forms that cannot be done on the computer.) On the half wall are three large pieces of heavy paper that the students use for impromptu writing, a kind of "democracy wall."

A yellow couch and two easy chairs sit under the long windows. A coffee table with yesterday's *New York Times* stands in front of the couch. In the far right-hand corner of the room are a conference table, four padded chairs, and a large bookshelf that runs almost the entire width of the room. Near the door is another desk that contains the appointment book, telephone, pads, and pencils, ready for the next conference.

Maria picks up an empty pop can and throws it into the recycling bin under a table, files the comment sheets left from the day before, and checks the appointment book for her first appointment of the day. Andrew, a timid freshman, approaches the desk. "Is this the Center for Writing Across the Curriculum?" he asks.

"Yes, it is," Maria says with a smile. "Come on in and have a seat." Maria pulls a white 8 1/2" × 11" conference form from the drawer and records the student's name, date, major, and address, all the time chatting with the student to put him at ease. As she finishes, she looks up, smoothly making the transition to the conference, "What brings you to the center this morning?"

The student pulls out a handwritten draft of a Humanities 102 paper, apologizing for it being "so messy." Maria smiles and says, "Don't give it a thought. We don't care if it's messy; after all, it's still a draft."

The telephone rings. Maria answers it and makes an appointment for a student later in the day.

Maria finishes reading the student paper, makes several positive comments about the topic and the examples the student has chosen, and then moves on to respond to the paper's focus or lack of it.

The telephone rings again; it's a student wanting an appointment. With only a nod to Maria, another student comes in to drop off a paper for the Hearst Writing Contest, another to read the *New York Times*. Almost intuitively, students understand how the center works, and they know that it is their place for reading and writing.

With a "thank you" and "I'll be back," the humanities student loads his backpack and leaves for class. Maria writes a one-paragraph evaluation of the appointment, which includes the kind of paper, its strengths and weaknesses, what suggestions she made to the student, and what the student intended to do with the paper after the conference; she then pulls the file on her next appointment—a freshman she has worked with before.

During the class break at 10 a.m., Shannon and Tara (two other writing advisors who will work in the afternoon) stop by to check their appointments, and Tara makes an appointment with Maria to go over rough drafts for a fiction class. All peer advisors are required to have at least two appointments each semester with another advisor.

Maria spends the next forty minutes with Sandra, who is working on a paper for English 101. Sandra's professor required everyone in her class to visit the center. Sandra fulfilled the requirement reluctantly the first time; now she visits the center regularly. When Sandra leaves, Maria has time to write the description of the visit and to work on a center announcement for the *Tattler*, the daily campus bulletin.

The 11 a.m. slot is free, so Maria also has time to read through the "info/file," a collection of memos and recent articles the director left for the writing advisors. But the telephone rings with students requesting appointments; two different students stop by with grammatical questions; and Bob, a student confined to a wheelchair, arrives to use the center's computers. (The center's computers are the only ones on campus that are accessible to students in wheelchairs.) The director stops in after her class to check the appointment book, to pick up messages, and to ask how things are going. (She has appointments booked for 1 p.m. and 1:30 p.m.)

At 11:55 a.m., Maria leaves for class. Shannon, a junior business major, arrives at noon. She has an appointment with a student who is having trouble getting started on a religion paper. Shannon goes over the assignment line by line with the student and, through extensive questioning, helps him brainstorm possible topics for the paper. The conference ends at 12:40 p.m., and she has time to record the visit before leaving for class. The director returns for her 1 p.m. and 1:30 p.m. appointments, both with students from her news writing class. From 1 p.m. until 2 p.m., all of the peer writing advisors are in class, so the director's time is spent conducting appointments, answering the telephone, and helping drop-ins.

At 2 p.m., Tara, a junior English major with a professional writing emphasis, arrives for an appointment with Matt from her advanced poetry class. She takes over the desk and telephone, and the director moves to the couch, staying on to talk to a student about a Rotary scholarship. Just before three, Brandon, a senior English major, reports for work. Because Tara does not have a scheduled appointment, she takes care of the telephone and the appointment book, and Brandon takes his student, Andrew, who is working on a review of literature for a physical therapy class, to the table.

At 4 p.m., Tara is ready to leave. Brandon moves to the appointment desk to hold his 4 p.m. and 4:30 p.m. conferences: one for an American History 351 student, another for a senior business major taking an American literature class. The center closes at 5 p.m., but reopens again at 7 p.m., when Shauna, an MAT candidate, comes in for evening hours. While Shauna conducts her conference, other students drift in to use the computers, and at 8 p.m., Brandon's writing group arrives for its weekly meeting on the yellow couch. At 9 p.m., Shauna finishes her last appointment and closes the door to signal that conferences are over for the day. She finishes at the desk and joins the writing group still in progress. The discussion continues late into the evening.

Writing Center Activities and Events

This typical day does not include all of the activities for which the center is responsible. In addition, we are responsible for the following activities and events.

Hearst Writing Prizes. Each spring, the center sponsors writing prizes funded by the Hearst Endowment for Writing. These cash prizes of $175 each are awarded to students who have written papers for courses in the humanities, social sciences, and natural sciences and mathematics. One prize is awarded for the best paper written in a Freshman Writing Seminar. The contest not only rewards good writing but also benefits the center in other ways. Dropping off papers in the center and picking them up after the contest brings all kinds of students into the center. The division faculty who judge the contest have the opportunity to discuss the qualities of good writing with their colleagues, something that seldom happens, even in the English department. They also see what kinds of writing assignments are being given in other departments and how students are responding to those assignments. Each year the committees change to give as many faculty as possible a chance to participate.

Workshops. The center sponsors workshops during the year for students engaged in special kinds of projects or with special needs: "How to Write Your Marshall, Mellon, Fulbright, or Rhodes," "Thesis Writing," "Thesis Revision," and "Strategies for Writing Essay Exams." These workshops, put on by the center director and faculty members, allow the center to work closely with the Honors Program and with other departments that require a thesis for graduation. Students get to know center staff and, as a result, often come in for individual conferences. In a small school, students know who the scholarship candidates are likely to be, and when they see a Fulbright candidate working in the center, they know that it cannot be a place for remediation.

Guest Speakers. The center sponsors or co-sponsors visiting writers, who come to read their stories or poems or to talk about the writing they do. In the past few years, the center has co-sponsored novelist Itabari Njeri; CBS News correspondent Lyn Brown; CBS/KIRO consumer reporter Herb Weisbaum; and author of *And the Band Played On*, Randy Shilts. The guest speakers let students and faculty know that there is more to writing than a paper for a class; writing is a human activity, not just an academic one.

Library. The center has almost 1,000 books about writing and publishing that are available to students. The reference books must be used in the center; other volumes can be checked out. Most, though not all, were donated to the center by members of the English department or friends of the university. The most popular of these are the dictionaries, handbooks, and the Associated Press (AP), American Psychological Association (APA), and Modern Language Association (MLA) style books. Other books include *The Writers Market, Writing in the Social Sciences, Handbook of Technical Writing, Business Writer's Handbook,* and *The Chicago Manual of Style.*

Writing-Across-the-Curriculum Activities. The center's director has helped faculty understand that writing is a way of learning course material as well as a way of communicating information. Because faculty members see the need for writing assignments in their courses, they seek the director's assistance when they are incorporating writing into their courses or into department curricula.

Strategic Campus Alliances

The center has been successful, in part, because its director has built strategic alliances within the campus community that have affected everything from the acquisition of new space to the recruitment and training of writing advisors. Many of the projects the center is involved in have grown out of these campus alliances.

The variety of students attending the center on a typical day is due to the enthusiasm with which most faculty members support the center. At least some of this support grows out of faculty involvement with the center; faculty members are asked to refer students for the writing advisor positions, and they are asked to come to training meetings to talk to the writing advisors about the writing in their courses and in their discipline. Some of these faculty members bring their classes into the center; others invite center faculty to come into their classes.

The director has also built campus alliances by participating in the activities and programs of other departments. One of the most important alliances was the one forged between the center and Academic Computing, which eventually solved the problem of space for the center. From 1985–1990, space was one of the center's biggest problems. In 1985, the center was fortunate to be stationed on the main floor of a centrally located building across from the Student Union. Unfortunately, it had only an alcove inside the Learning Center, although administratively it was not affiliated with this program (figure 1).

The Center for Writing Across the Curriculum alcove was separated from the Learning Skills Center with only half walls and no door. The greatest difficulty was the actual size of the alcove. When the university photographer came to the center to take a picture for *Arches*, the university's alumni magazine, the photographer had to stand on a chair outside the center and peer over the partition in order to photograph a conference in progress. It was so small that even when standing, the director and peer writing advisors could not all be in the center at the same time. Thus center meetings, writing groups, workshops, peer advisor training, and some conferences were held in rooms other than the center. The center had two computers, but only one fit in the center; the other was in storage.

When the center opened, space was not a significant problem. But as it grew, the number of students who used it and the six peer writing advisors who worked there presented significant problems for both the Center for Writing Across the Curriculum and the Learning Skills Center. Even so, by the 1989–90 academic year, the center conducted almost 1,100 conferences in the original alcove. To accommodate the clients, however, conferences spilled into the Learning Center, taking up space at tables generally reserved for quiet study.

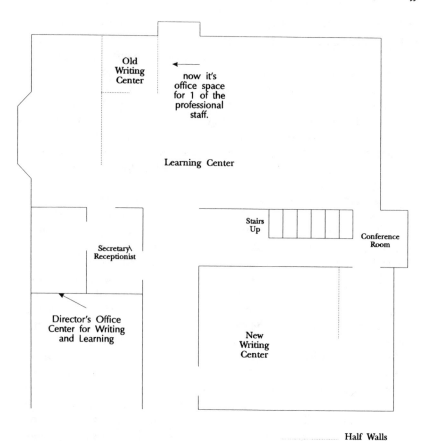

Fig. 1. The former location of the Center for Writing Across the Curriculum at the University of Puget Sound.

The center conferences sometimes included loud, enthusiastic conversations, which were irritating for the Learning Center and its four staff members.

The center's hours were also dictated by Learning Center hours, which were limited to 9 a.m. to 5 p.m., Monday through Friday. Because the center was so small, the director had an office in the English department, which meant that supervision of the peer advisors was often spotty.

By the fall of 1989, the deans realized that the center had outgrown its space. However, appropriate center space apparently did not exist at a school which had outgrown its existing buildings.

The first floor of Howarth Hall continued to be a desirable location for the center because of its central location and because it was an area that belonged to several departments: the Honors Program, Academic Computing, the Learning Center, and educational psychology. A solution to the center's space problem finally grew out of informal conversations between the director of Academic Computing and the director of the Writing Center. On the first floor of Howarth, next to the Learning Center, the academic computing department had a large room that had originally been two classrooms. Several years earlier the wall had been removed. The director of academic computing proposed that the center be given half of that large room in exchange for supervising at least six computers. This alliance was formed during several conversations about the need for students to make better use of computers. "They need to see them as more than smart typewriters," complained the director of Academic Computing.

"We can teach them strategies for revision, but we have only one computer because we don't have space for more," I replied. The center director agreed to work closely with Academic Computing to optimize the use of the computers, and in return, Academic Computing agreed to give the center half of its space.

The deans agreed to make the restoration of the wall a priority item in the following year's budget. By the beginning of the next fall term, the center had its own space and its own computers (figure 2).

The director collaborates with other departments, too. At the beginning of the year, the director participates in the training of the Peer Advising Associates, an academic advising program, the training of the new admissions counselors, the residence assistants, and the campus tour guides. One of the strongest alliances is with the Office of Academic Advising. The director sits on the ad hoc faculty committee to Academic Advising, works closely with the advising counselor who looks after at-risk students, and participates in transfer orientation.

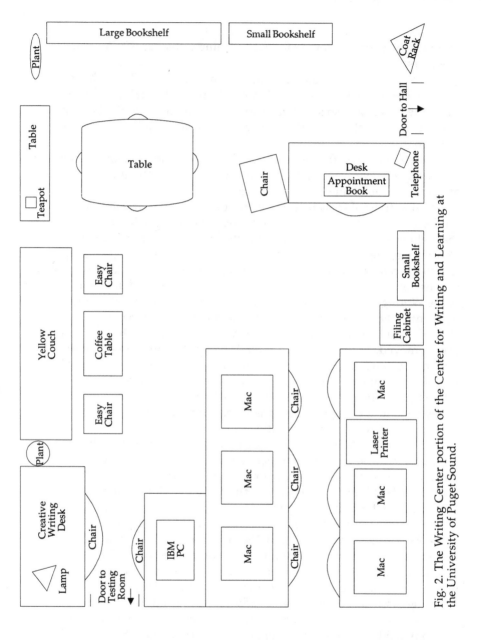

Fig. 2. The Writing Center portion of the Center for Writing and Learning at the University of Puget Sound.

The center works with career advising to see that application letters and graduate school personal statements are as clear and accurate as possible.

The alliance with the Honors Program has also been strategically important. The center director works with the director of the Honors Program and his assistant to conduct workshops and to support the students as they work on their honors theses. This connection allows the center to avoid the remediation label.

Another important alliance has been with the office of the dean of students. The director meets regularly with the counseling staff to establish lines of cross referral. Occasionally, the students' writing problems grow out of emotional, social, or academic problems that the writing advisors should not handle. On the other hand, counselors sometimes see students whose lives would improve if they had help with their writing. Establishing open lines of communication with this office has been essential for referring students to the appropriate places and for the center's success. To stay abreast of student concerns, the director joined the faculty Student Life Committee. The committee, composed of the dean of students, the dean of the university, three other faculty members, and two student members, gives the director one more way of making sure the center continues to be in the mainstream of university life.

Selecting the Writing Advisors

Brandon is just one of seven writing advisors who was selected the previous spring from about sixteen applicants. To apply, students send a letter of application, which includes their interest in the center, their writing classes at Puget Sound, their grade-point average, why they want to work in the center, what they intend to contribute, their major and minor areas of study, campus activities, and a sample essay that has been turned in for a class.

The director reads all of the applications and then calls colleagues in a variety of disciplines for recommendations and asks the current peer writing advisors for their recommendations and observations about the candidates. Many of the writing advisors know the candidates through class work or campus activities. The key question to the peer writing advisors is, "Would you take a paper to this candidate for a response?" Because this center is run primarily by the student advisors, they must be reliable and trustworthy. If they are, they will survive even the most chaotic days.

The director also tries to maintain various kinds of diversity in staffing the center: gender, race, age, major, activities, and learning style. But most important, the writing advisors must have three qualities: they must be good writers, good students, and nice people. The center faculty has discovered that students who are arrogant make poor writing advisors no matter how bright they are or how well they write. They have also discovered that students who are familiar with writing groups and collaborative writing are easier to train and generally make better advisors than those who are familiar with only the lecture model.

As the center has grown and as faculty and students have become familiar with its work, the number and quality of the advisor applicants have grown. The center positions are considered to be among the most desirable student employment opportunities on campus. Although the center tries to use work-study students, it has the option of hiring non-work-study advisors, if they seem to be the best qualified. Students usually work about ten hours a week and earn from $5.90–$6.40 per hour, depending on their length of service. Although the center occasionally hires a sophomore, the advisors are usually juniors and seniors.

Training the Peer Writing Advisors

For all seven writing advisors, training begins the day that classes begin. The director and the other faculty writing consultant meet with the peer advisors for two to four hours each day of that first week, depending on the students' schedules. After the first week, training continues on an individual basis, with experienced advisors working with new ones until the new advisors are comfortable and the veteran advisors think they are ready to do their own conferences. Throughout the semester, training continues at weekly meetings attended by everyone in the center.

The training includes the history and mission of the center; get-acquainted activities; an assessment of the advisors' attitudes toward writing; discussions of writing evaluation and writing pedagogy; conference demonstrations; a Learning Styles Inventory; a grammar diagnostic test; a tour of the center's files and bookshelves; and numerous practice sessions with both peers and the faculty who work in the center.

Follow-up training deals with specific problems the students are encountering in conferences, discussions about ethics, and other issues of composition theory and pedagogy as it applies to the center. The director usually schedules faculty from other disciplines to speak during the spring term.

The Future

In the summer of 1990, the dean of the university combined the Learning Center and the Center for Writing Across the Curriculum and gave the director of the Center for Writing Across the Curriculum responsibility for both. "Make the Learning Center like the Center for Writing Across the Curriculum," the associate dean said. The center director took this directive to mean "make it lively, vital, creative, and student-centered."

In September 1990, the combined centers opened under the new name of the Center for Writing and Learning (figure 3) with the redefined mission of helping every Puget Sound student make the most of his or her education. However, the specific mission of the Center for Writing Across the Curriculum remained the same: to promote writing as a tool for teaching and learning in every discipline.

The combining of the two centers has worked to the advantage of the Center for Writing Across the Curriculum. It has meant more resources for the center in terms of budget, secretarial assistance, and staff. Because the center director took on more administrative responsibility, the deans agreed to let the center share an additional faculty position with the English department.

The Learning Center benefited, too, as it became a friendlier, livelier place that attracts all kinds of students, not just the ones in academic trouble. The combined center benefits from the alliances that the Center for Writing Across the Curriculum had built over the years. The Learning Center has also benefited from the centrality of the Center for Writing Across the Curriculum. The new center works closely with a variety of departments, to the advantage of all students.

The Center for Writing and Learning will continue to explore ways in which it can increase and improve services to students and to faculty. The center has been working closely with academic advising and academic departments to identify and help at-risk students before they find themselves in academic trouble. At the same time, it has become increasingly active in helping students who are writing theses or applying to graduate school. The center also continues to look for ways to build strong ties between itself and academic departments so that it can be of assistance not only to students but also to faculty.

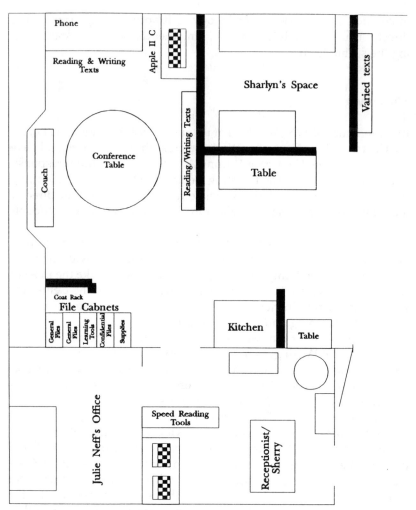

Fig. 3. The Center for Writing and Learning at the University of Puget Sound.

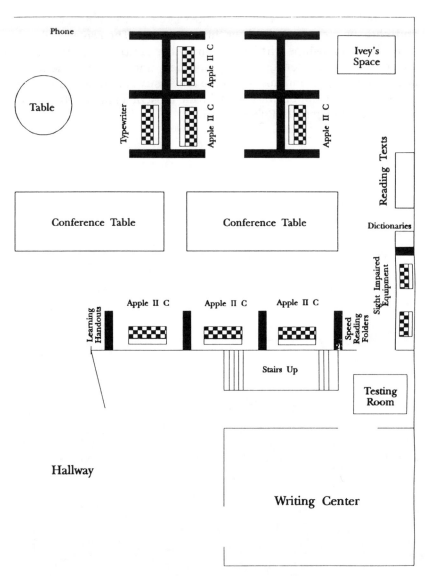

Fig. 3. *Continued.*

In the long run, the center will most likely have more computers and perhaps a computerized writing classroom. The center will improve its relationships with faculty and other campus departments to ensure that the Center for Writing and Learning will continue to be central to the goals and mission of the university and to provide every student with the opportunity to make the most of a liberal arts education at the University of Puget Sound.

8 Establishing a Writing Center for the Community: Johnson County Community College

Ellen Mohr
Johnson County Community College, Overland Park, Kansas

Founded in 1967, Johnson County Community College is located in the heart of one of the wealthiest and most prestigious suburbs in the United States. Johnson County is south of metropolitan Kansas City, just over the Kansas border. Once mostly farmland, in the past twenty years the community has consistently been a rapidly growing suburb, not only in population but also in business and industry. To meet the needs of the community, the college was established first in various office buildings and then later on a beautiful campus, which epitomizes the affluence and pride of its community.

In its short history, the college has established itself as an excellent educational institution, winning nationwide recognition for its nursing and dental hygiene programs, the hospitality management and chefs apprenticeship programs, the computer technology division, and the staff development program. Recently, the college was selected as one of the top twenty community colleges in the country. Its enrollment of over 16,500 daytime and nighttime students is made up of traditional students, who are recent high school graduates and will be transferring to four-year institutions, and nontraditional students, ranging from ages 22 to 82, who are upgrading technical information, polishing skills, earning new degrees or certificates, or simply acquiring knowledge. The quest for excellence, which has always been an ongoing mission of the college, includes writing proficiency in each of the disciplines. To assure that all students receive support in acquiring these writing skills, a writing center has been provided.

The community college philosophy provides an open-door policy to students at all levels. The Writing Center assesses, prepares, and supports these diverse levels of skills. This service aids in retention and helps ensure the success of most students.

Furthermore, the community college atmosphere of innovation and humanism provides the setting for teacher-student interaction and student-student collaboration. The community college does not have the red tape or bureaucracy that many universities have. Students may seek help on their own, or they will be referred to services where help is available; these services are free and do not require the student to qualify or enroll to take advantage of them.

The community college frequently attracts returning adults and others who might not have otherwise attempted furthering their education. A diversity of clients is to be expected when students know they will have encouraging instructors, class loads are small, and services are available to help them review and upgrade skills. Many of these students excel in the community college atmosphere, becoming peer tutors themselves, going on to succeed in universities, and even becoming teachers.

The Johnson County Community College Writing Center focuses on individualized instruction; provides student writers with an audience; encourages collaboration; puts the student at the center of the learning; maintains strict guidelines about proofreading and plagiarism; promotes writing across the disciplines; offers programs, both computerized and traditional, to help improve writing skills; and connects computer literacy and the writing process as essential lifelong skills.

History

Realizing that many students have difficulty writing well, a problem that requires more than classroom instruction, instructors in Johnson County Community College's English department agreed in 1977 that a writing center would be an asset. A survey of students enrolled in composition classes, as well as feedback from counselors, confirmed the need for a writing center, a need that was further substantiated as standardized test scores for students dropped and as students enrolled in composition classes without the prerequisite skills. Once the need for a writing center was established, two instructors with substantial release time began planning the center in the spring of 1978. The center was opened on a limited basis in the summer of that same year and was opened on a full-time basis the following fall semester. Also at that time, the Grammar Hotline was established to serve the community. Shortly after the hotline was installed in 1979, *Time* magazine published a short article about it.

In the beginning, the center primarily provided assistance to students from English classes who needed help with their writing skills. Today, the center's services have expanded to include aid to other disciplines by helping instructors design writing assignments and write sabbaticals, résumés, and other related material, and by assisting students with interdisciplinary writing assignments. Another attraction of the center has been the addition of one-credit courses.

The philosophy of the English department is the underlying philosophy of the Writing Center: (1) that writing is a process, (2) that through writing we discover more about ourselves and others, (3) that writing is a way of learning, and (4) that writing is an important lifelong skill which can be learned. Furthermore, we believe writing and reading are so interrelated that to help students improve their writing skills is to help them improve their reading skills. The synthesis of reading and writing is most pronounced when students read literature and write about it.

The primary concern of the Writing Center is to give personalized instruction to college students who need to refresh, review, and/or improve their grammar and writing skills. Students can improve their writing skills if they are willing to seek help and work. Furthermore, the philosophy is that the way to improve writing is to actually *write*. To this end, the center provides individualized instruction for students who seek assistance. The instruction is geared toward helping students improve actual pieces of writing. Tutors do not proofread; instead, they show students alternatives to overcome their writing problems. Based on the feedback from students, the center is living up to its philosophy that students can improve their writing and that writing is a tool for learning.

In the fall of 1987, the JCCC Writing Center was honored by the Kansas State Department of Education with the Excellence in Education award. In 1990, the center received an excellence award from the National Association of Instructional Administrators. As a recipient of these awards, the Writing Center has become a model for new and existing centers. For example, a number of new high school and middle school writing centers have been established in the Kansas City area. As a result, the JCCC Writing Center has been visited frequently by the directors and coordinators of those centers. The director has lent her support by sharing professional readings and materials as well as answering questions. Existing writing center personnel and people interested in starting writing centers have been brought together, first at JCCC's Writing Center and then, more recently, at the University of Missouri in Kansas City and Longview Community College.

At JCCC, the Writing Center has served not only the English department but also the students and instructors throughout the campus. The growing number of students from other disciplines and the support of instructors, staff, and community have helped to maintain the financial commitment of the school to this program.

Physical Description

The Writing Center is located in the building that houses the school library and is close to other student services, such as the Academic Achievement Center, Math Lab, and Apple Alliance Computer Lab. When students first enter the room, they notice at once that it is not a traditional classroom. Although somewhat crowded with numerous bookcases, filing cabinets, and vertical files, the room's most noticeable features are the friendly faces seated at the round tables throughout the room. Apple and IBM computers and printers for student use frame the room. Large bulletin boards display composition instructors' current assignments. A small bulletin board near the secretary's desk holds current complimentary notes and snapshots of tutors in meetings and social gatherings. A notebook with notes from tutor meetings and suggestions for newsletter articles keeps tutors abreast of the center's activities. Available on top of several low bookshelves are materials about the Writing Center's services and the current newsletter produced by the peer tutors. Students also take advantage of the numerous notebooks, which contain assignments and model student papers for specific courses across the disciplines. These books are especially helpful to the Writing Center staff when they work with students from courses with which they are unfamiliar. The furniture was selected to create a comfortable learning environment, and colorful posters and plants help to put the visiting student at ease. A smaller room is connected to the Writing Center and is large enough to house filing cabinets and to store computer software, while providing a quiet room for students not needing a tutor or a computer (figure 1).

Chronology of a Typical Day

A typical day in the JCCC Writing Center begins at 8 a.m. with the arrival of several peer tutors, who sign in and usually have time to discuss problem students from the day before or exchange pleasantries before the first client arrives. Around 8:30 a.m. clients begin to stop by. The secretary-receptionist greets students, makes each a folder with information about course and instructor, determines the reason for the visit, and then assigns them to the waiting tutors or instructors. If a

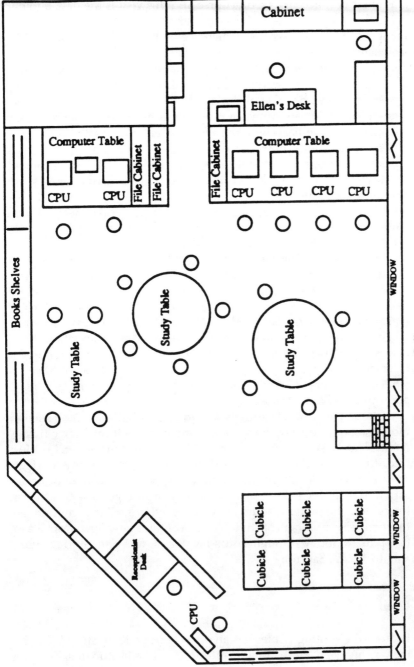

Fig. 1. The Writing Center at Johnson County Community College.

student is enrolled in a credit course and this visit is the first, a folder is filled out and a writing skills assessment given. Usually the assessment is a diagnostic writing which is evaluated by an instructor. The instructor then assigns appropriate materials, making sure all pertinent information is recorded in the student's folder. Thereafter, students will refer to the study guide in the folder each time they visit the center. However, because of the nature of individualized instruction, students may deviate from the program, if necessary, as long as they work on a regular basis with the Writing Center instructors.

Drop-in students, however, do not have a set program. They may work on assignments with tutors, who give them feedback on content and style; they may work on computer programs; or they may work alone on assignments, using Writing Center resources. A brief chat with a student usually establishes his or her immediate needs. When students leave the Writing Center, their time of departure and activity for the day are recorded in their folders.

The busiest time of the day is between 8:30 a.m. and 2 p.m. After a lull from 2 p.m. to 4:30 p.m., activity in the Writing Center increases around 5 p.m., when working students, who comprise an important part of the college population, come to the campus. Some days as many as 90 students seek help in the center. All of this activity is logged carefully so that the secretary can enter the information into a database program (*Smart*). She runs an individual monthly report for instructors so that they will know which of their students have attended the center and for how long. A statistical report is sent to appropriate administrators.

Although over 1,000 different students visit the Writing Center more than once during the semester (most return three to five times), no student is ever turned away or has to wait long for help. Most tutoring sessions last fifteen to thirty minutes, and many students remain to work alone on their writing. Appointments are not necessary, and plans are to keep this policy, as it encourages students to visit the center. The center's hours were increased in 1987 to accommodate the increasing numbers of students; the center is now open from 8 a.m. to 8 p.m., Monday through Thursday; 8 a.m. to 2 p.m., Friday; and 9 a.m. to 1 p.m., Saturday.

Clientele

Because the Writing Center has an open-door policy, it strives to serve the writing needs of the total institution, staff, and students. The ages of the over 4,000 students served each semester range from 16 to 70, with an average age of 28. Because the wide cross-section of students represents varied educational as well as ethnic backgrounds, the Writing Center also has programs geared for specific audiences, including the nonnative students and the hearing impaired. A one-credit course, Practical Writing Skills, focuses on sentence structure, vocabulary, and idioms in a program for the ESL and hearing-impaired students, two important and growing groups attending the Writing Center. Because JCCC is a satellite school for Gallaudet University, and located near the Kansas School for the Deaf in Olathe, many hearing-impaired students attend. In addition to providing materials and programs created especially for this audience, the Writing Center tutors receive special training, and interpreters are scheduled in the WC at specific times. One-credit courses are also offered in such areas as proofreading, sentence-pattern skills, paragraph skills, and research techniques. However, many students do not wish to take the credit courses but simply elect to receive individualized help on specific assignments or to work on correcting specific problems or weaknesses in their writing.

Another source of clientele is through instructor referral. Checklists are provided so that instructors may send their students with a tally of the skills they need to improve. The teacher is notified as to what was accomplished during the referral session.

A writing center is often shaped by its clientele. An obvious influence on an institution such as Johnson County Community College is, of course, the community. Our Writing Center meets the needs of the public by providing materials which address business or technical writing, hours which are flexible to meet work schedules, and the Grammar Hotline, which gives quick, direct answers to writers' questions. More specifically, the JCCC Writing Center has been influenced and challenged by three special groups: the adult learner, students whose English is their second language, and hearing-impaired students. As the college grows, so do these populations, and finding strategies to meet their needs while still providing quality service for the rest of our students is not always easy. At the risk of generalizing or stereotyping, I will discuss briefly each group's needs and how our Writing Center meets those needs.

The profile for the returning adult is frequently a middle-aged female whose children are grown and who would now like to pursue a career put on hold fifteen to twenty years ago or who has recently been divorced and must upgrade her skills for the job market. She comes to the Writing Center on the pretext that she needs to review her writing skills before taking composition classes or classes in which writing is assigned. Actually, she needs to build up her confidence. She needs a place where she feels she can belong. By writing in a comfortable, no-risk environment, she builds confidence in her ability to compete in an academic world with younger students. The tutors review the basics, explain the writing process, and offer her the opportunity to write in a variety of rhetorical modes. As she works through the process, she is encouraged with positive reinforcement. It is interesting to note that the JCCC Writing Center has later recruited some strong tutors from this group. Women who have begun in the Writing Center, moved through the composition program successfully (often as peer critique leaders), and then been referred to the Writing Center as tutor candidates are especially attuned to student writing problems, and the center's clientele enjoys working with them.

Forming a sizeable portion of the Writing Center population are the students for whom English is a second language. These students often come to the center with little knowledge of English. JCCC does not offer credit courses for the ESL students, so the task of teaching them often falls to the center. Working with these students takes special training for the tutors. Knowing how to assess their skill level and how to find the appropriate materials is difficult. Generally, the center's instructors do the initial diagnosis and set up a plan which may include not only drills in sentence structure, idioms, verb tenses, noun endings, and vocabulary, but also lots of writing, speaking, and reading. *Copy Write* and similar books are often used. The student copies an essay, which she then reads aloud. The tutor helps with pronunciation and vocabulary. As the student progresses, she makes changes in articles, pronouns, plurals, etc. Many of the ESL students admit that the only English they speak is on campus. At home and in their own communities, they speak their first language. These students are willing to spend long hours in the center, but the staff must be careful not to let them get mesmerized at the computer, where they sometimes feel the most comfortable. The interaction with the tutors is very important, but because there are so many other students, the tutors cannot afford to sit long hours with an ESL student working individually. Thus, a balance of writing, conferencing, and computer drill is beneficial. Although these students are often demanding, they are hardworking and genuinely thankful for the tutor's time. The center's staff senses their impatience in learning a new language and strives to encourage their work and to praise their accomplishments. Tutors in a writing center must be aware of and sensitive to cultural differences; they also must be aware of the embarrassment these students may feel about their lack of English language skills. Some hold degrees from their native lands or are even professionals. This embarrassment, I believe, is why they often insist on working at the computers. And although the computers can be helpful by teaching and reinforcing basic skills, the one-on-one socialization may be the most beneficial strategy used in the Writing Center.

The third type of student challenging the writing center services is the hearing-impaired student. As noted earlier, JCCC has a connection with Gallaudet University and works closely with the Kansas State School for the Deaf; as a result, JCCC provides a wonderful program for these students. For many of these students, the Writing Center is their first mainstream experience. How they are greeted, the materials they are provided, and the staff's demeanor are all very important in that initial visit. Again, staff training is crucial. An instructor/interpreter from JCCC's special services talks to the staff about the unique needs of these students, gives them some simple sign language, and helps them all to understand better these students' needs. Many of the materials and strategies used are similar to those used with ESL students because the hearing-impaired student's first language is usually American Sign Language and English is his second language. An interpreter is usually present for the tutor sessions. Learning to work with someone signing behind them and yet supposedly not there can be disconcerting to the tutors. Working without an interpreter forces the student to communicate with the tutor, and that interaction can be rewarding. Regardless of whether an interpreter is present, working with these students can be very tedious. Patience, empathy, and understanding are important traits for the tutors.

All three of these groups represent an important component of the JCCC Writing Center community. Providing the kind of atmosphere where learning takes place, recognizing individual skill levels, and selecting and training staff who will be empathetic are strategies which help us meet the needs of these special audiences.

Course Placement

Student placement in freshman composition courses is first determined by ACT or ASSET tests. Once students are placed in composition classes at the appropriate level, instructors require a writing sample to validate the appropriateness of the initial placement. In some cases, students are transferred into a higher- or lower-level composition class. Other students are directed to the Writing Center, where one-credit courses or individualized programs are offered. Further-more, an assessment can be administered in the Writing Center, if the instructor desires another opinion. Houghton-Mifflin has a computer-ized program—*MicroLab*—which assesses the proofreading skills of individual students. Then, specific modules dealing with the various grammatical problems are offered through the *MicroLab*. Another means of assessing students' skills is working with their graded es-says, a strategy which enhances the value of editing and revising. Checklists and score sheets which tie into composition assignments have been created through the combined efforts of the composition instructors and the Writing Center staff.

Peer Tutors

The Writing Center is staffed with both peer tutors and part-time instructors; there is at least one instructor on duty at all times. The instructor serves as the main resource, answering troublesome ques-tions and handling difficult students. The instructor on duty is also in charge of assessing, diagnosing, assigning, and grading the written work of students enrolled in the one-credit courses. The tutors' pri-mary responsibility is to conference with students about their writing assignments, which are generally in the rough-draft stage of the writ-ing process. The instructors, of course, also conference with students. We try not to distinguish between tutor and instructor conferences in the Writing Center, and we emphasize the importance of keeping the conference writer-centered so that the writer is in control of his or her own revision. Sometimes students coming to the center ask for an instructor or refuse to work with a peer tutor. According to the circum-stances, we may oblige them, but at the same time, we let them know that there is no difference.

Selection

Two important parts of the writing program at JCCC are the peer critique groups, in which students share rough drafts with one another and offer suggestions for revision, and the teacher/pupil conferences. To carry this collaborative pedagogy into the Writing Center is only natural because the peer tutors function in much the same way as the members of a class critique group. The practice of involving peer critique groups in composition classes also affects the selection of students as peer tutors. One of the primary means of selecting tutors is through instructor recommendations. All peer tutor applicants must have completed Composition I and II at JCCC, so instructors who make recommendations do so on the basis of their knowledge of each student's performance. The best peer tutors were often leaders in the peer critique groups in the composition classes; however, the best writers are not always the best peer tutors. Good writing skills are important, but so are strong interpersonal communication skills, which are easily detected during the interview with the Writing Center director. Thus, peer tutors are selected because of their writing skills, as verified through instructor recommendations and their interpersonal communication skills.

After students have been recommended and have applied for the position of peer tutor in the Writing Center, they are interviewed by the Writing Center director. The interview is typical in that basic questions which help to reveal the candidate's aptitude and attitude are asked. Included in the interview are questions such as "Why do you want to be a peer tutor?" "What are your goals for the future?" "What do you think are the duties of a peer tutor in the Writing Center?" Following the interview, the director lets the candidate ask questions, and a short exam is given. The exam is made up of brief student writings that display various writing problems. The candidates identify the aspects of the writing they think need to be improved. The test reveals the candidate's writing skills and helps us to make a final decision.

Peer tutors are an important part of the JCCC Writing Center program. Their presence assures students that with time and practice, they, too, can write. The fact that the tutors have written the very assignments that the students bring to the center makes the tutors seem reliable, human, and honest.

Training

The training of the peer tutors begins soon after they are hired. The first training workshop, for which they are paid, is usually in the late spring. Experienced tutors also attend to lend support, answer questions, and help in mock tutoring sessions. The first session of the workshop is divided into two parts. In the first hour and a half, the Writing Center is described: its materials, services, history, and school-wide impact. The second hour and a half is an informal discussion about clientele and typical tutoring sessions. Each new tutor is given a tutor handbook to study during the summer.

Just before classes begin in the fall, another daylong workshop is held that includes other tutors employed across campus. This workshop begins with an overview of each center (Academic Achievement Center, Math Center, and Writing Center). Then, speakers from student services, computer labs, the Learning Strategies Program, and counseling talk with the peer tutors about their respective areas. The first in a series of videotapes from *The Tutor's Guide,* a program developed by UCLA, is also shown and discussed. In the afternoon, tutors retire to the centers for which they were hired and learn about their respective center's rules and procedures, such as dress code, behavior, computer use, etc. All of these regulations are listed in the handbook, too, so the tutors have already had the opportunity to familiarize themselves with them. The secretary-receptionist helps during the workshop to explain the importance of keeping accurate records of each client's program.

The second part of the afternoon workshop covers the writing process. Another videotape, which specifically addresses the Writing Center tutors, is shown. It is a review for the tutors but necessary because students seeking help in the Writing Center can be at any stage of the writing process. Tutors are asked to become familiar with the writing assignments and the materials, such as handouts and computer programs. At this time, tutors are asked to keep a journal of their Writing Center experiences—observations, frustrations, successes, etc. They are also told about the Writing Center newsletter, which is published twice a semester and includes stories written by the tutors. The tutor's journal can be a good resource for the newsletter and for group discussions.

Soon after classes are under way, monthly staff meetings are held to answer questions, finalize the semester's schedule, and evaluate sample essays. The tutors practice grading the essays holistically, and the tutor considers various rhetorical problems in the essay.

Both workshops and meetings are important to the training of the peer tutors, helping to set a comfortable atmosphere, which is both professional yet warm and friendly. Also, the instructors and the peer tutors are encouraged to exchange ideas and approaches so that they can learn from one another. Differences in personal interactions become clear and thus do not settle into a "let-me-do-it-my-way" attitude. The airing sessions help hold down the burnout rate, too. Frustrations along with successes are vented in a cheerful, informal atmosphere. These meetings are not a panacea but reinforce the ongoing training and evaluation.

During infrequent slack times, tutors study a checklist that reminds them of the materials—such as the computer programs, handouts, and resource books—available in the Writing Center. Students are also asked to stay abreast of the current assignments from teachers, which are posted in the Writing Center.

Besides the checklist, other activities help the tutors become more proficient in their tutoring skills. A box of essays is available for tutors to evaluate and discuss with the Writing Center instructors; in addition, reading material—mostly professional articles about various methods and strategies of teaching writing—helps tutors understand theory. To further understand teaching strategies, students are asked to sit in on tutoring sessions between Writing Center instructors and clients, thereby allowing the peer tutor to see in practice how to individualize instruction. Later, the peer tutor and instructor can discuss the session. Teachers from all divisions at the college are encouraged to visit the Writing Center so that they can meet the peer tutors and the peer tutors can get to know them. Many of the instructors bring their classes to the Writing Center for a brief orientation. As an added learning tool, the peer tutors can visit classes and talk with instructors about problems unique to the course or the students attending the course. This kind of exchange is valuable for everyone.

Although the evaluation of the peer tutors is a constant charge, a more extensive evaluation comes at the end of the year. Besides the director's evaluation, tutors are asked to write a self-evaluation of their experiences in the Writing Center.

Types of Services

Overview

Students may either use the Writing Center facility on a voluntary basis, or they may be referred to the center by an instructor. Making an appointment is not necessary; students may drop in at their convenience or schedule a time to come in weekly. Many students come with writing assignments from their English classes; however, a growing number of students come to get help on lab reports, practicums, book reports, critiques, annotated bibliographies, or research papers assigned from a variety of courses such as biology, business administration, psychology, nursing, history, or computer science.

Clients in the Writing Center may work with a tutor on a writing assignment during any step of the writing process, or they may want to review their writing skills by taking a diagnostic test or working on the many handouts provided in the center or on the computer. The center does not proofread papers, however.

Students who need a more intensive review may take one of the center's five one-credit courses. The Sentence-Pattern Skills course helps students to master the grammatical structure of the English language. The Proofreading Skills course enables them to proofread and correct errors in their own writing. The Composing Skills course gives students the necessary tools for developing and organizing good writing. The Practical Writing Skills course provides approaches to writing correctly when English is a student's second language. The Research Skills course presents a practical and reliable process for writing the research paper.

The Writing Center also offers assistance to the college staff. Of course, instructors and office staff are encouraged to use the Writing Center resources for their own writing needs, but they may also ask instructors to come to their classes to talk about the organization of specific writing assignments. Because the Writing Center is not just a branch of the English department but reaches out to all areas of the college, it is the nerve center of the instructional services of the college.

Providing a vital part of and being consistent with the community college philosophy (that is, to enhance community lives), the Writing Center provides a Grammar Hotline, which people of the community can call to have specific grammar questions answered quickly. From the time that this service was initiated ten years ago, the Grammar Hotline has been kept busy. Tutors answer questions about word usage, spelling, punctuation, and sentence structure. Institutions and organizations like IBM, Southwestern Bell Telephone, and the FBI have used the Writing Center Hotline from time to time.

Students, staff, and community are further assisted with work-related writing. The center offers help with writing skills needed for the work world, such as writing résumés, letters of application, reports, or resignations.

Above all, the tutorial system of the Writing Center has been effective in meeting the needs of clients. Students returning to school after many years have found that the individualized instruction provided by the Writing Center helps them to cope with out-of-practice skills and get back into the mainstream of education. Other students like the individualized program because it focuses on their particular needs and allows them to learn the basics at their own speed. The success of the program stems from the philosophy that each student has individual needs and should be taught accordingly.

Computers

Coming into the Writing Center, a visitor immediately sees a row of computers framing the busy room. These computers are multipurpose, providing assessments of students' proofreading skills, an efficient way to review grammar, usage, and mechanics, and instruction in sentence and paragraph composing. In addition, all of the credit courses have been integrated with software materials, giving students a choice of working through written materials created by the Writing Center director or working on comparable computer programs. Writing programs such as *Writer's Helper*, *Think Tank*, *Term Paper Writer*, and *Grammatik IV* promote a writing process and emphasize revising strategies. Although the computer programs enhance learning, they will never replace the individualized instruction which is the priority of the Writing Center.

Because of the small number of computers in the center, word processing is virtually impossible; however, students do bring their data disks with their stored papers for help with revision, as several word-processing programs are available. In the fall of 1989, eleven instructors began teaching their composition classes in a collaborative computer classroom (CCC), where computers are networked. The software used in the classroom is also available to students in the Writing Center, an arrangement which is especially helpful to CCC students who are first-time computer users.

In the future, plans are that the computers in the Writing Center will be linked to the computer classroom and will have access to the electronic bulletin board on this campus and on other campuses. In addition, electronic mail and conferencing will soon be a reality.

Writing Across the Curriculum

The Writing Center has played an active role in writing-across-the-curriculum (WAC) programs: first, by helping to create and present the in-service workshops given for all staff members; second, by continuing to be an ever-ready support for instructors and staff working on specific writing projects; third, by talking to all divisions on campus about the Writing Center services; and fourth, by visiting classes across the curriculum to acquaint students with the Writing Center and to discuss strategies students might use for specific writing assignments.

The JCCC Writing Center has become the focal point for writing across the curriculum at the college. Among the ways that the Writing Center supports WAC are the following:

1. Samples of formats of specific writing assignments are kept in the Writing Center. Generic handouts provide a guide for writing assignments such as book reports, research papers, essay exams, and lab reports.

2. The director of the Writing Center visits classes to talk about writing assignments and assists instructors with designing and evaluating writing assignments.

3. Writing Center instructors provide class instruction for specific assignments and explain the appropriate documentation style.

4. All of the major styles of documentation (MLA, APA, CBE, etc.) are kept in the Writing Center for student reference. Also, a research handout is available for student and faculty use. The one-credit course, Research Skills, is also offered as a support to research writing in all the disciplines.

5. The Writing Center keeps instructors' current assignments and good student writing samples on file for student reference.

Outreach

Another important role of the center is to serve the community in various ways. One way is through the Grammar Hotline mentioned earlier in this description. Information about the Grammar Hotline and the services of the Writing Center is published in bulletins and class schedules, credit and noncredit, which go out to all residents of Johnson County. All calls to the Grammar Hotline are dated and described in a log kept on the secretary's desk.

The Writing Center staff is always improving its resources to adapt to the needs of a changing community. Community members may have a program designed for their needs or may take any of the courses in the Writing Center for credit or noncredit. For example, the Writing Center has served a retired railroad man who wanted to research retirement villages; an eighty-four-year-old gentleman who wanted to write his memoirs as a legacy for future generations; a retired Scout leader who wanted to share camping experiences in delightful vignettes; a lawyer who wanted to write more colorful, meaningful prose; and a ten-year-old girl whose mother wanted her to work through computer grammar drills and get a view of academe. All of these people represent the Writing Center's diverse role in the community. Yet it is the Writing Center which is enriched by their presence.

Administration

Personnel

At the present time there are ten part-time instructors working in the Writing Center. The full-time instructor who directs the Writing Center teaches at least one composition course each semester and coordinates the Writing Center by (1) hiring and training student tutors, (2) selecting and assessing materials and software, (3) writing and evaluating individual student programs of study, (4) overseeing the recordkeeping and analyzing the evaluations, and (5) acting as a consultant to other Writing Center directors through sharing of ideas and materials. The director also acts as a liaison between the English department and the Writing Center and seeks to gain support from all divisions and the community. Some part-time instructors are also instructors who teach composition classes and then work with Writing Center students on a one-to-one basis. They must hold at least a master's degree in English. They are compensated at a ratio of 2 to 1; in other words, for the equivalent of one three-credit course, they spend six hours in the Writing Center each week. At this writing, two of the instructors work twelve hours in the Writing Center in lieu of two composition classes while the others work six hours each. Beginning in the fall of 1989, newly hired full-time instructors began working several hours a week in the center during their first year at JCCC.

Meanwhile, a full-time secretary does all the clerical work and prepares the reports. She types all of the materials and handouts used in the center and the newsletters and memoranda which go out to instructors. She also logs hours and keeps track of the folders for the students visiting the center. The secretary prepares a monthly report which is sent to instructors, the program director, the division director, and the dean of Instruction (figure 2). A part-time secretary covers the evening hours from 5 p.m. until 8 p.m., answering the telephone and handling the clerical load for those hours.

As mentioned earlier, peer tutors also work in the Writing Center. To qualify, they have to complete Composition II at JCCC and be recommended by their composition instructors. Tutors work approximately ten to fifteen hours a week and are paid on an hourly basis. At present, there are ten students working as WC peer tutors.

Budget

As early as 1975, the college recognized the need for a Writing Center and was philosophically supportive of it. That support is still there

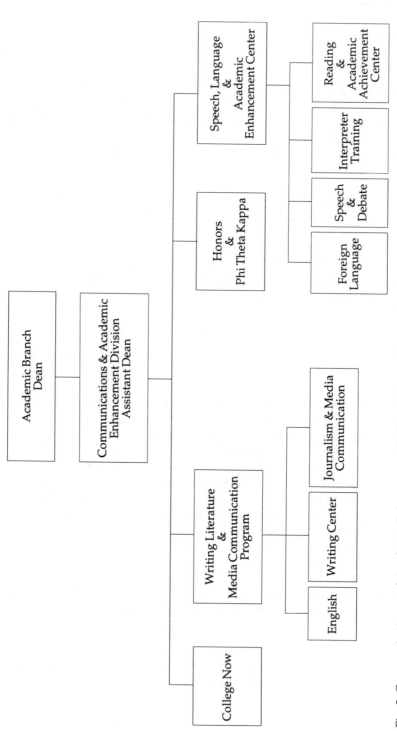

Fig. 2. Communications and Academic Enhancement Division, Johnson County Community College.

now, not only philosophically but financially, as shown by the level of staffing, materials, and computer hardware and software provided. The annual budget for the Writing Center is approximately $65,000, which includes salaries, office supplies, and educational materials. The ultimate proof of the college's support of the Writing Center is that its success is based not on student credit hours generated but on the quantity and quality of services provided.

General funds are used to finance the Writing Center; however, any big budget projects must be substantiated in reports that document needs assessments, total costs, and values. In the fall of 1988, the Writing Center budget became part of the English department budget.

Records

Over a thousand visits to the center are made monthly. To document this information, careful records are kept. All students coming to the Writing Center sign in and sign out. Each walk-in student has a file that includes not only an attendance record, but also a progress report on the activity of the session and the course and instructor for whom she or he is working. Enrolled students also have folders, which not only record attendance and activity but also document test scores and writing assignment grades. At the end of each day, the secretary enters all information from the folders into a computer database program. At the end of each month, a comprehensive computer list of students, indicating the number of times they attended and the referring instructors, is compiled and distributed to instructors. Totals for the month are generated into administrative reports. At the end of the semester, the total number of students, total visits, total Hotline calls, and comparisons to the preceding semesters are gathered for an administrative report. Also, information about enrolled students is collected in a semester report, which indicates attendance, test score averages, essay grades, etc. Accurate records are essential, both for instructional as well as budgetary purposes.

Research and Evaluation

Another reason for keeping impeccable records is for evaluation and research. Collected data are used to determine traffic patterns for scheduling staff; to note the implications of writing across the curriculum; to understand clients; to improve/update materials, software, and resources; and to use as a reference to support Writing Center theories and practices, which are then shared in published papers or at professional conferences.

Research for JCCC's Writing Center director means keeping professionally fit by reading professional journals and attending and presenting at conferences. The director must also be in tune with instructor demands and assignments, new software advancements, and recent publications.

Another important part of research is the evaluation of the Writing Center. Evaluation of the program is multifold. First, an evaluation is given at random to all walk-in students during a specified period. Another evaluation is filled out by students taking the one-credit courses. Both of these evaluations are summarized by the office of institutional research. A third evaluation is computerized and asks all Writing Center students specific questions about their work in the Writing Center; this evaluation is considered by the Writing Center staff in improving services offered or acquiring new software. A fourth evaluation is a questionnaire posed to instructors who use the Writing Center as a resource, not only for themselves but also for their students. This survey provides the staff with vital information to help in ordering resource materials, hiring peer tutors, and improving services generally. Finally, every three years the Writing Center, as part of the English program, undergoes the college's program review.

In the future, research studies will document student success in writing skills improvement and retention in mainstream courses.

The Future

The Writing Center has established itself as a vital part of the educational support system at Johnson County Community College. Future plans will focus on strategies to make the center even more effective and to reach more students, especially those enrolled in classes other than composition, by increasing the enrollment of adult learners in the one-credit courses, talking to counselors, and rewording course descriptions to suggest that writing skills are lifelong skills. Furthermore, more specific goals will include the following: extending the Grammar Hotline to provide electronic bulletin board access for networking with other institutions, locally and nationally; consulting with area high schools to encourage the establishment of quality and quantity writing in the various disciplines; and seeking innovative methods for reaching reluctant writers.

The JCCC Writing Center of the future could be pictured as a giant wheel with the hub being the tutoring sessions or the conferencing. The spokes would include a computer lab for computer-aided instruction and revising on a word processor, a classroom for interdisciplinary seminars, a library with resources for instructors and students, and a quiet room for writing. By continuing expansion of the center's outreach programs and writing-across-the-curriculum program, we hope to keep alive the awareness of the importance of writing. The Writing Center will play an increasingly important role for the college and the community in years to come.

9 Redefining Authority: Multicultural Students and Tutors at the Educational Opportunity Program Writing Center at the University of Washington

Gail Y. Okawa
Indiana University of Pennsylvania

> I view the Writing Center as a place of learning not only in the
> intellectual sense, but in the broadest sense of learning—I see it as
> a place for nurturing.
>
> —George Hunter

George Hunter, to whom this chapter is dedicated, was a tutor who represents in his words and insights the achievement and complexity of the Educational Opportunity Program (EOP) Writing Center's students and tutors. Born in Korea, George moved to the United States with his family at an early age and grew up in Tacoma, Washington. He earned a B.A. in English from the University of Washington (UW) and was a tutor at the UW's EOP Writing Center for a year and a half before he fell ill and passed away in February 1991. His mixed heritage—he was African American, Native American, and Asian—both complicated and enriched his life, and sensitized him to the struggles of other students of color.

In the piece of writing reproduced above, George continues:

> From my undergraduate experience here at the university, I know
> that this place can be very alienating for [one of] any race, but
> especially so for the minority student. I think it would prove very
> beneficial if somehow we could extend our "nurturing" to other
> minority students who are not so much lacking in instruction as
> they are in faith and confidence, being minorities in an academic
> setting like the University of Washington.

This chapter is a collaborative effort. I want to thank Donna Bolima and the Writing Center tutors who provided their insights and energy in developing the tutoring program; the Hunter family for permission to quote from George's journal; Virginia Chappell, Alphonse Keasley, and Bennett Rafoth for helpful critiques of this essay; and Nadine FabbiShushan for permission to reproduce hand-drawn charts based on her originals.

George's words define the context of the UW's EOP Writing Center—its setting, a large research university of approximately 33,000 students, and its clientele, the less than ten percent of the student body who are admitted through the EOP and are eligible to use this Writing Center. His words also highlight "nurturing" as a significant ingredient in our center's philosophy and operation, fundamental to redefining sources of authority among writers, tutors, and tutor-trainers during my involvement there. As an instructor in this Writing Center from 1980 until I entered a doctoral program in the summer of 1990, I witnessed and participated in its fluctuations and struggles. I developed what evolved over six years as the Multicultural Tutoring in Writing Program and coordinated the activities in the center for three of those years. It is from this perspective that I write about this Writing Center's responses to a complex institutional and student context.

Historical and Institutional Setting

The EOP Writing Center was the first writing center to be established at the first state-assisted institution of higher education in the Pacific Northwest. Founded in 1861, the University of Washington had its beginnings on a 10-acre wilderness forest that is now Seattle's downtown business district. Later, it was relocated to a 680-acre campus four miles away, bordered on two sides by residential communities and on two others by Lake Washington and Lake Union. For over 100 years after its establishment, the university educated those who could afford to attend, predominantly white middle- and upper-class students. This practice virtually closed off educational access to many students of color and other economically disadvantaged students.

In response to the mounting civil rights activism of the 1950s and 1960s, however, the Special Education Program was established in 1968 as a program for minority and economically disadvantaged students. Roger Sale (1976) writes about UW President Charles Odegaard's farsighted response to community pressures in the late 1960s:

> Rather than ... treat the matter as one strictly between students and administration, Odegaard made the University involved as it had never been before in seeing its obligation to the black, minority, and poor communities. He told the students, in effect, to go out into the community and recruit.... He told the legislature and faculty, in effect, to pay for whatever it cost. He established the Special Education Program out of an Office of Minority Affairs with a university vice-president to run it. At the same time, then, that the Panthers were marching and the police helicopters were

circling, recruiters were out doing their best to convince the disaffected that the University was open to them. (221)

In 1969, the Special Education Program became the Educational Opportunity Program; over twenty years later, having survived budget cuts and reorganization, it continues to be run out of the Office of Minority Affairs under a university vice president.

Having these sociopolitical origins, the EOP Writing Center evolved as a unit of the Reading Study Skills Center, the initial academic support facility for EOP students. Writing instructors worked there one-on-one with students as early as the mid-1970s. But the development of a writing center as such resulted only after a number of staff from the Reading Study Skills Center attended a conference on learning centers at the University of California at Berkeley in 1978, learned about the work of Charles Cooper and Thomas Reigstad at SUNY at Buffalo on concepts of individual tutoring and self-sufficiency, and visited the writing center at Berkeley run by Thom Hawkins. Together with other units in science, math, and reading, the Writing Center began to assume an identity of its own in what was renamed the EOP Instructional Center (IC).

In the context of an imposing research university, which Sale (1970) describes as being initially "ill equipped to respond well to the sudden arrival of less-than-well-educated minority students" (222), the EOP Writing Center has gradually assumed a complex function. Not only has the writing staff worked with students on their writing and addressed other linguistic issues, but these instructors have also taken on the sociopolitical role of student advocates, helping the institution to understand and cope with the students and the language issues that confront them in the academy.

A more specific example may serve to illustrate this latter function: At a monolithic university like the University of Washington, the English department is also monolithic, with first-year composition courses being taught primarily by graduate teaching assistants (TAs). These instructors are supervised according to the style and involvement of the faculty member who runs the writing program. During the academic year, the English department offers English 104–105, a multisectioned, two-quarter writing course nicknamed "EOP English." All sections are taught by teaching assistants who are seasoned by at least a year of teaching freshman composition, and the program is coordinated by a veteran TA. While I worked with this program, this structure alone—predominantly Caucasian doctoral students, many interested primarily in literature, teaching composition to ethnic

minority and nontraditional students—sometimes generated a disso-
nance which produced both extremely rewarding and extremely frus-
trating experiences for teachers and students alike. On more than one
occasion, the Writing Center staff and tutors served as a bridge and
helped to diffuse this tension between student and teacher, and between student and institution, or helped to celebrate their successes.

Clientele

The EOP students, who provide the second element in the Writing
Center's context, are of culturally and linguistically diverse origins:
ethnically and racially, they are admitted to the university under the
rubric "African American, American Indian, Asian and Pacific Is-
lander, Chicano/Hispanic, or economically disadvantaged White,"
but come from even more diverse subcultural backgrounds; linguistically, they may be from as many as twenty language groups, including
Spanish, Korean, Mandarin, Thai, Tagalog, Vietnamese, English and its
various dialects. These students also may range in socioeconomic
status from those at the poverty line to those from the upper middle
class, and in scholastic performance from erratic to consistently successful. They span the spectrum of ages from recent high school graduates to returning adults.

Beyond these bureaucratic descriptions, each student, of course,
comes from complex and unique circumstances quite hidden from
those who would teach him or her. For example, Kay was an African
American woman in her thirties, widowed by the Vietnam War,
mother of two children, who wrestled constantly with economic survival and her dream of finishing her bachelor's degree. Jaíme, newly
immigrated from Mexico, spoke mainly Spanish when he was first
introduced to us at the center; working part-time and attending school
full-time, he not only mastered English but was also admitted finally
into the engineering program of his choice. Janice was a second-generation Chinese American, working diligently toward academic success in the competitive communications field—despite family
disapproval. As a freshman in his mid-twenties, Stan wrote powerfully
about his experiences as an alcoholic and his mentors at Alcoholics
Anonymous, but dropped out of school after a few quarters to support
his family. Having grown up on the Makah Indian Reservation on the
Olympic Peninsula, Irene was a single parent, determined to finish her
degree in psychology so that she could go on to law school, as she

finally did. These students reflect diversity in its richest form—beyond statistics and stereotypes.

Concept

Perhaps one of the Writing Center's more overt responses to the imposing monocultural university structure and environment, on the one hand, and to the diverse EOP student population, on the other, was also one of our most instructive ones: whether a writing center is expressly charged to serve multicultural/multilingual/nontraditional students, as is the case with the EOP Writing Center, or happens to do so because of the structure, needs, and politics of its institution, it has the potential to serve these students well or ill. If a center focuses on using computerized grammar drills, for example, it is not likely to work with issues central to the composition strategies of the novice writers that Patrick Hartwell (1984) discusses in his essay on the paradoxes of written-down speech. If the people working with students have a patronizing attitude toward minority student learning, if they merely punch the clock to collect their paychecks, if they are oblivious and insensitive to the writers' needs, and if they irresponsibly appropriate student texts, their attitudes and practice would render them ineffective with, if not destructive to, student writers.

Given the concept of a writing center as defined by Stephen North (1984), any center might choose to be student-centered and process-oriented. The EOP Writing Center, however, should be not only a student-centered and process-oriented place where students of color and nontraditional students can go to discuss their writing, but a place where these students can also feel comfortable discussing their experiences with language as well as their thinking on any subject with people who might share their complex experience in the academy. Such a center would have the potential to cultivate a safe and enriching environment for multiple views of reality so that students could feel free to take risks. It could encourage student writers to find voices that would serve them in their private and public worlds. And it would have the potential to provide revised perspectives about where authority *should* lie in writing so that students assume true authorship of their work.

Our center had this potential for cultivating the writing experiences of students from diverse backgrounds, particularly those who felt dissonant with academic culture. Ironically, the perennial budgetary constraints under which the writing center worked provided us with an unexpected opportunity: we came to rely more heavily on peer tutors for staffing, and in the mid-1980s, it became apparent to some of us on the Writing Center staff that reexamining the existing tutor recruitment and training program might help us to realize more fully the Writing Center's potential.

Tutoring Program

Rationale

Issues concerning student diversity, authority and voice—themes critical to the setting and students of the EOP Writing Center—converge in the relationships among the writers, the tutors, and the tutor-trainer/teacher. Working through the process of revision, I found that three factors proved significant in this regard: first, at a writing center like the EOP, which serves multicultural and multilingual students, peers or other tutors who mirror the students' diversity and who are themselves learning to take on challenges in the academic world can become important role models for less experienced writers. Second, as a tutor-trainer, I learned that those tutors can best serve the students they work with if they develop their own critical awareness of personal, cultural, educational, and sociopolitical issues related to literacy. And third, I found that tutors can develop that consciousness more readily when those who train them work with them dialogically and collaboratively, as Paulo Freire (1970) and Kenneth Bruffee (1984) suggest. It is these issues and relationships that I will turn to briefly.

At the beginning of the previous section, I used the examples of grammar drills and insensitive tutor attitudes to illustrate how a writing center might potentially serve its students ill. These practices and attitudes are not simply misguided; the underlying assumptions are related to the complex problem of authority in writing and tutoring. In my differing roles as college professor, writing center instructor, and writing center tutor-trainer, roles in which authority can take different forms, I learned that working with ethnic minority and nontraditional students in a writing context does not raise simply an academic issue of text ownership, that is, *who* has ownership of a text being written? Rather, it raises a critical social and political issue of identity and authority, that is, who has the *right* to control ownership of a text? Who has the *right* to write in the academy?

If a student is reasonably confident about her ideas and comes to the Writing Center for collaborative feedback on a text, issues of authority and hierarchy may be less applicable. She knows she has the right to express her ideas in the academic community, and that sense of authority, as Shirley Rose (1989) defines it, is her voice: like the speaker's voice in spoken discourse, the writer's voice, most importantly, manifests the writer's right or opportunity to express an opinion or desire (111–12). I would add to this the student's right to express complex and reflective thoughts and beliefs. In a writing conference, the writer and her tutor can negotiate a balance in their relationship. However, if we in the Writing Center encounter anxious, abused, and inexperienced writers—silent, silenced, marginalized voices—*how* we choose to work with them is what John Rouse (1979) calls "a political act" (1). Our choices reveal where we believe such students are predetermined to be in society's power structure. The Asian ESL student who nervously pushes her paper in front of the tutor and asks that her errors be corrected or who religiously takes down the tutor's every word as though receiving dictation is absolving herself of any responsibility for her writing. The tutor who takes the pen and corrects "the errors" because "her English is so bad" or who becomes enamored of his own ideas on a subject and talks endlessly without interacting with the student is absolving himself of his responsibility as a tutor by assuming the authority she is giving away. Whether and how students develop their authority and voices over and through language depends ultimately on their own choices, but, in the context of a writing center, depends on the choices of their tutors and teachers as well.

In the early years of the EOP Writing Center's history, some excellent tutors were hired, but they did not reflect the diversity of the students we served. Cultural issues were discussed as a one-time seminar topic, and problems arose resulting from cultural differences and insensitivity to them. With these problems in mind, I worked with tutors and others inside and outside the center—including the director and teachers in EOP English and academic counselors in the EOP—to reshape both the recruitment and training of tutors. Together we constructed the Multicultural Tutoring in Writing Program, the name emerging out of our collective efforts.

The process of revision was an evolutionary one. First of all, my instincts told me that role modeling is important: growing up in Honolulu and majoring in English at the University of Hawaii, I recalled that all my English teachers were Caucasian except one, an Asian American man who made Shakespeare come alive for me. Although my mentors were Caucasian and this man played only a momentary role in my life, he was physical evidence that someone who looked like me could "teach English" at a university. EOP students also could benefit from such role models among their tutors. Although other units in the Instructional Center realized and considered this point in their tutor hiring, the Writing Center made minimal progress through the early 1980s. Some of us understood that hiring primarily English majors who mirror the near cultural homogeneity of most English departments visually perpetuates the myth that most people of color and other outsiders "can't write" precisely because they are outsiders, that a hierarchy in fact exists. At least in the writing center context, EOP students need to see that students from diverse backgrounds like theirs have become good, decent, strong writers. The language of power does not have to remain beyond their reach.

A second step in the reshaping process was that it made sense that shared experience and cultural sensitivity might also enhance collaborative relationships between tutors and nontraditional, ethnic minority, and working-class students. Scholars and practitioners like Thomas Reigstad and Donald McAndrew (1984), Kenneth Bruffee (1984), Muriel Harris (1986), Stephen North (1984), and others have clearly established how effective peer tutors can be, pedagogically and affectively, with student writers. Patrick Hartwell (1984) expresses a great deal of faith in tutors (as opposed to teachers) working with novice writers, as does Thom Hawkins (1980), who points out that "the unofficial closeness of the peer relationship" (64–65) opens up the academic code to inexperienced and insecure writers. Thus, to maximize the possibility of these relationships developing in our center—to give students more options for such relationships—we needed to do two things: (1) actively recruit and hire tutors to reflect the cultural, linguistic, gender, age, and class diversity of our student clientele, to provide physical evidence for the sharing of language ownership; and (2) provide a training program to foster the tutors' willingness to grant writers authority over their own texts.

Recruitment and Selection

We advertised for tutors campuswide, using posted fliers and job announcements in the university work-study office and the campus newspaper. More successful sources for tutors were referrals from the English department instructors who taught EOP writing sections, from Writing Center instructors and tutors who saw potential in writers using the center, and from faculty. Applicants were screened and selected according to their existing awareness of the writing process and their openness to learning the complexities of tutoring—their *potential* to become strong, sensitive, responsible tutors.

Hiring from the EOP population across the disciplines as well as non-EOP undergraduates, graduate students, and volunteers, we developed a committed multicultural cadre of tutors. By 1989–90, two-thirds of the tutors were students or former students of the Educational Opportunity Program, and 86 percent of them represented different non-European ethnic, cultural, and linguistic backgrounds. Many of them had used the center for their own work in the past and continued to discuss their writing with their peers and other writing instructors while they worked there. Their use of the center provided an added benefit in that it quite naturally modeled for our student clientele the ideas that collaborating on writing need not be a sign of weakness and that authority could and should remain with the writer as collaborative roles shifted.

Tutor Training

Structurally, we had two groups: trainees/interns and veterans. The trainees, who joined the program at the beginning of a given quarter, attended a training seminar which met weekly for one hour through the ten-week quarter and in which we discussed basic theoretical issues. These tutors also joined the veteran group (generally, tutors who had completed the training seminar) in a weekly staff meeting in which we discussed current issues and concerns of interest to fifth-year veterans as well as new tutors, topics arising rather naturally and organically. Trainees were consistently and continually folded into the existing group by way of these meetings, observation triads, and collaborative projects such as composing group essays and staffing the *EOP Writing Center Newsletter*.

Trainees generally were not paid during their internship period (the initial quarter) unless they had work-study funding. English majors with junior status could earn variable (2–6) internship credits through the English department, while students in other disciplines could earn variable (2–6) field study credits through the Independent Fieldwork Program administered by the College of Arts and Sciences. Those who wanted the experience but not the credits volunteered their time, a considerable weekly commitment. Tutors who completed the one-quarter training seminar were invited to return on an hourly wage, credit, and work-study basis, depending on their potential as tutors and their commitment to the students and program.

The mere existence of a diverse group of tutors did not, of course, assure their working effectively with student writers or with one another. Cross-cultural issues can often increase the complexity of existing writing center relationships. We needed to consider the tutors' relationships within and among themselves and, most important, with their trainer. Furthermore, we needed to revise our definition of authority among ourselves so that the tutors could develop productive relationships with their student writers.

Developing a training program for multicultural tutors and working jointly with tutors toward that end, we ultimately tapped into our collective creative resources and engaged our sense of social responsibility as tutors, teachers, and learners. The training program evolved, based on theory, our intuition, and our previous experience with student attitudes toward writing, writing classes, and writing teachers, as well as on our awareness of the academy's traditional exclusionary stance with reference to disadvantaged, ethnic minority, and nontraditional students.

For me, it became increasingly clear that the training of tutors is a political act, as is the tutoring and teaching of writing. What I call "self-discovering" had to begin with the trainer and the tutors and our views of learners and learning. In our training program, then, the pedagogy developed along a collaborative, egalitarian model, where we (tutors and trainer) saw ourselves as teachers and learners/researchers—coexistently—as advocated by Paulo Freire (1970), Dixie Goswami and Peter Stillman (1987), and others. I developed this perspective out of necessity, especially because of our complex multicultural writing center setting: we trainers/teachers do not and cannot have all the answers, and we must be willing to relinquish authority, to take risks ourselves. We must start from the supposition that we are all equally ignorant and equally knowing. As Freire (1970) asserts, "the problem-posing educator constantly re-forms his reflections in the reflection of the students. . . . The teacher presents the material to the students for their consideration, and reconsiders his earlier considerations as the students express their own" (68). Thus, where possible, I used a dialogical, nondirective approach in training, modeling the reflective method that the tutors needed to use with their students. Perhaps my greatest responsibility was to be ever-watchful of my own assumptions. In a tutoring program built on diversity, it was essential that I foster a sense of community rather than competitiveness among the tutors—the "nurturing" that George referred to in the opening quotation—so that we could support each other in this complex learning process (Okawa et al. 1991, 15).

For their training to be liberating—in order that they might have choices—our tutors also needed to develop some sociohistorical, sociopolitical background for multicultural literacy and their tutoring.

They benefited by understanding why writing centers exist, why their particular center existed, and its social as well as academic purposes. The civil rights movement, open admissions, and demographic changes, for example, gave the center a different purpose from that of a grammar fix-it shop or an aid station. In this enriched context, we raised questions regarding writing issues, current writing theory, writing anxiety, tutoring methods, learning styles and theories, academic culture, and sociopolitical issues and events impacting our education and educational system. We discussed and practiced the "hands-off" approach to tutoring outlined by Virginia Chappell (1982) as a way of encouraging the independence rather than the rescuing of writers. Chappell, a former EOP Writing Center instructor, developed and articulated the "hands-off" metaphor while she worked with EOP students at the center. Shana Windsor (1991), an American Indian EOP student who grew up on the Yakima Indian Reservation, was a second-year tutor at the center and an English education major when she described this approach in a paper presented at the 1990 Conference on College Composition and Communication (CCCC) annual convention:

> In addition to literally keeping our hands off the students' papers, we respect the writer's ... personal space, keep our dialogue as open as possible, and constantly reinforce in the writer that the work is his or her own. ... The most important part of the hands-off style of tutoring is that it lets the writer know that the way he or she chooses to manipulate language is a personal statement about the writer, no matter how formal the text is. The writer knows, then, that the text is his or her own, and that no one has the right to infringe upon that space. ... The student is no longer a student attempting to write, but a genuine *writer* with the power to write academically in a style conducive to his or her culture. (20)

In addition to tutors and trainer sharing a philosophical, pedagogical, and historical perspective, of critical importance in our multicultural tutoring program was my commitment as trainer to explore cultural, racial, social, gender, political, and class issues, specifically in relation to a question raised earlier: Who has the *right* to control ownership of a text in the academy? I needed to encourage our writing tutors to develop an understanding of and respect for the culturally based experience and the expectations that they and their students brought to each tutoring session. Developing such sensitivities required that the tutors be critically reflective. For example, they needed to explore and critique their own attitudes toward language, their cultural and socioeconomic values, and their worldviews (see Okawa, et al. 1991 for our use of Bizzell). We confronted such issues head-on, discussing difference, identity, stereotyping, ethnicity, and learning styles, among others. In doing so, we made unconscious assumptions more conscious. This increased consciousness helped us work with students with greater sensitivity and respect.

In this way, tutors could respond not according to prescribed rules of writing center behavior ("when this happens, do this"), but according to their own sense of social responsibility based on their own informed decisions, each unique to the writer and the writing conference. Laura Henderson, a tutor of mixed Asian/Caucasian heritage, was majoring in anthropology and English when she wrote the following about her training experience:

> I have been challenged on all different levels—from the theoretical to the practical to the very level of my own conscience and sense of who I am. The value of both group commitment and individual contribution is repeatedly affirmed and encouraged, and has led me to see the different dimensions of my impact on minority education, and thus its impact on myself.

Such a newly developed sense of responsibility directly affected the quality of tutoring that students received. In a paper presented with Shana at the 1990 CCCC convention, Lucy Chang (1991), an EOP student, English/art history major, and third-year veteran tutor, shared her encounter with mutual learning between student and tutor provided by writing conferences and the Writing Center experience:

> Working at the Writing Center with many students like me has taught me to examine the world around me as a Korean-American, to validate my cultural perspective. In turn, by validating and acknowledging the world that the students see and live in, I am essentially empowering them to own their writing, own their experiences, and call their perspective their own and worth having. I believe that the ownership of these things produces powerful and visionary writers (17).

In the essay cited above, Shana also writes about her experience with cultural loss and rediscovery and how that translated into her tutoring.

Based on an egalitarian, holistic, and dialogical approach, the training method and our awareness of it continued to evolve with new tutors and under new circumstances. For example, when I knew that I would be delivering a paper about our tutoring program at a CCCC convention, I worked closely with interested tutors on both my paper and the handout and diagrams that I would use to clarify our relationships. Nadine FabbiShushan, an Italian Canadian woman who began tutoring with us when she was a graduate student in comparative literature, worked from a chart that I had developed describing our training process and relationships, thereby clarifying and defin-ing both (figure 1). She portrayed perceptively the intricate learning experience of trainer, tutors, and students (figures 2 and 3). Her dia-grams are an attempt to capture what happens in the complex proc-ess—how the tutor, being a person with a home culture and identity (often taken for granted), may come to understand that personal worldview and, in turn, his or her relationship to the often over-whelming values and influences of the dominant culture represented by the university. This awareness of a dialectical relationship presents the tutor with choices—a power which is ultimately liberating— and helps him or her to interact constructively with the student writer. George, who had also been an EOP student as an undergraduate, wrote about an early experience that he had working with an African American student:

> I think it is important for the tutor to understand that he or she has as much potential to learn from each conference as the stu-dent. . . . I noticed a diversity in approaches to language and writ-ing, the issues and themes. This made me even more sensitive to and aware of the individuality of every student. In particular I recall having a conference with an African-American freshman that I think was my very first conference. She . . . had an assign-ment to write about a person whom she admired in the past. Surprisingly, she chose an aunt who ostensibly did not appear remarkable but, through the eyes of this student, she was a tower of strength, optimism and love. What I was struck and moved by was this young girl's natural respect for charity, integrity and humor, all embodied by her aunt. . . . She clearly knew what her ideas and feelings were and had a natural way of illustrating them. All she needed from the tutor was the "approval" that her feelings were good to give her enough encouragement to feel confident about her paper. I think she would have felt the way she did regardless of what I thought. However, I also knew that it was important to her to know she was on the right track academically. This I was able to do for her, and also helped her with some organizational and grammatical problems. I felt good when she left because I knew she had enough encouragement to continue to write and produce the best paper she could.

The benefit was thus reciprocal between tutor and student and, in effect, passed back and forth among tutor, student, and tutor-trainer.

Beyond this, what tutors learned in the Writing Center translated directly into their own classrooms when they became teachers. Karen Witham, a graduate student in English when she worked with us, earned her M.A. degree from UW and her teaching certificate at San Francisco State University. In her training journal, she wrote:

This is the second time in my life where I, a pure white Anglo-Saxon, have been a minority; and it has taken some adjustment. Our very first training seminar challenged my intentions in tutoring when we discussed the connotations behind "help" and "helping." I wanted to tutor because I wanted to help students be better writers. I now know that to strongly independent students "Can I help you?" can suggest a hierarchy and a superiority that I don't intend to suggest. . . . I will be a high school teacher in less than a year. I know I will take a greater sensitivity toward the minority experience into my classroom. I will bring in an attitude that recognizes the validity and richness of varied worldviews and cultural patterns. I am learning how to incorporate, not eradicate, this diversity.

Donna Bolima (1989) began working in the Writing Center as an EOP undergraduate and continued to work with us as a senior tutor after she graduated with a degree in English and women's studies. Coming from a bicultural background (Japanese American/Caucasian), she is the mother of two teenagers and spent many years in a small village in southeast Alaska. When she was in her fifth year at the Writing Center, she was also teaching in Upward Bound, a program for disadvantaged high school students. In a paper presented at a Pacific Coast Writing Centers Association conference, she reflects on how tutoring influenced her views of education and learning:

The biggest motivator . . . that I've found for some of these students has been my willingness to validate them by giving them the authority for their learning, in much the same way that I was given that opportunity through the Peer Tutor Training. Not only have I seen how collaborative learning and respect for diverse learning styles can empower students and other tutors, but I have found value in striving to be an educator who is willing to be a learner. Text ownership, I believe, belongs with the owner of the text because learning is always in the present tense for all concerned. And [the teacher's] giving up authority to the student does not mean complete anarchy, but rather the transference of responsibility to the learner to be his/her own context for learning development. It is a process that is best fostered through allowing individuals lots of validation, lots of support, lots of respect and, most importantly, lots of personal voice.

Tutors evaluated themselves and one another on an ongoing basis and in a nonthreatening and constructive manner in seminars and individual conferences with their training supervisor. Journal writing encouraged their continual self-evaluation and introspection as well. Tutors earning credit through the English Internship Program and Independent Fieldwork Program were given a formal written evaluation requested by those two offices. In turn, tutors had the

A TRAINING/LEARNING PROCESS

Trainer's Role   **Critical Reflection**   **Tutor's Role**
                              (ongoing)

sees herself/himself and tutors as
  researchers/learners (Goswami,
  Freire)

uses collaborative, dialogical
  approach, more egalitarian
  relationships, reveals own
  thinking/writing process

uses "hands-off,"[1] nondirective
  approach in writer and tutor
  conferences

provides same tools for critical
reflection—discussion of:
  writing theories, issues
  learning theories
  tutoring methods
  authority
  conditions in education

confronts cultural issues directly:
  difference, identity, values,
  stereotyping, worldviews[2]

provides different modes
of learning:
  talking in seminar discussions
  reading (journal articles, etc.)
  writing (journals and essays)
  observing/participating in
   conferences with veteran tutors
   and writing center instructors

uses validation, positive feedback
  on individual insights, learning
  styles, cultural awareness,
  worldviews:
   through journals, conferences,
   seminars

takes on authority for own
  learning, become "subjects" in
  Freire's sense

responds to collaborative
  relationship by taking more
  responsibility for own learning:
  models this with students

can learn according to individual
  learning styles (personal
  and/or cultural)

makes the unconscious conscious:
  personal assumptions
  values
  worldview

personalizes, subjectifies,
  internalizes concepts leading to
  growth, empowerment

learns to demystify the academy

develops personal definition,
  authority, ability to
  perceive/respect multiple
  worldviews, sensivity to others'
  experience, confidence in
  writing, voice

Fig. 1. The training/learning process. [1]Chappell, Virginia. 1982. "Hands Off!" *Writing Lab Newsletter* 6 (6): 4–6. [2]Bizzell, Patricia. 1986. "What Happens When Basic Writers Come to College?" *College Composition and Communication* 37: 294–301

opportunity to evaluate their trainer and training program using a questionnaire distributed to them at the end of the quarter.

Ultimately, the tutor training process evolved along a community/family-building model, with the underlying attitude being one of nurturing, as George observed with characteristic insightfulness, the underlying pedagogy being one of redefining the writer's, tutor's, and trainer's authority, and the underlying spirit being one of commitment—to the students, to one another, and to the program. The mentoring between senior tutors like Donna and the trainees extended the important nurturing relationship to new generations of tutors and established bonds that continue to be vital years later.

Chronology of a Typical Day

Especially during the autumn and winter quarters, almost no day in our writing center was ordinary. Since we conducted one-on-one conferencing on a drop-in basis, we never knew what to expect, and that was, perhaps, what kept life and the job unpredictable. But a typical day might have the following rhythms.

Sometime after 8 a.m., one or another of the professional staff saunters through the reception area of the Instructional Center, through the maze-like hall into the Writing Center, a very ordinary rectangular room off of which are four modest staff offices, two on each side. The room is decorated simply, mainly with posters from museums and recycled art calendars. Turning on lights and possibly straightening chairs and tables, the instructor becomes absorbed in writing a memo or engaging in conversation with a colleague from the chemistry or math drop-in center.

Nearing 9 a.m., a sleepy tutor arrives, clutching a café latte from the Last Exit downstairs, a throwback from the 1960s, or a more bitter version with a doughnut from Arnold's next door, a video arcade that sells cheap food cheap. While waiting for a student to come in, he cracks open his American literature text; he is taking the course because it is his sophomore year and he is seriously considering majoring in English, something we at the center have been encouraging him to do because he is such a talented writing tutor. An Alaska native in his thirties, he is a Vietnam veteran who returned to school as an EOP student after considerable alienation from academe. I have seen the red pen marks circling grammar errors on papers he wrote at a community college. Early experiences in a massive class at UW were also upsetting and provoking. Somehow he ended up at the Writing Center

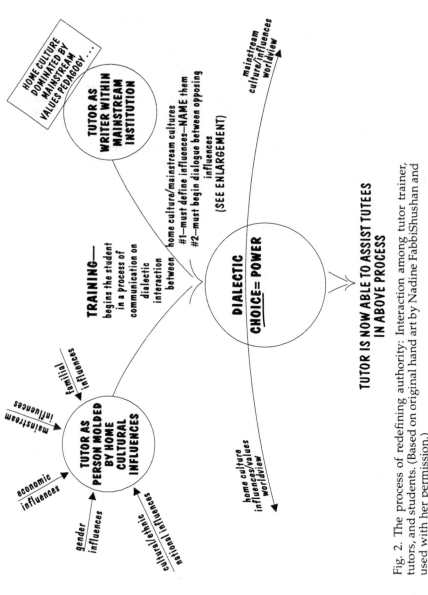

Fig. 2. The process of redefining authority: Interaction among tutor trainer, tutors, and students. (Based on original hand art by Nadine FabbiShushan and used with her permission.)

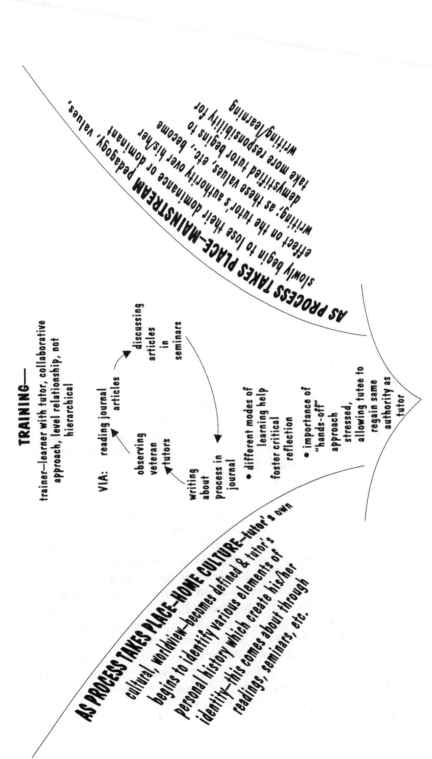

Fig. 3. The training/learning experience. (Based on original hand art by Nadine FabbiShushan and used with her permission.)

because he was in English 104, which some viewed as a course for basic writers. One look at his writing, however, and we knew he had a unique sensitivity to language and people and would be a good tutor.

After a few minutes, a Mexican American student currently in English 104 enters hesitantly. The tutor greets her casually in his low-key manner and asks her if she is registered to use the Writing Center. He then shows her how to fill out the Writing Conference Report (WCR), a form designed to encourage the writer's self-sufficiency and decision making, so that she can tell him what she wants to work on. She is a bit timid at first, but his encouraging manner puts her at ease, and she begins to talk to him about the experience she is trying to describe, the idea she wants to convey.

Since students are generally in classes during the mornings, traffic is usually light until late morning; staffing is abbreviated accordingly—two staff members and a tutor. At 10:30 a.m., the pace changes: a staff member working on a doctoral degree leaves for class or a meeting, and a couple of tutors arrive. One, a young Asian American woman, electric in personality and energy, swings into my office, drops her book bag at the door, and plops into a waiting chair. She talks excitedly about the script she is writing about a tutor-student conference—about what goes on in the tutor's mind. An Asian American student comes to the door to ask her if they can continue discussing a paper they had conferenced on the day before, and the tutor retires with the student to a table in the center. Other students enter the center, fill out their WCRs, and soon all of us, instructors and tutors, become absorbed in writing conferences, some lasting fifteen minutes, some thirty-five to forty minutes, depending on the needs and purposes of the writers. Though the lunch hour is often a difficult time to staff the center, we never close down.

At times during the day, there are several students at each of the six tables in the quickly congested room, some writing intently, some talking with a tutor or instructor about a class assignment or a graduate school application. At one table, a veteran tutor is working with a student and a tutor-trainee in an observation triad and will discuss the conference with the trainee after the student leaves. During especially busy times, instructors and veteran tutors move more quickly from student to student so that waiting students can confer with someone before too long. Working intently with a writer, a tutor finishes a conference and "comes up for air" to find that it is already 3:30 p.m.; a part-time instructor has left for the day while other tutors have arrived and are at work with students.

At 4 p.m., as the traffic begins to wind down, an African American man—who knows us well because he has used the center in the past—dashes in to work on a research paper; he has just gotten off work. Our senior tutor greets him with a smile and sits down to work with him while jokes and teases fly back and forth among us. The 5 p.m. closing hour arrives and most tutors and instructors leave, but the senior tutor works with the student until he feels confident about where he is going with his research and writing. After he leaves, those remaining talk about the events of the day or how things are going in general before they themselves are ready to turn out the lights and leave.

Services

Tutoring

An interdisciplinary center, the EOP Writing Center provides primarily one-on-one tutoring for registered EOP students daily from 8:30 a.m. to 5 p.m. Although inadequate staffing at one time forced the instructional staff to experiment with conferencing on an appointment basis, usage of the center dropped, and we resumed a drop-in format after several quarters. This open drop-in system serves more directly the needs of EOP students, many of whom work and find scheduling difficult. Students come in with ideas, sometimes no ideas, with assignments and papers from courses across the disciplines—from anthropology to engineering to English, from history to forestry to nursing and sociology. Many are in EOP English sections (see below), although the ratio of these students to students in other courses fluctuates from quarter to quarter. In addition to class assignments, they come to work on job, graduate, and professional school applications, letters to scholarship committees, members of Congress, and so forth. They work with any tutors or professional staff who are available at a given time, or come in to work with specific people when they are scheduled to be on duty.

Ties with the Instructional Center's Computer Lab

The Writing Center does not have its own computers, but the Computer Lab at the Instructional Center is available for all EOP students' use. Through the spring 1990 quarter, the formal arrangement between the Writing Center and the IC Computer Lab (ICCL) involved instruction and staffing: one of the Writing Center instructors offered workshops on word processing for a few quarters after the ICCL began operating, while writing tutors worked in the Computer Lab several hours per week, both to provide writing assistance and to help the Computer Lab with coverage. Also, not infrequently, a tutor in the Writing Center might disappear momentarily into the Computer Lab to confer with a student who is word processing a composition or research paper.

Linkage with the English Department

Outside of individual conferencing, perhaps our greatest staff effort in the 1980s was to serve as a link to the English department's writing program, especially EOP English. Coordinating its own admissions program with that of the university, the EOP also administered its own testing and placement program for entering students. In the spring quarters, Writing Center staff served along with others (usually other Instructional Center reading and study skills instructors and veteran TAs) as readers for the writing placement test, using a holistic scoring method. In this way, they brought their expertise to bear on EOP students' writing from the onset. Students were generally placed in one of three levels of English classes: English 131 (standard freshman English for students reasonably comfortable with the conventions of academic writing); English 104–105 (EOP English); and English 103 (primarily for EOP and other students in the federally funded Student Support Services Program who are nonnative users of English).

In September, before autumn quarter classes began, Writing Center staff members also worked closely with the director of EOP English to plan the orientation and training of new instructors. Again, the Writing Center staff's expertise in working with ethnically, linguistically, and socioeconomically diverse students served as a resource for the English department. The nature of the Writing Center's influence on the instruction of the TAs in a given year depended on the relationship between the center's staff liaison, the director, and the teaching assistants themselves. Throughout each quarter, a Writing Center staff member regularly attended the EOP English staff meetings to provide a continuing Writing Center perspective on issues that might be raised.

Writing Center instructors also provided a series of support workshops for EOP English classes on verb usage, research writing, and analysis of literary works (autobiographies, novels, etc.). Student attendance at the Writing Center and at these Writing Center workshops was reported to the English 104–105 teachers on a weekly basis and was sometimes discussed with the teachers at the joint staff meetings.

At times, highly charged, complex political and professional questions were raised at these meetings. Regarding issues of a multicultural or student advocacy nature, my colleagues or I might be asked to speak to one group of TAs or administrators or another group about the needs or perspectives of the students with whom we worked so closely.

Outreach

Outreach activities during the 1980s primarily targeted EOP students in English 104–105 sections, in other courses like ethnic studies classes, and in ethnic student organizations. For example, EOP English teachers could request a class tour of the Instructional Center and a specific orientation to the workings of the Writing Center or a class visit by Writing Center staff. Writing Center instructors and tutors participated in these classroom visitations, with instructors making presentations to EOP English and other classes on topics such as research strategies or study skills and tutors urging students to come and work with them in the center. Although initial outreach activities were somewhat sporadic, one instructor became the conduit for these efforts, establishing and maintaining contacts with selected faculty and departments and serving as the primary contact person for such outreach activities.

Administration

Professional Staff

In the 1980s, EOP Writing Center instructors held nonfaculty positions ("exempt staff/professional staff" classifications) at the university and ranged in academic qualifications from holders of Ph.D. degrees on down through baccalaureate degrees. Most of us held masters degrees in English or education; some were working toward a masters or doctoral degree at different times. Counting full-time and half-time instructors, we totalled 2.5 to 3.5 Full-Time Equivalent (FTE) positions during that period and considerable collective teaching experience, both domestic and overseas. As employees of the Office of Minority Affairs (OMA), instructors served on EOP committees and sometimes represented the OMA on universitywide committees in addition to our regular duties. Because of the Writing Center's location—structural and political—serving EOP students while serving the needs of the English department and the university at large, the types of services provided by the Writing Center staff shifted over the years, depending on the expertise and motivation of the individual staff members and the needs of the students and writing program.

Budget and Records

Because of its structural and political location as a minority support program, the Writing Center necessarily sought to keep relatively careful and detailed records and a relatively close rein on its budget. Prior to 1990, the coordinator/unit leader worked with the Instructional Center director and other unit leaders on budget allocations primarily for tutor training and publications. Another instructor coordinated recordkeeping efforts, which culminated in quarterly and annual reports reflecting total student visits by quarter, as well as an alphabetical list of students by race and ethnicity, language, class standing, course, and number of visits. These statistics also provided separate breakdowns by variety of courses students came from, by student ethnicity and class standing, by student language groups, and by the number of visits from each EOP ethnic division. They show, for example, that in 1988–89 the Writing Center served students from over 160 different courses, in addition to providing assistance on job, departmental, and graduate/professional school applications, financial aid appeals, résumés, and scholarship statements. Also, they show that we served students from all class levels and from all ethnic groups represented in EOP, including over twenty language groups (Okawa 1989, 2).

Evaluation and Research

Throughout the 1980s, the areas of formal evaluation and research were the least developed in the Writing Center. Although the staff developed a satisfactory evaluation instrument for EOP English instructors to provide feedback on our services to their students, and the Instructional Center at one point developed a centerwide survey of all units, no systematic practice of evaluation by students was established and carried out on an ongoing basis. Measures of success seemed to be based on student usage, and much effort was spent in clarifying and quantifying this usage both in the Writing Center and in the Instructional Center as a whole. Being primarily a service-oriented operation in a highly political context, the Instructional Center, generally, and Writing Center, specifically, focused on identifying student needs and refining services for its students in the face of fluctuations in budgetary and administrative support.

Needless to say, the potential for ethnographic and other forms of research in such an environment as the EOP Writing Center is rich and limitless, particularly in light of current and progressive educational theory and research methods like narrative inquiry (Connelly and Clandinin 1990). Because some instructors would be rightfully protective of EOP students being used as objects of exploitative research, I see in retrospect that one of the most productive forms of study would be a collaborative inquiry involving students and teachers as researchers, not unlike the critical reflection that Writing Center tutors developed in their training program. Much could be done in this context to teach others about the real education of students of color.

The Future

Although many of us were overjoyed when the Writing Center received a paint job and were exuberant when it was carpeted, we agreed that, clearly and simply, the people make the place—the students, the tutors, the staff. George extends the metaphor of nurturing to healing in order to convey what he as a person of color experienced with the people in the Writing Center:

> What the Writing Center has given me on a personal level, I feel, is a very important learning experience. It has literally brought me in from the cold of feelings of racial isolation. Here at the center, I have been able to discuss issues freely with other students of diverse racial backgrounds. What I find most important is that every one of them is willing to acknowledge and discuss . . . the problems of prejudice, racism, and sexism in our society today, in a manner which is honest and intelligent. Up to this point, I have never had the chance to talk seriously with my own peers about these ugly issues. . . . Because of my academic pursuits as an English major, I have often (almost always) found myself to be the only minority in a classroom. It seemed that very few minorities were attracted to English. Though I love the English language and its literature, strangely enough, I have never had the occasion to discuss in depth the very human issues of racism, I think partly because of the discipline itself. Here at the Writing Center . . . I have been able to unite two very important parts of myself—the mind, or the intellectual stimulation of English, and the heart, or the social issues which I feel are most relevant to my condition. I no longer feel, emotionally, that I have to take a back seat, behind another race or class of people, because I can surround myself with people here . . . that feel as I do . . . .
>
> Working at the Writing Center in a way has been a healing process for me. I feel as if the rift between being a minority and studying English literature . . . is narrowing; and I realize now that

I need not be alone in this, that there are others who have the same struggle as I do, and most importantly, we can meet at a place which encourages discussing such issues and finding solutions. I am very grateful for this.

And El Mundo Berona, a young Filipino American undergraduate, who first came to the Writing Center as an English 104–105 student, whose name was given to me by his English instructor as a person having potential to be a good tutor and who indeed worked there for three years, who glided through the center some days and bounced off the walls on others, who earned the exasperation and affection of almost everyone there as kid brother to us all, reflects on his experience as an EOP student in the center:

I've benefitted greatly from the Writing Center environment. The staff, the peer tutors and students have made me more conscious of how to relate to the university and to the outside world. The Writing Center tutor seminars continually reflect on issues regarding how we (minorities in particular) face many obstacles in life and at the university—yet my thoughts have become more optimistic about the future.

From the vantage point of one who was intensely involved in the workings of the EOP Writing Center and who has the perspective of time and distance, I see that such optimism about the future—in all its complexity—among the Writing Center's students, tutors, and staff is, in effect, the future of that center. Efforts to maintain that optimism must be vigilant and ongoing. Vision, not cynicism, will build a strong and viable program and will sustain it for EOP students and tutors who come to redefine their own authority over those "obstacles in life and at the university."

Works Cited

Berona, El Mundo. 1989. Peer Tutor Journal. University of Washington. Seattle, Washington. Spring.

Bizzell, Patricia. 1986. "What Happens When Basic Writers Come to College?" *College Composition and Communication* 37: 294–301.

Bolima, Donna Y. 1989. "Speaking from Silence." Paper presented at the Pacific Coast Writing Centers Association Annual Conference. Tacoma, Washington. October.

Bruffee, Kenneth. 1984. "Collaborative Learning and 'The Conversation of Mankind.'" *College English* 46: 635–52.

Chang, Lucy J.Y. 1991. "The Spirit of Vision: Writing from the Inside/Outside." In "Multi-Cultural Voices: Peer Tutoring and Critical Reflection in the Writing Center." *The Writing Center Journal* 12: 15–18. (Originally presented at the 1990 Conference on College Composition and Communication Annual Convention. Chicago, Illinois. March.)

Chappell, Virginia. 1982. "Hands Off!" *Writing Lab Newsletter* 6 (6): 4–6.

Connelly, F. Michael, and D. Jean Clandinin. 1990. "Stories of Experience and Narrative Inquiry." *Educational Researcher* 19: 2–14.

Freire, Paulo. 1970. *Pedagogy of the Oppressed.* New York: Continuum.

Goswami, Dixie, and Peter Stillman, eds. 1987. *Reclaiming the Classroom: Teacher Research as an Agency for Change.* Upper Montclair, NJ: Boynton/Cook.

Harris, Muriel. 1986. *Teaching One-to-One: The Writing Conference.* Urbana: NCTE.

Hartwell, Patrick. 1984. "The Writing Center and the Paradoxes of Written-Down Speech." In *Writing Centers: Theory and Administration,* edited by Gary Olson, 48–61. Urbana: NCTE.

Hawkins, Thom. 1980. "Intimacy and Audience: The Relationship between Revision and the Social Dimension of Peer Tutoring." *College English* 42: 64–68.

Henderson, Laura. 1989. Peer Tutor Journal. University of Washington. Seattle, Washington. Spring.

Hunter, George. 1989. Peer Tutor Journal. University of Washington. Seattle, Washington. Winter.

North, Stephen. 1984. "The Idea of a Writing Center." *College English* 46: 433–46.

Okawa, Gail Y. 1989. EOP Writing Center Annual Report, 1988–89. Statistics provided by J. Morley. University of Washington. Seattle, Washington. Spring.

Okawa, Gail Y., Thomas Fox, Lucy J.Y. Chang, Shana R. Windsor, Frank Bella Chavez, Jr., and LaGuan Hayes. 1991. "Multi-Cultural Voices: Peer Tutoring and Critical Reflection in the Writing Center." *Writing Center Journal* 12: 11–32.

Reigstad, Thomas, and Donald McAndrew. 1984. *Training Tutors for Writing Conferences.* Urbana: ERIC and NCTE.

Rose, Shirley K. 1989. "The Voice of Authority: Developing a Fully Rhetorical Definition of Voice in Writing." *The Writing Instructor* 8: 111–18.

Rouse, John. 1979. "The Politics of Composition." *College English* 41: 1–12.

Sale, Roger. 1976. *Seattle, Past to Present.* Seattle: University of Washington Press.

Windsor, Shana R. 1991. "Writing and Tutoring with Bi-cultural Awareness." In "Multi-Cultural Voices: Peer Tutoring and Critical Reflection in the Writing Center." *Writing Center Journal* 12: 11–32. (Originally presented at the 1990 Conference on College Composition and Communication Annual Convention. Chicago, Illinois. March.)

Witham, Karen. 1988. Peer Tutor Journal. University of Washington. Seattle, Washington. Winter.

10 The Land-Grant Context: Utah State University's Writing Center

Joyce A. Kinkead
Utah State University

Located in a northern valley along the Wasatch Mountain Range, Utah State University is the land-grant university for the State of Utah (enrollment 17,000). The symbolic "A" atop Old Main Tower marks this as an "Aggie" school, where applied science has dominated curriculum since its founding in 1888. At that time, Utah had not yet achieved statehood, locked as it was in battle with the federal government over the polygamy issue. Anti-Mormon sentiment ran high in the legislature as its members passed first the Edmunds Act (1882) and then the Tucker Amendment (1887), which virtually divested the LDS Church of its funds, turning the monies over to public schools (which had replaced the ward schools a decade earlier). Only when the church president passed what became known as the "Woodruff Manifesto" (1890), prohibiting plural marriage, did Utah become a candidate for statehood, which was granted in 1896. The fight for a theocratic state by its settlers was lost.

The Morrill Act of 1862 provided for support of a college in each state "where the leading object shall be, without excluding other scientific and classical studies, to teach such branches of learning as are related to agricultural and the mechanic arts." Certainly this emphasis is reflected in the colleges that are considered most prestigious today: natural resources, science, engineering, and agriculture. The primary mandate of the Morrill Act is "to promote the liberal and practical education of the industrial classes in the several pursuits and professions of life." Although educating students in the liberal arts is a concern for land-grant institutions, the emphasis resides in the sciences. For instance, the largest college on the USU campus, the College of Humanities, Arts, and Social Sciences (HASS) is considered primarily a "service" unit of the university.

In addition to its origins as an agricultural school, the university has good reason to favor the sciences over the humanities: over one-half of the university's budget is derived from "dollarship"—grants from the U.S. Department of Agriculture, the U.S. Department of Defense, NASA, and so on. University resources are distributed accordingly, a fact that creates some tension. While this underlying conflict might appear to pit scientists against humanists, the opponents are actually those who see university education as vocational preparation versus those who see it as enlightenment. Not surprisingly, the former equate writing with skills (the bottom-up approach) while the latter prefer a process methodology. These conflicting approaches, which parallel the dollarship/scholarship standoff, provide a challenging environment for the Writing Center at Utah State University.

In spite of these different stances, the entire academic community strongly supports writing: the written communications requirement includes both freshman and sophomore writing classes; furthermore, 80 percent of the departments on campus require an additional one or two writing classes at the upper-division level. One might say that the liberal arts are enforced at USU. Writing is required throughout a student's career so that a graduate of engineering "won't embarrass us by writing fragments and misspelling words," an attitude that puts writing on a par with using the correct fork. In other words, writing is perceived by most of the faculty as a set of discrete skills and the Writing Center as a service program where students acquire those skills.

From another perspective, though, the concept of a writing center should mesh well in an agricultural school since the mission of a writing center parallels the original mission of a land-grant university; that is, writing centers originally came about because of open admissions for students who had traditionally not sought post-secondary education. Likewise, the Morrill Act targets the "industrial classes."

History

Dramatic changes have occurred in the fifteen-year history of the Writing Center. In the early 1970s, a budget-conscious administrator decided that students learn to write during their public school days; logically, then, writing should not be a university requirement. Rather than wipe out writing entirely, the English department opted reluctantly to try an experimental writing program (actually, only one class) in which students could test out at the beginning of the course or any time thereafter as they passed an objective exam called the

English Department Composition Exam (EDCE). This program required fewer instructors since it enabled the department to offer large sections of seventy-five to ninety students. As a result, the department lost about one-third of its faculty—those without tenure and/or without doctorates.

Enter the writing lab. Initiated as an adjunct to this writing program, the lab was staffed by English faculty. After only a few years, faculty across campus began complaining about their students' writing skills; as a result, the Faculty Senate investigated the writing program, deciding that a more traditional program would improve student writing. Appalled that students could graduate without a single writing class by passing the EDCE, the faculty and administration supported the creation of a vertical writing program distributed over three years of a student's undergraduate coursework.

The writing laboratory changed, too, beginning in 1978, with the introduction of the vertical writing program. At that time, the director of composition also administered the lab. Instead of serving just the needs of students enrolled in freshman composition, the lab broadened its scope to the entire writing program. Soon, students from across campus were seeking help at the lab, which was staffed by graduate assistants as well as undergraduates. Frankly, the faculty—who did not feel comfortable with the nontraditional EDCE approach to teaching writing and who had not yet converted to the student-teacher conference approach—wanted nothing to do with the lab and retreated to their offices. Instead, the center was supervised by a person who held a clerical position. A Writing Program Administration (WPA) evaluation of the writing program in 1981 recommended hiring a full-time, tenure-track, writing lab director. This recommendation was implemented, thus creating a new tenure-track faculty position in the department and acknowledging the growing importance and clientele of the lab, which soon became the Writing Center. Since 1981, the goals of the center have remained fairly constant: helping students improve their writing through tutor-writer dialogue, expanding clientele, and educating university faculty in process pedagogy.

Physical Description

Until 1990, the center was housed in the same building as the library and the English department, conveniently located. When the department moved to a separate building, the center moved, too. Three rooms constituted the USU Writing Center then and now: a reception area (with adjoining offices for the administrators); a large tutoring room with tables, chairs, and study carrels; and a computer room (figure 1 is an illustration of the former layout and figure 2 of the current one). The tutoring room is staffed 32 hours per week while the computer room is open 60 hours. In the reception area, tutors greet students as they enter and ask them to sign in. Students may seek immediate help from tutors, request materials, or work individually on a piece of writing. At several desks in this room, tutors and students sit together to go over papers, exams, or exercises. Bookshelves hold professional publications for the tutors' use. Several large metal closets contain supplies, cassette recorders, and materials. Four filing cabinets hold the center's records, practice and mastery tests, and student exams. A high rise of baskets offers various modules, and bulletin boards announce meetings and tutor schedules.

Formerly used for classes, the adjacent tutoring room contains six rectangular tables with four chairs each. Around two walls are twelve study carrels. A filing cabinet holds free handouts plus student files. Four bookshelves contain reference books, ranging from basic writing texts, dictionaries, and handbooks to technical writing, business communication, and ESL texts. A chalkboard with screen and overhead projector is available for use in basic writing classes and workshops.

Originally, this large room was used for tutorials between tutors and students; however, in evaluations of the center, students noted that the noise level of this room was too high for them to work comfortably on drafts or exercises. As a result, as much tutoring as possible was moved to the smaller but more private reception area, where tutors and students could sit side by side at desk chairs or desks. The larger room is now used primarily for quiet work such as composing, drafting, and revising.

Activity characterizes the computer room, visible through a picture window between the two larger rooms. In 1983, the size of the Writing Center was doubled to accommodate a new computer room that houses twenty-three "dumb" terminals hooked into a campus mainframe, five personal computers, a dot matrix printer (for rough drafts), and a laser printer (for final drafts).

The arrangement of computers in this room did not seem of consequence initially. The important thing seemed to be the center's getting on the technology bandwagon and purchasing hardware. In retrospect, we realized that *how* a room feels to writers is just as important

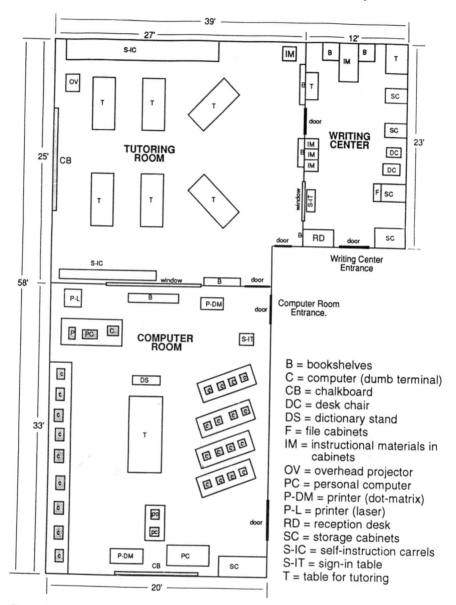

Fig. 1. Former layout of the Writing Center at Utah State University.

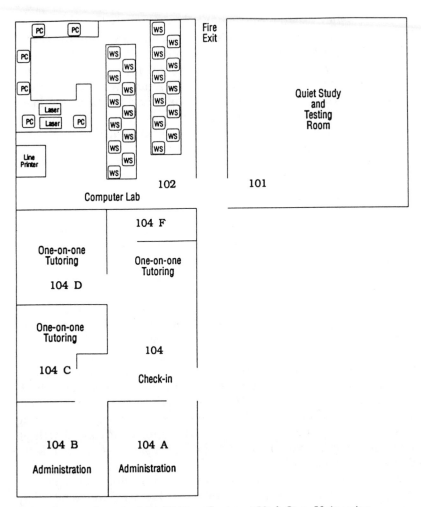

Fig. 2. Current layout of the Writing Center at Utah State University.

as the tools they use to write. Having the computers lined up against bare walls lasted only a few months as even the staff found this layout less than user-friendly. Given the constraints of wiring and the dimensions of our tables, we rearranged the computers in a less regimented order. In the center of the room is a table for writers who want to revise their printouts. In the best of all possible worlds, there would be several round tables for writing and group work. In addition, hindsight tells us that more space around each computer for books and drafts would also be desirable.

Chronology of a Typical Day

Because instruction is spontaneous in a writing center, with no opportunity for advance planning, we are never sure what will happen on a given day. The following description is an amalgamation of events.

At 8:30 a.m., a basic writing class taught by the director meets in the center, moving between lecture room and computer room; meanwhile, the assistant director works on records. An hour later, the Writing Center opens for tutoring and computing; the first clients are holdovers from the basic writing class plus technical writing students; three tutors show up for work. At 10:30 a.m., two of the tutors leave for classes, and two new tutors show up for work; one tutor looks over mastery test results and confers on further study; a second tutor finds time to finish a literary criticism paper after conferring with the center's assistant director; the director stops by on her way to a meeting with ESL faculty; there is a rush at 11:20 a.m. as advanced writing students come in after class for response; business students ask for *English 3200* exercises.

At 11:30 a.m., three different tutors come on duty, replacing the others; they chat about the upcoming Shakespeare test while they scurry to get materials for technical writing students; fifteen minutes later there is a breathing space for two of them as they share chocolate chip cookies for lunch; they read the latest issue of *Writing Lab Newsletter* and talk about the tutor's column, wondering if what they are writing for their tutor seminar would be appropriate.

At 12:30 p.m., the director and assistant director go to lunch to discuss the afternoon's tutor seminar. While they are gone, a secretary from soil science calls with a question about punctuation; a Salt Lake City community college teacher phones shortly afterward to arrange a visit to the computer room; the dot matrix printer runs out of paper; students swarm the center needing various responses (one student just wants to "drop off" his paper for proofreading—which requires an explanation of how the center operates).

The assistant director returns from lunch to pick up materials for teaching a technical writing class at 1:30 p.m. (her role description includes teaching one writing class each quarter); a graduate student working on a thesis needs help with a chapter (she is told tutoring is limited to one hour but given a list of professional editors); two tutors try to figure out alternate schedules for days they will be absent; three students from a WAC class in agriculture bring in papers; a freshman composition instructor comes in to check his students' records; a secretary from the College of Education calls to arrange an evaluation session; the director of Admissions calls to invite the staff to discuss the importance of writing skills during "Parents Day" on campus; the computer center calls to ask if it's okay to "take down" the mainframe for maintenance (answer: NO); a student drops by to report a successful grade on an essay which received tutorial help.

During the last operating hour of the tutoring room for that day, a tutor calls in sick (leaving only two on staff); an ESL student brings in a 101 essay for help; a reference librarian drops in to discuss a future workshop on researching and writing; a group of 101 students meets for additional peer work.

At 3:30 p.m., the tutoring room of the Writing Center closes (students move from the tutoring room to the computer room to work on drafts); at 3:35 p.m. a student comes by for "just five minutes of help"; the assistant director collects records to be entered on her computer; officers of Sigma Tau Delta meet to discuss next month's meeting and speaker. The tutor seminar begins ten minutes late.

By 4:30 p.m., the computer room has begun to empty as students go to dorms for dinner; the "electronic" tutor looks at requests for the day and answers them; the computer goes down for fifteen minutes. An hour later, the evening rush begins in the computer room as freshman composition students revise drafts. By 6:30 p.m., it is SRO in the computer room, and the computer consultant suggests students try another computer station on campus.

At 7:30 p.m., the consultant trains three new computer users; the dot matrix printer runs continuously as drafts spew out. Some students complain that the tutoring room of the Writing Center is only open two nights a week. Gradually students leave terminals, signing out as they go; when the consultant closes at 9 p.m., some students rush off to computer rooms that are open twenty-four hours; the door closes at 9:15 p.m., just after the last printout. When the assistant director tallies the number of student visits the next morning, she will find that 160 students used computers during the twelve-hour day of the computer room while 44 students received assistance in the tutoring room.

Clientele

USU's Writing Center provides individualized tutoring to all students at all levels. Consequently, the center serves the basic writer as well as the Ph.D. candidate. By far, the majority of students who use the center are enrolled in English classes. Given the number of writing classes offered, this is hardly surprising. Outside the department, as within, students may be referred to the center by an instructor or may come voluntarily. Students learn about the center from several sources: an orientation session in their writing class, bulletin boards, brochures, teacher referral, the campus newspaper, and, most commonly, word of mouth. Although writers often visit the center to learn "skills," what they find is a responsive reader for their writing.

The distinctive characteristic of the community of writers that the Writer Center serves is its homogeneity. Because one religion—the Latter-Day Saints, popularly known as the Mormons—dominates the state and because the majority of students who attend USU are Utah residents, the values of this church influence all arenas. For instance, education is highly regarded by the LDS Church; consequently, Utah ranks first in the nation in the percentage of bachelor's degrees held by its adult citizens. A tangible effect of this emphasis is a small remedial program with only three sections of basic writing offered during an academic year; consequently, the Writing Center sees very few students who could be termed basic writers. And while a brewing coffeepot is typically a sign of warmth and welcome in writing centers, it is taboo in Utah.

The absent coffeepot is symptomatic of other issues that are unique to a Utah university. Although the nineteenth-century leaders of the state finally capitulated to the desires of the national government, many contemporary non-LDS residents feel that the state still is a thinly veiled theocracy. Certainly no other state has as its "minority" a group of WASPs. Faculty on campus often complain that the 1960s directive to "question authority" never reached Utah. One of the goals of USU—or any university for that matter—is for students "to develop skills of critical thinking and reasoning and to foster the process of intellectual discovery," a goal which smashes head-on with a reliance on faith.

Tutors: Selection and Training

Where do our tutors come from? Some are English majors, while others come from other disciplines. All tutors write an essay as part of their application. Basically, our tutors fall into four groups: undergraduates paid an hourly wage, undergraduates serving an internship as a tutor (without pay), graduate teaching assistants, and computer/writing tutors hired because of their computer expertise. Those tutors serving an internship tutor two hours a week while enrolled in a teacher education course called Diagnosing Basic Writing Problems. These students enthusiastically endorse the internship as one of the few hands-on experiences available before student teaching. The initial tutor training occurs during the first week of the quarter before the center opens officially. During this training, tutors learn about writing center procedures such as greeting students and filling out visit records. They also participate in the first of many role-playing activities that replicate tutorials, "trying tutoring on for size." Weekly one-hour seminars follow for which students earn one credit each term; enrolling in this practicum quarterly is a requirement of employment for the paid undergraduate tutors (the other three categories of tutors are not required to attend the weekly meetings).

Tutorials are shaped by the training tutors receive. Just as freshman composition students are taught to subordinate surface features to global issues, so, too, are tutors. It is imperative that a tutor's reaction to a given text mirror composition faculty reaction so that writing program philosophy and pedagogy are reinforced. Our writing program uses conferences, portfolio grading, and peer-response groups to emphasize collaborative learning. Likewise, tutors are directed to respond to a student writer collaboratively rather than hierarchically. They are advised to follow the three principles Thomas Reigstad and Donald McAndrew (1984) suggest: establish and maintain rapport, allow the writer to do the work, and maintain high-order concerns over low-order concerns (1). By helping students articulate and expand their knowledge, tutors also share in learning and, ideally, become learners themselves.

Typically, tutors practice tutorial dialogues through role-playing; during the "real thing," they keep logs in which they analyze sessions. A typical log entry might analyze what worked in the tutorial and what the tutor would have done differently, given the chance. Besides the log, tutors write other assignments such as case studies or essays that summarize and evaluate their tutoring experiences. They may also design modules or workshops. Required readings include Muriel Harris's *Tutoring Writing* (1982) and *Teaching One-to-One* (1986).

Types of Services

By far, the bulk of the services offered lies in the tutorial program, one-on-one instruction. Tutor-designed materials back up this coaching. A third, problematic service is testing. In addition, word processing and text analysis are an integral part of the Writing Center.

Tutoring

Opting for a casual rather than a formal atmosphere, the center operates on a drop-in basis. Since students do not schedule appointments, few go through what we would recognize as a "sequence of instruction." Rather, the typical student brings in a near-to-final draft of an essay for response; while the impetus for the visit may have been an awareness of a surface problem (e.g., "I need some help with commas"), each text is responded to on a global level before possible surface errors are identified. This philosophy reinforces the pedagogy of writing classes, where holistic review precedes matters of editing. Tutoring sessions are explicitly designed to suggest the hierarchical nature of writing skills.

Computers

All English 101 students are required to learn word processing (now a mainframe version of *WordPerfect,* although the original program was a *VAX VI Editor*). Freshman composition students also have the option of using the text-editing program *Writer's Workbench* to analyze their texts (fewer students use *Writer's Workbench* now than when we first started the computer writing room since we no longer strongly promote its use). Using *Writer's Workbench* prompts students to be more curious about style; as a result, they ask for help in interpreting the stylistic analyses (e.g., passive voice, types of sentences, expletives). Students may consult with a tutor in the tutoring room. The center has avoided purchasing "skill-and-drill" exercises for the computer room.

The addition of computers to the center has doubled both space and student use. That being the case, some background on computer integration into the writing program will be helpful here. At the time we purchased computers for the center, it was less expensive to use dumb terminals as opposed to personal computers although this would no longer be the case. Hooking into a campus mainframe also meant students could use *Writer's Workbench* (which at that time ran *only* on su. h large machines). The primary advantage of the decentralized computer access we chose is that students can log on twenty-four hours a day at various locations across campus or via modem and personal computers; as a result, the Writing Center can keep its "8 to 5" hours. The disadvantages of this setup include the mainframe's slow response time and unfamiliar text-editor program used for word processing (*VI Editor*). The purchase in 1986 of a dedicated microvax for the writing program quickened response time, while the latter problem was solved when a mainframe version of *WordPerfect* was developed.

An advantage we did not foresee was access to electronic mail (Kinkead 1987b), which provides networking for students, instructors, and tutors. Jack Jobst refers to computer mail as the "New Golden Age of Correspondence," a term true for USU students who enjoy sending and receiving electronic mail. The writing program has made use of the popularity of e-mail in several ways. In the Writing Center, the "electronic tutor"—nicknamed "E.T."—is available to answer questions about writing (Kinkead 1988a). Students mail their queries—and perhaps the text in question—to E.T. and can expect a response within a day's time. E.T. operates much as a regular tutor in the center, following the same guidelines for response. Often the E.T. correspondence is the first step in getting the student writer to the center in person. The over 3,000 electronic mail messages sent each term suggest that it's a popular mode of communication. In addition, e-mail provides yet another medium through which the Writing Center can reach and help students.

Because students are required to use a word processor (their own or one on campus) for drafting and revising, the demand on the computer room does not allow classes to meet there—except during the early-morning hours. However, all classes go to the Writing Center during the first week of each term for a computer orientation given by the assistant director. From that point, students rely on the computer manual (written by Writing Center staff) and the computer consultants on duty. Each instructor, having learned about this particular computer program during a week's orientation prior to the fall quarter, is able to field questions in class and suggest writing methods that are especially appropriate for this technology. For example, students trade essays electronically and "mail" back critiques using the mainframe's electronic mail.

The addition of several personal computers allows students to create documents by using them or to bring disks from their personal computers to transfer files to the mainframe. Using *Uniform* and *Kermit* software, computer consultants help students upload and download files between machines.

How is such a comprehensive computer system funded? *All* students on campus pay a $20 "computer user fee" to a university computer-use fund each quarter which contributes to the purchase of hardware, software, and paper as well as maintenance. Students enrolled in writing classes pay an additional $5 "lab" fee to the English department since it bears the cost of computer manuals, paper, ribbons, and tutors for its own lab (one of the few on campus dedicated to a particular discipline).

Ironically, the addition of computers to the Writing Center caused some unwanted attention from the university administration, which provided initial funding for the computers in the hope that they would improve writing on campus. They also hoped that computers might increase what the state has termed "productivity," which translates as larger classes. Similarly, they also purchased *Writer's Workbench* because they visualized writing instruction without teachers. So far, however, class sizes have not been increased, nor has the number of teachers been decreased.

Testing

The Writing Center also serves the department and university by administering tests. The center administers *challenge exams* to students whose maturity and writing experience suggest that, for them, freshman composition might be superfluous. Unlike the former EDCE test, the challenge exam requires a writing sample. Only a very few students attempt or pass these exams, but offering them gives the writing program flexibility.

At one time, the center evaluated the writing proficiency of students as a service to other departments and colleges. For example, the College of Education requires that all teacher education students write a proficiency essay. This used to be evaluated by a combination of writing center staff and education faculty. Since 1990, the testing has taken place in the education building. Students who are found wanting in writing skills work through specific modules to remediate these problems and prepare for a retest.

Providing such services fosters cooperation between writing specialists and faculty from other content areas. That advantage was offset, though, by the negative connotations of being considered a *testing* center—especially in the minds of those students who are "punished" with remediating exercises for being "deficient."

Materials

Re-educating students about what makes good writing is part of the center's mission. Some students still believe that if they just do enough exercises on comma splices, they will solve their writing problems. For them, the center has self-study *modules* that focus on common problems such as paragraph development, parallel structure, subject-verb agreement, or pronoun usage; these modules include short exercises in workbooks, followed by practice tests and mastery tests. Students determine how much of a module they want to complete, and tutors may suggest during consultation that they skip ahead and try a practice test if they seem to understand the concept being studied. Most of the mastery tests ask the student to write at least a paragraph using the concept learned. During this work, tutors encourage students to produce their own texts to demonstrate their mastery of a concept.

Least used of the materials available to students are the tape-recorded programs in vocabulary and spelling purchased during the early days of the center when buying commercially produced materials seemed essential. Only a few students—those who do not seem to mind regimented drill—seek these tapes. Nonnative speakers of English most often ask for these because they serve as language tapes, reproducing the sounds of English words.

Writing Across the Curriculum

Besides working with faculty across campus to evaluate their students' writing skills, the Writing Center director and assistant director are frequently invited to classes to talk about specific writing assignments or problems. Faculty request workshops for specific classes on prewriting; writing essay exams, research papers, or abstracts; or peer editing. Tutors have initiated workshops for a broader audience—held after hours in the Writing Center—on MLA style, punctuation, and point of view.

Improving writing in the content areas has taken various forms over the years. Individual faculty members provide specific information packets for their students in the center. For example, the instructor of a film studies class created guidelines and sample critical reviews for his students to use while visiting the center. A biology instructor worked with the center in setting up small response groups for lab reports. To get students to visit the center, others offer incentives, such as adding ten points to papers that have received tutor response.

Outreach

Because teacher education is a strong program within the Department of English, the Writing Center has collaborated with the university and public schools on several projects (Kinkead, Smith, and Stoddart 1986). For example, a high school English class visited the center, bringing with them essays and receiving feedback from tutors (faculty and English education majors). Center instructors are also frequently invited to public schools for guest lectures and to meet with university and high school teachers to discuss evaluation standards for writing. Other collaborative projects include pen-pal correspondence between university and high school students to discuss young adult literature (Kinkead and Stoddart 1987). The pen-pal project transferred from the post office to electronic mail when the university and high school writing and computer centers were linked (Kinkead 1988b).

Administration

Although the center's patrons come from across campus, the administration and budgeting of the center remain in the English department.

Faculty and Staff

As part of the department's writing program, the Writing Center is supervised by a director who reports to the director of writing, who in turn, reports to the department head. (The department head oversees the budget, deciding on how much money can be allotted to tutor salaries, computer equipment, and supplies.) The current director is the fourth since the founding of the center.

Besides serving on departmental and university committees that focus on writing or general education, the director of the Writing Center is responsible for ensuring that the philosophy of the writing program is mirrored in Writing Center policies and practices. These decisions influence how the center is perceived by students and faculty within and outside the English department. A more tangible responsibility is training tutors, a responsibility shared by the director and assistant director. Another task they share is interviewing and hiring tutors. They are responsible also for publicizing the center through orientations, brochures, and newspaper articles. In addition, the director reports annually to the English department chair on the state of the center. Traditionally, the director's teaching assignment of seven hours per quarter is drawn from the following courses: Basic Writing (English 100), Diagnosing Basic Writing Problems (English 405), Practicum in Tutoring (English 492), or Rhetoric and Basic Writing (English 605). Using a conference approach, the director also offers writing instruction (one credit) to students who need additional practice before or during their required writing courses.

In addition to the responsibilities already noted, the assistant director is accountable for the day-to-day supervision of tutors and operation of the center (e.g., scheduling, keeping records, and organizing materials). Tutoring is another part of the assistant director's job. This nontenure track, professional slot is filled by an experienced writing teacher with an M.A. in English.

Records

Although keeping records sometimes seems to exist on the same level as error-hunting, we know that records keep the center in operation. Recordkeeping begins when students enter the door and are asked whether they would like a single tutorial or a series of visits. The short-term student simply fills in a timecard and logs in on a sign-in sheet; the student who expects to visit the center several times during the quarter fills in a time card and sets up a folder where work in progress and tutor notes can be filed. The first time a student visits the center, an "initial visit" notice is filled in, which is later sent to the instructor. The timecards and folders are color-coded to indicate the course in which the student is enrolled (e.g., 101, 200, business, education). At the end of each day, the assistant director adds each student's name to a computer list, noting how much time the student spent in the center, and then puts the visit forms in instructors' mailboxes to alert them that one of their students has attended the center. At two-week intervals, teachers receive a computer printout—divided into tutorial visits and computer visits—listing the students in their classes who have used the center and giving the number of hours logged there. Faculty may also look at student files in the center. At the end of the term, faculty receive a final printout that reports the total hours each of their students spent in tutorial sessions.

The directors of the Writing Center and writing program receive a more detailed report indicating the number of students using the tutorial services of the center (faculty referral and self-referral), attendance in hours, and names of faculty making referrals. This latter item, for instance, helps the director identify teachers who recommend the center to their students. The report also includes information on total use of the computer room. Records like these help the center justify its existence to the central administration. For example, we typically report 8,000 tutorial sessions annually. This type of data is understood and appreciated by administrators.

Evaluation

Students evaluate the center at the end of each quarter. (The center uses the evaluation form developed by Phyllis Sherwood in Harris 1982, 281.) Knowing why students come to the center, how often they visit, and how successful the tutorials are help the staff plan tutor schedules and training. Student input was especially important when the computers were added to the center; following student suggestions, we rearranged the room, modified the schedule, and revised the computer manual.

Faculty do not hesitate to offer advice either. They often ask for additional topics such as plagiarism, résumés, or proofreading to be covered during tutor training. One of their continuing concerns is the writing skills of nonnative students.

Outside evaluations of the center by WPA evaluators take place about once every five years. Their advice in 1982 included major staff changes, while a 1987 evaluation found little to change and much to applaud.

The Future

The opportunities for field research in the center have largely been overlooked in a department grounded in a traditional literature program. That scenario is changing with the influx of writing specialists (the department now offers an M.A. emphasis in the theory of writing as well as technical writing). Thus, graduate students are beginning to look at the center for qualitative research studies. A study on the influence of gender on the writing center tutorial (Kinkead 1987a) involved videotaping tutorial sessions and analyzing transcripts and tapes for verbal and nonverbal behavior.

The Writing Center will increase its role in the WAC program of writing-intensive and writing-emphasis classes. Required visits to the center will be included in those classes. But some storm clouds still hover on the horizon. An area of continuing concern is the growing number of ESL students who are drawn to USU's engineering and science programs. Concern over adequately serving this population might be alleviated by recruiting successful nonnative speakers of English as tutors or establishing a separate ESL tutoring center. Since the level of written English proficiency of nonnative speakers is a campuswide concern, the center will need to plan carefully for its future role in this area.

State legislators continue to ask that faculty and programs at universities do "more with less," which threatens the quality of instruction. Unlike other states, Utah has a burgeoning population, and the result has been a 10 percent increase in student enrollment in each of the past few years. In spite of these problems, the Writing Center staff retains its energetic and enthusiastic outlook. It enjoys its reputation in the state as a place where future teachers receive practical hands-on training in one-to-one teaching. But because of its context, the USU Writing Center will always have to be wary of the bottom line in a land-grant university that pays more attention to soil science than to short stories.

Works Cited

Harris, Muriel. 1986. *Teaching One-to-One: The Writing Conference*. Urbana: NCTE.

———. ed. 1982. *Tutoring Writing: A Sourcebook for Writing Labs*. Glenview, IL: Scott, Foresman.

Kinkead, Joyce. 1987a. "Authority, Gender, and Tutors," Paper presented at the 77th Annual Convention of the National Council of Teachers of English. Los Angeles, California. November 21.

———. 1987b. "Computer Conversations: E-mail and Writing Instruction." *College Composition and Communication* 38: 337–41.

———. 1988a. "The Electronic Writing Tutor." *Writing Lab Newsletter* 13 (4): 4–5.

———. 1988b. "Wired: Computer Networks in the English Classroom." *English Journal* 77 (7): 39–41.

Kinkead, Joyce, William E. Smith, and Patricia Stoddart. 1986. "Northern Utah's English Articulation Program." In *School-College Collaborative Programs in English*, edited by Ron Fortune, 105–10. New York: MLA.

Kinkead, Joyce, and Patricia Stoddart. 1987. "Pen Pals and *I Am the Cheese*." *ALAN Review* 15 (1): 40–43.

Reigstad, Thomas J., and Donald A. McAndrew. 1984. *Training Tutors for Writing Conferences*. Urbana: ERIC and NCTE.

Sherwood, Phyllis. 1982. "Evaluations from Students." In Harris, *Tutoring Writing*, 281.

11 Taking Tutoring on the Road: Utah State University's Rhetoric Associates Program

Joyce A. Kinkead
Utah State University

> November 7: I began to write suggestions on the papers. I hadn't realized how hard it would be. I'm just another student like them, and I began to worry how they'll take the comments I make. I ran into another problem. I could see where they had made mistakes, but I wasn't sure what suggestions would be helpful for them. I knew that I needed to point out good things in their papers, but I had a hard time finding anything good about some of them.

This is the tenth entry in Mary's tutoring log. She is a "rhetoric associate" (RA) in a new program at Utah State University which takes tutoring to the people. Although the RA program is based on the same principles as those used in the USU Writing Center, the two are not connected administratively or physically.

Drawing upon Brown University's successful decade-long Undergraduate Writing Fellows Program, created by Tori Haring-Smith, USU's College of Humanities, Arts, and Social Sciences established its Rhetoric Associates Program (RAP) in 1990 in order to increase and improve writing in its thirteen departments and to help professors with the increasingly heavy paperload. Unlike the Writing Center, RAP is administered through the college office by an associate dean. In fact, the director of writing has a 50 percent position in the Department of English and 50 percent in the College of HASS to oversee writing across the curriculum.

The college climate for writing programs is indeed an enviable one; the dean of the College of HASS encouraged and—more importantly—funded RAP, an innovative program that relies on students helping students. The dean and the writing program administrator (WPA) worked together to design a program that best suited the institutional needs. As any WPA understands, administrative support is integral to success.

210

Program Description

As envisioned by Haring-Smith, a rhetoric associates program is a cross-curricular peer-tutoring program that places tutors who are excellent student writers within the context of classes—not in a centralized writing center. RAs work directly with faculty under the supervision of a director. Given the fact that many faculty will never jump on the writing-across-the-curriculum bandwagon and attend the workshops necessary to introduce them to principles of effective writing, this program provides instruction in more subtle ways. The peer tutors are trained to serve as "educated lay readers" who comment on students' papers *before* the instructor evaluates them; Mary's log entry at the beginning of this chapter describes her initial contact with these assignments. Students then have the opportunity to revise and hand in both the critiqued draft and the final version to the professor.

Brown University has funded its program to the extent that eighty writing fellows from across campus are chosen annually and paid $400 per semester for working with fifteen students on two assignments. Using this formula, the Brown program can work with over 2,500 students annually (Haring-Smith 1985).

Tutors: Selection and Training

In its pilot year (1990–91), the USU program selected thirteen outstanding students, nominated by faculty within the college. Each year the student applications include a writing portfolio and a sample critique of a student essay. Students are selected as RAs not only on the basis of their writing skills, but also on the basis of their willingness to help other students. (As all writing center directors know, sometimes the valedictorian does not make the best tutor.) During the fall quarter, RAs enroll in a three-credit English internship course in which they learn how to be sympathetic and careful readers of student essays. A common misperception is that the RAs will be teachers, not readers— an attitude often shared by the students with whom they work.

How can undergraduates become effective agents of change? First, their own attitudes about writing must be revised. For example, this past fall, during the initial meetings of the RA seminar, John and Shawn, two of the RAs, kept talking about "correcting" student essays. By discussing which comments on their own essays proved most helpful to their development as writers, both were able to redefine their notion of "teaching writing." Analyzing sample student essays and making a trial run at comments also helped them to build confidence in their own abilities and to avoid any destructive approaches to tutoring.

The attitude of the RA is most important. RAs find Donald Murray's *A Writer Teaches Writing* (1985) inspiring because is often gets them thinking for the first time about *how* they write. Other helpful texts for RAs include Meyer and Smith's *The Practical Tutor* (1987) and Lindemann's *A Rhetoric for Writing Teachers* (1987). In the seminar, our RAs discuss writing theory, assignment design, student essays, and logistics.

Faculty and Student Participation

Faculty must meet certain criteria in order to qualify for participation in this program: (1) require at least two writing assignments, one before mid-term and one after; (2) evaluate the course using the program's forms; and (3) meet with the RAs to discuss goals and assignments. We encourage faculty to see writing as a developmental process occurring over the course of the ten-week term. The two-assignment requirement is directly aimed at changing the last-day-of-the-quarter research paper, which students often find a futile exercise since they may never see it again, or if they do, at some point after the course concludes.

Students enrolled in RAP-coordinated courses have several due dates for each essay: the first one is the date on which students submit drafts; once the RAs comment on the essay in writing, students meet individually with the tutors to discuss their comments. For the second due date, the students revise their assignments and hand in both drafts to the professor.

Too often, our students whip out "midnight wonders," essays that require more time for the professor to evaluate than it took for the student to write. One result of these sloppy assignments is that professors from around the campus blame the English department for "not doing its job." The Rhetoric Associates Program helps faculty see that the problem of teaching writing is more complex than merely making and evaluating assignments. When instructors participating in RAP compare the two drafts handed in, they are astonished at the differences in content, organization, and proofreading. One professor of an introductory liberal arts class, surprised at the impact of a reader, conducted an experiment with a second section of the same course by using peer-response groups. The result? The scores on their writing assignments also jumped. As a consequence of this experiment, he uses peer-response groups regularly in his classes. This is one way that the principles of effective writing instruction are demonstrated without benefit of faculty development workshops.

Naturally, the participating faculty influence the quality of the RA experience. We advertise that RAs are not graders but readers who will respond to content and structure primarily and will proofread should the draft need only polishing (according to RAs, few drafts are ready for refinement but instead require major rethinking and restructuring). Before the term begins, the RAs meet as a group with their cooperating professors. The most enthusiastic faculty invite the RAs to act as a sounding board for the assignments, to provide input on scheduling, and to evaluate their syllabus statement on the program. In this scenario, we have the apotheosis of the program: faculty and students collaborating for the common good of undergraduate education. RAs who function in this manner get an insider's view of academe and what good teaching can mean; as a result, several RAs have chosen to pursue graduate studies in preparation for careers in the professoriate. These are our best examples.

Likewise, faculty who do not take RAP seriously can have a deleterious effect not only on the RAs but also on the students in the course. A professor who drops early writing assignments, relies solely on the traditional final-day research paper, does not speak of RAP in positive terms to the class, and does not communicate writing expectations clearly to the RAs or the students will not be invited back for participation. Even with faculty orientations and RA-faculty conferences, some instructors still commit these sins.

Evaluation

The successes and problems of the program are addressed in three evaluations: student, faculty, and RA. From the students, we hear:

> I was skeptical at first, but I was surprised about how much I learned.

> I really enjoyed talking with my RA. She was willing to work with me and gave me a lot of encouragement and advice, which made me feel more confident. The grades on my papers were much better.

> Even if I don't have an RA in the future class, I'm going to always have someone else read my papers and respond. My RA gave me different insights I hadn't thought about.

Faculty noted the "dramatic difference" between the two submitted pieces and commented that they spent less time evaluating papers because "they were so much better." The RAs discovered that they learned about their own writing by commenting on other students' drafts. The improvement on student essays became visible between conferences on the first and second papers: "Students implemented the writing techniques we'd talked about in the initial meeting." Their students were honest about the lack of labor they had put in on previous assignments, too: "Many of the students with whom I worked said they often just turned in the first draft; now they see the value of re-drafting and putting more effort in their writing."

During the pilot year, RAP worked with 553 students and eighteen professors in courses that ranged from Society and Law (sociology) to Site Planning and Design (landscape architecture). In the second year, four expert RAs served as mentors to the novice RAs. Eventually, our goal is for this program to become universitywide—similar to parent programs at Brown, LaSalle, Western Washington, and Swarthmore.

Already, RAP has inspired an offshoot: the Undergraduate Teaching Fellows Program, a plan designed to recruit the promising under-graduate students who may have future careers in the professoriate. Affiliated with faculty mentors—themselves exemplary teachers—teaching fellows serve as discussion leaders in classes, lead review sessions, and hold office hours for questions.

Although it strains credulity, the students who are nominated to become RAs are often insecure about their own writing skills. At the beginning of the year, these tutors require quite a bit of hand holding as they must be persuaded that they can actually provide help to their peers. In the RAs' synthesis essays for the first term, this issue of insecurity is a frequent topic. In Sandi's essay, entitled "A Letter to Mr. Bassett," she castigates a former teacher for setting up students to fail and for instilling negative attitudes in them toward writing. Another RA, Melody, created a precedent for the program as the first artist to be nominated; her insecurity is evident in her essay title: "An Art Student's Survival Handbook to the Rhetoric Associates Program." She cautions future RAs who are art majors:

> You may be inordinately nervous, 'cause let's face it folks, we don't write very much. Part of that is the structure of the studio experience. The focus is on developing one's skills and eye, not conjugating verbs.

Ironically, Melody's insecurities are not indicative of her abilities; she is a sterling and conscientious tutor.

Certainly there is some evangelical zeal associated with programs such as RAP that rely heavily on students' taking responsibility for their own learning. And no wonder. The brochures about the RA program give prime consideration to improving the writing of students in classes. Secondary to that—but no less important—are the unadvertised benefits. One is that the RAs note the improvement in their own writing skills. As Chalyce blurted out one day in an RA seminar, "I thought this program was for other students, but now I see it's really for us." From an administrative point of view, the college wanted a program that would provide a paying, academic experience for students, so they would not have to take jobs as baggers at the local supermarket. Finally, professors are introduced to effective principles of incorporating writing as a way of learning. Not only do the RAs provide insights into student attitudes and perceptions, professors in the program share writing assignments and strategies that work with one another, providing a kind of cross-germination of ideas.

A decentralized tutoring program simply provides some benefits that cannot be matched by a writing center rooted in one place. This high-profile tutoring program provides students and professors with productive, efficient writing instruction in their own contexts.

Works Cited

Haring-Smith, Tori. 1985. *A Guide to Writing Programs: Writing Centers, Peer Tutoring Programs, and Writing-Across-the-Curriculum.* Glenview: Scott, Foresman.

Lindemann, Erika. 1987. *A Rhetoric for Writing Teachers.* 2nd ed. New York: Oxford University Press.

Meyer, Emily, and Louise Z. Smith. 1987. *The Practical Tutor.* New York: Oxford University Press.

Murray, Donald M. 1985. *A Writer Teaches Writing.* 2nd ed. Boston: Houghton-Mifflin.

12 Moving toward an Electronic Writing Center at Colorado State University

Dawn Rodrigues
Colorado State University

Kathleen Kiefer
Colorado State University

Colorado State University (CSU) is a land-grant university located in Fort Collins, Colorado, approximately sixty miles north of Denver. A comprehensive research university, CSU enrolls roughly 18,900 full-time equivalent students. Although the university's reputation is based primarily on its research in the sciences and engineering, its largest college is the College of Liberal Arts, which houses the English department, including its Writing Center as well as its Computer-Assisted Writing Lab.

Although faculty across campus have long agreed with their colleagues in the English department that writing is essential for students completing undergraduate degrees, institutional support for writing programs was minimal throughout the 1970s and 1980s. There was, however, support for computer-assisted writing during this same period. The university eagerly invested in hardware and software, encouraging some cynics to suspect that the university as a whole valued computers over personal instruction. Nonetheless, despite tight budgets for new or expanding programs of other kinds, the trend toward more spending on computer hardware has translated into positive results for the English department—allowing faculty to experiment with technological approaches to teaching and to writing center design.

The long-term indifference of many faculty toward writing and the recent changes in attitude can be explained by a closer look at our institutional contexts. For many years, faculty across campus have felt that CSU students do not need the kinds of services traditional skills-oriented writing centers provide. Admittedly, with admission standards relatively high (average ACT scores are 24), there are few seriously underprepared writers at CSU; however, each year a limited number of underprepared students is admitted under special admissions programs. The English department has been expected to meet those students' needs in appropriate ways—previously, through a basic writing course and, currently, through a specialized tutorial program implemented through the Writing Center. In addition to helping the students it serves, however, the Writing Center and writing program at CSU have had much larger goals, goals which, until recently, have been unattainable.

During the last two years, there have been many signs of a renewed interest in writing skills across the entire campus. One example of this change in outlook is the central administration's recent support of a research center for writing. In fall 1991, as part of a new strategic planning and budgeting process, the university designated selected programs in the university for enhanced funding. A joint project of English and technical journalism, the Center for Research in Writing and Communication Technologies was identified as one of these programs. The research agenda of this interdisciplinary program includes writing in the disciplines and the development of computer tools for writing.

Other signs across campus also point to an improved attitude toward writing. Science and engineering faculty have begun to realize the importance of communication skills in their students' careers and are demonstrating considerable interest in incorporating discipline-related writing tasks into their curricula: they have asked the English department to address the communication problems of an increasing number of upper-level undergraduate and graduate students, many of whom are nonnative speakers; they have invited English department faculty to speak to their students; and they have begun to collaborate with the English department on grant proposals to support writing in the disciplines.

Shifts in computing at CSU have also, indirectly, improved the status of the English department. With a switch from mainframe to distributed computing, our computer center has changed in both name and function: formerly called the University Computer Center (and formerly a facility that primarily supported scientific and administrative computing), the computer-support facility is now referred to as Academic Computing and Networking Services, and it now supports labs in each of the university's eight colleges—all of which can access the computers in the English department's Writing Center and in its Computer-Assisted Writing Lab through a campuswide computer network.

With this positive atmosphere emerging on campus, what have we done to extend writing support services to more students? The capabilities of computer networking and the increasing respect for writing have led us to develop plans for an Electronic Writing Center, a place for on-line tutoring and writing assistance, including a library of faculty-developed cross-disciplinary writing software. We envision students accessing on-line writing help from any networked computer on campus, including computer labs in residence halls and in different departments and colleges across campus.

In effect, we hope to deliver writing center assistance directly and conveniently to all students through the campus computer network. We anticipate cooperation from administration and faculty in the eight different colleges in the development of an integrated, networked academic writing environment that would link the services of our traditional writing center with the resources of our computer-assisted lab. A more complete description of our current writing facilities—our Writing Center and our Computer-Assisted Writing Lab—should help establish a context for our emerging plans.

The Writing Center: History, Description, and Tutorial Support

The Writing Center was created in 1979, shortly after the university curriculum committee reduced the freshman English course requirement from four credits to three and increased sevenfold the number of students required to take basic writing. A small operation, the original writing center was "a moveable feast" for two years—housed in successive semesters in an office, a classroom, and a graduate teaching assistants' lounge. Eventually, the Writing Center moved into Johnson Hall, for most students much too far from most other classroom buildings on campus and a quarter mile from the English department.

The original Writing Center was staffed by three or four second-year teaching assistants and was open for fifteen to twenty hours per week. The primary role of this writing center was to provide tutorial support to students in basic writing and freshman English. After the first year of operation, tutors also worked with occasional drop-in students from other classes across the university, but the Writing Center could not advertise its services widely. In essence, it had a small staff and no way of supporting a growing clientele.

The Writing Center continued to operate according to this original model for ten years, with only minor changes. During this time, the university's enrollment went up, but the English department's faculty size remained the same. With a growing backlog of students unable to schedule their required freshman English course during their freshman year, the critical issue for the English department was finding the money to staff a sufficient number of composition classes. In this climate, expanding the Writing Center was simply not possible.

Then, in 1989, the situation changed. The Colorado Commission of Higher Education (CCHE), the governing board for all state colleges and universities, informed us that as a research institution, we could no longer offer basic writing as a credit-bearing course. This decision was part of a statewide attempt to shift remedial courses to the community colleges. We considered our options: we could send our students to the local community college for a basic writing course; we could revise the basic writing course, making it clearly a college-level course; or we could try an alternative approach—making one-on-one tutoring in the Writing Center available to students whose placement exam results suggested that they would struggle to complete college composition.

Because creating a new course would take more than a year, we decided to try the tutorial approach temporarily. The tutorial program we developed was tailored to the needs of the students who would have taken basic writing—students underprepared for college, largely first-generation college students and minority students.

These changes required internal support from the central administration, since the tutoring program could not be counted toward regular academic credit. Fortunately, we received that support. The central administration had begun to understand the urgency of providing adequate writing support to all of our students, basic writers included.

The central administration's support allowed us an unanticipated benefit: now we could actively advertise. We were able simultaneously to extend the Writing Center's services to students in all courses and to establish a visible presence on campus.

Expanding the Writing Center made it necessary for us to make other changes internally. We needed additional staff, a new training program, and a larger room to house the Writing Center. We also needed to extend the Writing Center's hours of operation from twenty to forty hours per week.

Staffing changes included additional teaching assistants and a Writing Center director. With basic writing no longer required, our second-year teaching assistants, who typically taught one freshman composition course and one section of basic writing, could now be asked to tutor in addition to teaching freshman composition. To coordinate the program, we received funding to hire a lecturer, a graduate of our M.A. program in TESOL.

The new foci of the Writing Center demanded a significantly different training program for teaching assistants. Previously, the director of basic writing could meet informally with the four teaching assistants who had been selected to staff the Writing Center. Now, with up to twenty teaching assistants tutoring in their second year and with a new target audience of not only underprepared students, but also students in upper-level courses across the university, a new training program was needed.

Beginning in 1990, second-year teaching assistants have been required to attend a week-long training session in August, before the school year begins. (During that week, first-year teaching assistants follow a different orientation program.) Because our tutors have already taught freshman English, they understand the kind of class that their clients must be ready to enter. What they do not necessarily understand is how to help immature, novice writers develop their confidence and their competence. Nor do they have the necessary orientation to academic writing to help them tutor students in different disciplines. By the end of the orientation, most tutors are eager to begin their new assignment and are relatively comfortable with their roles.

With an expanded Writing Center staff, we also needed more space. Again, we searched for a room. This time we located a large office area, previously used by temporary instructors. Located in the Vocational Education Building, this space became our new Writing Center. Much more inviting than our previous center, this well-lighted room, decorated with plants, provides students with a comfortable Writing Center. Moreover, donated equipment from the College of Business linked the center to the campus computer network.

The mandate from the CCHE which required us to drop our basic writing course thus took an ironic turn. Indirectly, the forced change in the composition program helped us move toward our long-range goal of developing a true universitywide writing center. Specifically, it gave us bargaining power with the administration because it was apparent that central support and funding are crucial for a writing center to serve not only the needs of basic writers, but also the needs of students across the university.

This change in our curriculum also encouraged us to continue thinking about where we are as a composition program as well as a Writing Center and in what directions we might want to move. As a result, we have decided to implement a peer-tutoring program in order to keep our Writing Center open for longer hours and to allow us to staff satellite Writing Centers in residence halls across campus. We have also decided to explore the potential for providing most Writing Center services on-line, along with the computer resources already available in our Computer-Assisted Writing Lab.

The Computer-Assisted Writing Lab: History and Description

As the Writing Center itself was evolving, a parallel "center" also emerged in the English department—the Computer-Assisted Writing Lab. Fortuitously, the English department managed to interest the administration in funding a computer lab for writers at a time when composition in general was underfunded. Although the services this lab provides to students have changed, the Computer-Assisted Writing Lab continues to play an important role in the university.

How did the English department manage to secure funds for a computer lab so early in the history of computers in education? In brief, key personnel in the Computer Center and in the central administration were aware of the increasing demands for word processing, and faculty and administrators alike were intrigued by the then unexplored potential of textual analysis programs such as the *Writer's Workbench* program developed by AT&T's Bell Labs. An English department request to conduct preliminary research on the use of text-analysis programs with college freshmen resulted in administrative funding for a large computer facility with computer access for up to 5,000 students per week.

The Computer-Assisted Writing Lab opened in 1982. It was the first large computer lab for writers in the country. The English department considered housing this lab in the same location as the Writing Center, but no available room on campus was—nor is—large enough for both facilities.

Originally, the focus of the Computer-Assisted Writing Lab was to provide a site for students to use text-analysis programs to analyze their essays. Soon thereafter, this lab was also used as a supplementary lab/classroom for students enrolled in basic writing and freshman composition.

The early years of the Computer-Assisted Writing Lab drew many visitors from different parts of the country to Colorado State University. Many came to see the software—the *Writer's Workbench* program developed by AT&T and modified by CSU faculty. Others, interested in developing their own computer lab for writers, came to see the physical layout of the lab and to learn about our method of administering the lab with a work force of "monitors"—English majors on merit work-study awards, who help writers use word processing and related software.

Originally, students in our basic writing course—which had a one-hour computer lab component—used the Computer-Assisted Writing Lab for their lab meetings. Class meetings took place two days each week in traditional classrooms and one day in the computer lab. The students' lab hour gave them time to work on drafts of their current assignment, to use prewriting files and revising files available in the lab, or to run the *Writer's Workbench* software on their completed drafts. Unfortunately, if they wanted to see a writing tutor for advice on their emerging drafts, they had to go to the Writing Center, at that time still located on the opposite side of campus in Johnson Hall.

No longer used by entire classes for class meetings (as a result of the CCHE mandate to eliminate developmental writing courses at research universities), the Computer-Assisted Writing Lab has evolved into a drop-in lab, a comprehensive environment for writers that is open from 8 a.m. to 11 p.m. every day except Saturday. The lab is available to students across the university for course-related writing assignments.

When we lost our basic writing course, we were concerned that with the strong link gone between the Computer-Assisted Writing Lab and the composition program, the department's storehouse of computer software and the technological expertise of its faculty might remain untapped by most students at the university. Not wanting to lose ground, we began paving the way for a technological link to our two "centers." Our goal is to develop an Electronic Writing Center to serve as a focal point for our burgeoning universitywide writing efforts. We believe that the university's recent commitment to providing writers across campus with writing support can be maximized by creative use of the English department's established computer resources.

Moving toward a Cross-Curricular Electronic
Writing Center: Current Plans

At a time when students have begun to depend on computers in virtually every discipline on campus, we feel it is essential that writing tools be integrated into the computer environments in which they do their discipline-related work. Students should be able to access tutors electronically, as they work on their computer-graphics program in art labs; while they explore their database programs in social science labs; during their use of CAD/CAM software for engineering; or while they are working on their writing assignments. We also feel that tutoring should not be the only form of writing assistance available. Students should also have easy access to a range of computer tools for writing.

Because the faculty across the university are interested in providing their students with writing assistance, we are enlisting their support in a collaborative project to develop computer-assisted software for writing in the disciplines. The resulting writing software, along with on-line tutoring and a bulletin board to facilitate electronic peer response to writing, will be available through a new on-line writing service, the Electronic Writing Center.

This menu-driven corpus of writing support will be accessible to students across campus through our computer network, CSUnet. It will include network access to the software collection now housed in the Computer-Assisted Writing Center. With writing tools available from computer networks in laboratories and residence halls, we will have enabled students to move back and forth between writing, seeking tutorial support, and conducting research (figure 1).

In the computer-rich environment at CSU, students who seek tutorial assistance in the Writing Center will be able to access computer software to help them with their writing, even if they never physically enter the Computer-Assisted Writing Lab. Students in the Computer-Assisted Writing Lab or in other computer labs across campus, similarly, will be able to receive tutorial help from Writing Center tutors without having to make the trip across campus to the Writing Center. If they prefer electronic tutoring, they need not ever meet with their tutors face-to-face.

Our approach will enable the Computer-Assisted Writing Lab to maintain its identity as a drop-in lab for writers; it will allow the Writing Center, with new connectivity across campus, to extend its services through electronic tutoring and electronic peer-response groups. And it will result in the creation of a new service, the Electronic Writing Center, a "virtual" reality, a place where students can "talk" in writing to one another or to a tutor, a place where they will also be able to locate appropriate writing software to help them with a writing assignment in any of their courses.

The Electronic Writing Center should be valuable not only to students at Colorado State University but, eventually, to students at

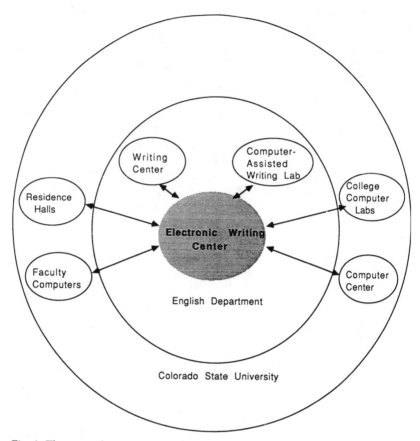

Fig. 1. The central position of the Electronic Writing Center at Colorado State University.

similar institutions across the country who will be able to access our collection of writing tools through the Internet. Thus far, our plans include:

1. Developing a database of guidelines for writing and a cadre of interactive software programs to assist writers as they generate and revise ideas.

2. Linking specially trained writing tutors with specific courses and specific faculty.

3. Providing individual students with on-line tutoring and peer response to their writing, whether or not they are enrolled in a writing course.

4. Inviting all faculty members to contribute assignments to the ever-expanding database of writing support.

5. Enabling students and faculty across campus to be a part of this dynamic writing environment.

6. Providing access from computer labs across campus, at remote sites, and (through Internet) across the country. (Components of the software would also be made available on disk for students and faculty who do not have convenient access to our computer network.)

7. Involving faculty and students across the country as partners in the testing and evaluation of the software.

Fortunately, we have already expanded our writing center staff. But to serve students in all majors, we will need additional resources, and we will need to expand the training program. Writing tutors from various disciplines will need to be trained to work with writers in their major; they will also need to become familiar with the software available for their clients. We hope that funding for these tutors will come from the colleges themselves, who will be asked to provide release time for faculty to assist with the project and to support graduate students who will be trained to tutor students in their disciplines.

We plan to collaborate with faculty in various departments to isolate the criteria for successful writing in their courses. By working with us to isolate the specific genres and conventions of effective writing in their disciplines and by helping to develop appropriate software for their students, faculty across campus should quickly recognize their importance to the success of a universitywide writing program. Our procedures for collaborating with faculty to develop the discipline-specific software include:

1. *Conducting Writing Institutes to Begin Software Development.* Faculty from representative disciplines across campus will be invited to attend writing institutes in which they help determine what kinds of writing support would be useful to students in their fields. We expect to develop writing aids with interactive prompts for students to use as they gather information and data for a given assignment or as they revise and edit their writing.

2. *Implementing and Evaluating the Software.* By involving computer center staff in the project from the onset, we feel confident that we will have their support when we reach the critical stages of implementing our software on the network. As a result of having

worked closely in the past with the University Computer Center (now the Academic Computing and Networking Services), we expect a productive relationship with them on this project.

Conclusion

Context determines so much of what we are able to do, including when we can make changes. In our case, we have wanted, from the start, a comprehensive Writing Center, but the institution was not ready to respond to our perception of student needs. Now, with computing and technical support in place, and with a new respect for writing developing on campus, we are confident that our timing is right.

Fortunately, our interest in developing a comprehensive Electronic Writing Center not only coincides with an increasing respect for writing on campus, with the availability of a collection of general writing software in our Computer-Assisted Writing Lab, and with an expanded Writing Center, it also coincides with an administrative decision to revise the undergraduate curriculum—in ways that include writing and critical inquiry as core skills. We have good reason, therefore, to be optimistic about securing university funding for our efforts.

The long-term results of early administrative support of computing in the English department have been overwhelmingly positive. The department continues to be recognized as a key player in technology development across campus. Even though many central administrators are unaware of the extent to which computer support for writing has shifted focus from limited research on textual analysis software to comprehensive support for student writers, they continue to support the English department's Computer Lab financially and symbolically. They have also demonstrated their commitment to our traditional Writing Center. And we anticipate their continuing support as we establish the Electronic Writing Center.

13 Epilogue

Joyce A. Kinkead
Utah State University

The institutional context of a writing center determines what it looks like, how it functions, and where it finds itself placed administratively, physically, and fiscally. The preceding case studies strongly support this notion. As Muriel Harris (1985) points out, "Characterizing writing centers, then, is difficult because it depends on our perspective. Viewed from one angle, they function too differently for us to find a common 'ideal'" (8). However, in spite of the dissimilarity between the assortment gathered here, we can still find some common threads.

When we sift through the examples from the case studies, we find that the writing centers fall within a variety of categories (see table 1). For instance, if we look at the types of institutions represented here, two obvious categories emerge: two-year and four-year colleges. If we filter the programs through that screen, then we get the following arrangement:

Two-Year Colleges:
Johnson County Community College
ComTech at the University of Toledo

Four-Year Colleges:
Purdue; Medgar Evers; University of Toledo; Lehigh University; USC; Harvard; University of Puget Sound; University of Washington; Utah State University; Colorado State University

In order to understand the four-year schools better, we need to see them sifted through an even finer screen. Land-grant institutions include Purdue, Toledo, Utah State, and Colorado State. Private schools include Lehigh, USC, Harvard, and Puget Sound. Using another filter, major research universities are exemplified by Washington, Purdue, and Harvard. An emphasis on engineering and the sciences is evident at Purdue, Lehigh, Utah State, and Colorado State. Although a liberal

Table 1. Writing centers at a glance.

School	Size of School	Type of School	Administrative Control
Colorado State University	18,900	land grant; research university	Head of English department
Com Tech at Toledo	4,600	two-year	Director for Developmental Education
Harvard University	18,000 (total)	private university	Director of Expository Writing Program
Johnson County Community College	16,500	two-year	Head of English department
Lehigh University	6,000	private; engineering emphasis	Associate Provost
Medgar Evers College	3,000	hybrid of 2- and 4-year degrees	Chair of Language, Literature, Communication & Philosophy
University of Puget Sound	2,800	four-year liberal arts college	Associate Deans of the University

Table 1. *Continued.*

Location	Audience	Computers	Tutors	Special Notes
decentralized by network; physical facilities in 105 VocEd and 300 Eddy	campus	access over campus net-work; 3 PCs in VocEd, 25 PCs & 20 terminals in Eddy	graduate and undergraduate	online tutoring; faculty-developed software
Learning Rescource Center	campus	32	undergraduate; instructors	collaborates with University of Toledo
Freshman Union with Writing Program	50% from writing program and others from undergraduate and graduate population	1 for director	undergraduate; graduates; ESL tutor; 1 faculty for senior theses	appointments only
Third floor of Educational Media Center	open-door	10	undergraduate; part-time instructors	works with Gallaudet and Kansas School for the Deaf
formerly Coppee Hall; now Drown Hall with English	self-selected, mainly from English	5	English graduate students	uses tutoring technique of "dramatized reader"
	mainly from Basic Skills	25	upper-division undergraduates and graduates	WAC outreach to high schools
Howarth Hall, near Academic Computing, Honors Program, and Learning Skills Center	cross-curricular writing program	6	undergraduate writing advisors	sponsors writing contests; hosts faculty workshops

Continued on next page

Table 1. *Continued.*

School	Size of School	Type of School	Administrative Control
Purdue University	35,000	land-grant; research university	Head of English Department
University of Southern California	28,000	large, private university	Director of Freshman Writing Program
University of Toledo	20,000	land-grant; comprehensive university	College of Arts and Sciences
Utah State University	17,000	land-grant; research university	Director of Writing— Head of English Department
USU: Rhetoric Associates Program			Dean of College of Humanities, Arts, and Social Sciences
University of Washington	33,000	research university	Office of Minority Affairs

Table 1. *Continued.*

Location	Audience	Computers	Tutors	Special Notes
English Department building	primarily for students in writing program	3	lab instructors (graduate); undergraduate teaching assistants; undergraduate writing consultants	3 categories of staff with 3 training programs
Taper Hall of Humanities	primarily for students in writing program	2 computer labs	graduate students; undergraduates	Researcher's Electronic Notebook
TuckerHall— shares with history, political science, and philosophy departments	60% self-referred	6	peer-tutors; graduate students; composition instructors; journalists; reading teachers	tutor-linked courses
Bottom floor of English Department	Primarily students in freshman– junior writing program courses	30 (open-acess) 21 (classroom)	peer tutors; English education interns; graduate assistants	home to Sigma Tau Delta, honor society
decentralized	tutors are linked with courses as requested by faculty		undergraduates nominated by faculty	modeled on Brown University program
Instructional Center	Solely students in EOP writing sections	Available through Instructional Center Computer Lab	86% representing non-European ethnic and cultural backgrounds; veterans of EOP	Center is restricted to use by the 10% of students in Equal Opportunity Program

arts focus might seem a better bedfellow for a writing center, there are advantages to being in a science/engineering institution. Lehigh is "open-minded about how to teach writing" because engineers can see multiple solutions to problems. At Utah State, where over 50 percent of the funding comes from grants and such, the overhead funds spill over into the humanities.

Cultural diversity is most apparent at urban schools such as Medgar Evers, formerly a two-year school. However, diversity as a theme is highlighted in the Washington and Southern California descriptions, too. Their emphasis on diversity is directly related to their urban locations. Other urban schools include Toledo, Johnson County (or, should we say, suburban), Puget Sound, and Harvard.

We can also categorize writing centers on the basis of their clientele. The clientele or student body often determines the types of services a writing center must offer. For instance, some campuses enroll grade-conscious, sophisticated students concerned with fashion, sports, cars; as Ed Lotto puts it, "They know something about good wine." In particular, the schools that fit this picture are Harvard, Lehigh, Puget Sound, and USC. Irene Clark calls the writing center at Southern California a "three-ring circus," a description we can all recognize; the USC receptionist thinks that her job is like working at a "trendy hair salon in Beverly Hills," a comparison that most of us probably cannot relate to.

We can also imagine a reader analyzing these descriptions chronologically. Some of the centers are nearing a twentieth anniversary, while others have more recent origins:

    1975: Purdue, Medgar Evers, Utah State
    1977: Johnson County
    1978: Lehigh, USC, Washington
    1979: Colorado State
    1981: Harvard
    1985: Puget Sound
    1988: Toledo
    1992: CSU Electronic Writing Center

It should be clear after this brief sifting and filtering that each writing center can be viewed from multiple perspectives. Therefore, it is impossible to make generalizations about writing centers. For example, people who believe that writing centers were created to help the underprepared student cope with college would be amazed to find centers housed at Harvard or USC. Although the directors at these centers acknowledge that their students are well prepared for writing, they also note that "every writer needs a reader." Harvard hires a special tutor each spring to read senior theses; another center holds workshops on how to write successful applications for Rhodes Scholarships, Marshall Fellowships, and Fulbright Grants.

Other centers state explicitly that their goal is helping students who are not academically prepared for college; falling into this category are ComTech, Johnson County, Medgar Evers, and the Educational Opportunity Program Center at Washington. Most students at Medgar Evers represent the African diaspora, while those at ComTech include many rural Ohio students, and those at Johnson County are often nontraditional suburban students. Johnson County is also a satellite school for Gallaudet University and is located near the Kansas School for the Deaf, which means they employ signing tutors.

Other ways of looking at these writing centers include focusing on where they are housed, to whom they report, and, more importantly, from whom they receive their funding. First, many of these programs are located within departments of English: Purdue, USC, Johnson County, Utah State, and Colorado State. Medgar Evers exists within the Humanities Division. Harvard reports to the Expository Writing Program, which offers the one required course in the Harvard curriculum. Other writing centers find themselves on a flowchart with reporting lines to the dean—Toledo, USU's Rhetoric Associates Program, Puget Sound—while Lehigh is administratively responsible to the provost. The University of Washington program described here reports to the Educational Opportunity Program.

When we talk about progress in writing centers, one of the visible signs of success is where the writing center is housed. As most of us know, many centers started out in windowless basements, broom closets, or stuffy alcoves. The floor plans and the physical descriptions of the writing centers included here indicate that these humble accommodations have changed. Who would not want to be located in the Lehigh Learning Center with its "cathedral ceilings" and skylights? Although the space at Toledo is not expansive at 619 square feet, its Tudor architecture is charming, especially in contrast to the more industrial-looking 3,700 square-foot Writing Center of its sister school, ComTech. USC spreads over a space equal to six classrooms, and Utah State has recently received a fourth large room to provide space for tutoring as its computer facilities spill over into what was known as the "quiet room."

Other writing centers are housed in thin air, so to speak. While many of the centers have satellites in dorms/residence halls or libraries, the Rhetoric Associates Program at Utah State (patterned after the

Brown University model) assigns tutors to specific classes. The University of Toledo represents another version of this decentered model with its tutor-linked program, while Purdue calls its version "Traveling Tutors." Finally, Colorado State's Electronic Writing Center provides for on-line tutoring over a vast network. For this program, software development is used as the impetus to initiate writing in the disciplines. CSU's commitment to a "computer-rich environment" provides the context essential for the success of this approach. In brief, students never have to enter the computer-assisted writing lab to receive help.

What's in a name? Seven of the chapters describe writing *centers* with only one writing *lab* weighing in. *Learning* is the key phrase in most other names: Learning Center, Learning Assistance Center, and Center for Writing and Learning. Finally, Colorado State's plan is for a Cross-Curricular Electronic Writing Center.

Although we immediately recognize the term *tutors*, not every center chooses to use that designation; two other appellations, consultants (USC) and writing advisors (Puget Sound), are also used. Where the tutors come from also varies. The Writing Lab instructors at Purdue are graduate students, while the undergraduates who tutor are writing consultants, unless they work with developmental composition, in which case they are called undergraduate teaching assistants. Medgar Evers draws its tutors from the Learning Center. ComTech uses peer tutors as well as part-time instructors (as does Johnson County); in a unique collaboration, ComTech tutors may also tutor at the University of Toledo, which draws its staff from a diverse group: undergraduates, graduates, journalists, and reading teachers as well as composition instructors. At Lehigh University, all of the tutors are graduate students in the English department, while USC draws its staff of 120 from various graduate and undergraduate programs. Colorado State employs only second-year TAs, wanting a staff that has taught in the writing program. Harvard provides a mix—a dozen undergraduate tutors, several graduate student tutors who work with other graduate students, a tutor for ESL students, and a faculty member who works with senior thesis writers. Puget Sound relies entirely on undergraduate students for tutoring, which is considered a prestigious job on campus. Utah State employs peer tutors as well as graduate students who work as part of their teaching assistantships. The University of Washington, which is charged to serve multicultural/multilingual/nontraditional students, reinforces that charge by employing tutors who mirror the diversity of the students; in fact, two-thirds of the tutors are former EOP students.

The roles played by tutors vary, too. At Toledo, the staff knows that "our most valuable materials for tutoring are paper and pencil." When a student emerges from a Toledo tutorial, she may well have in hand a large sheet of paper on which ideas are sketched. At USC, tutors come to understand that "talking, not exercises, is the essence" of the Writing Center. The Harvard center credits its reputation as being "an intellectually sound academic service." Puget Sound supports only process writing and bans grammar hotlines, grammar workshops, and any kind of testing. In the words of its staff, "conferences are primary." The center at Washington takes a political stand, asserting that this is the place students come to understand their own authority; tutors are not to "help" because this approach indicates a hierarchical relationship between tutors and students. They practice "hands-off" tutoring. Tutors receive training in the history of the civil rights movement and the development of writing centers. Gail Okawa calls their approach "egalitarian, holistic, and dialogical."

How computers are used—or not used—is also related to institutional context and philosophy. Harvard, for instance, prides itself on not having any technology in the Writing Center, except for one computer used for records. The University of Toledo features six computers while its counterpart at ComTech has thirty-two, largely a result of having more space. Johnson County Community College has a mix of Apple and IBM units. Purdue has only three computers in its writing lab, but that is due to the number of computers found in widespread use around campus. As at Purdue, Lehigh is a computer-sophisticate with jacks in every classroom, dorm, and office. Medgar Evers has twenty-five computers, and some classes meet in a computer-networked classroom. Likewise, USC and Utah State have a number of computer labs for drop-in use or for scheduled classes. Most ambitiously, Colorado State envisions an Electronic Writing Center not dependent on any physical space.

One of the most common features of writing centers is a concern for funding. Thus, most directors know how to raise institutional funds. Below, we offer a summary of the best ideas from the previous pages:

Have the president of the institution sit in on a staff meeting.

Send reports to administrators.

Host open houses and invite administrators.

Place satellite centers in the library, residence halls, etc.

Host visiting writers.

Hold writing contests (e.g., Hearst Prizes at Puget Sound).

Recycle paper.

Publish a newsletter.

As we read these descriptions, every once in a while we think we come across a characteristic that crosses the board. Coffee—instant, brewed, or café latte—seems almost universal, but then we remember the *verboten* coffee in the Utah State center. Likewise, the notion of a wine-and-cheese party to share writing assignments is enticing, but how many campuses allow alcohol on the premises?

To ignore institutional and cultural contexts is similar to ignoring audience when beginning a writing assignment. Ed Lotto points out that when he came to Lehigh he found a center "struggling to define itself." A center which does not have a clear picture of what it is and where it fits into its institutional environment is doomed to strain and stress. Only by knowing its contexts can a director decide whether to work *within* those contexts or *against* them.

Work Cited

Harris, Muriel. 1985. "Theory and Reality: The Ideal Writing Center(s)." *The Writing Center Journal* 5(2)/6(1): 4–9.

Names and Addresses of Contact Persons:

Irene Lurkis Clark
Writing Center, HSS201
Freshman Writing Program
University of Southern California
Los Angeles, CA 90089-0062
PHONE: 213-740-3691
E-MAIL: ICLARK@MIZAR.USC.EDU
FAX: 213-740-4100

Brenda Greene
Department of Language,
Literature, Communication Skills
& Philosophy
Medgar Evers College
Brooklyn, NY 11225
PHONE: 718-270-5079
FAX: 718-270-5126

Jeanette Harris
Department of English
University of Southern
 Mississippi
Hattiesburg, MS 39406-5037
PHONE: 601-266-5047
E-MAIL: JGHARRIS@USMCP6
FAX: 601-266-5757

Muriel Harris
Department of English
Purdue University
West Lafayette, IN 47907-1356
PHONE: 317-494-3723
E-MAIL: HARRISM@
 MACE.CC.PURDUE.EDU
FAX: 317-494-3780

Kathleen Kiefer
Department of English
Colorado State University
Fort Collins, CO 80523
PHONE: 303-491-6845; 491-6428
E-MAIL: KKIEFER@
  VINES.COLOSTATE.EDU
FAX: 303-491-5601

Joyce Kinkead
College of Humanities, Arts, and
  Social Sciences
Utah State University
Logan, UT 84322-0700
PHONE: 801-750-1706
E-MAIL: FATCG@USU
FAX: 801-750-1092

Ed Lotto
Department of English
Lehigh University
Bethlehem, PA 18015
PHONE: 215-758-3097
E-MAIL: EEL2@LEHIGH.EDU

Ellen Mohr
Writing Center
Department of English
Johnson County Community College
Overland Park, KS 66210-1299
PHONE: 913-469-4413
FAX: 913-469-4409

Luanne Momenee
Learning Assistance Center
University of Toledo—
  Scott Park Campus
Toledo, OH 43606
PHONE: 419-537-3140

Joan Mullin
Writing Center
University of Toledo
Toledo, OH 43606
PHONE: 419-437-4939
FAX: 419-537-2157

Julie Neff
Department of English
University of Puget Sound
Tacoma, WA 98416
PHONE: 206-756-3395

Gail Okawa
102 Essex House
1300 Oakland Avenue
Indiana, PA 15701
PHONE: 412-357-8237
E-MAIL: GXVLKAD@IUP
FAX: 412-357-6213

Dawn Rodrigues
Department of English
Colorado State University
Fort Collins, CO 80523
PHONE: 303-224-0023 (H);
  491-6428 (W)
E-MAIL: DRODRIGUES@
  VINES.COLOSTATE.EDU
FAX: 303-491-5601

Linda Simon
The Writing Center
12 Quincy Street
Harvard University
Cambridge, MA 02138
PHONE: 617-495-1655
FAX: 617-496-6864

14 The Scholarly Context: A Look at Themes

Joyce A. Kinkead
Utah State University

When the National Writing Centers Association was formed in 1983, it became the umbrella organization for two journals. The older and more widely distributed publication is the *Writing Lab Newsletter (WLN)*, which Muriel Harris started in 1976. Published monthly, except for July and August, this informal but informative newsletter finds its way into writing centers nationwide, informing, encouraging, and uniting its subscribers. The second national publication, *The Writing Center Journal (WCJ)*, was begun in 1980 by Lil Brannon and Stephen North; the second set of co-editors, Jeanette Harris and Joyce Kinkead, oversaw its next stage from 1985 to 1990 (Brannon, North, Kinkead, and Harris 1990). The current editors of the journal are Edward Lotto, Diana George, and Nancy Grimm, and the editorial office is now housed at Michigan Technological University. Published twice per year, the journal includes articles devoted to theory and research as well as practice, reviews of new books that might be of interest to writing center directors, and an annual bibliography of writing center scholarship. These two publications serve not only to provide important information about pedagogical, theoretical, and administrative issues, but also to keep subscribers abreast of current developments—conferences, materials, publications, and announcements.

In addition to those two publications, other professional journals regularly publish both theoretical and practical articles about writing centers. For example, writing center articles have appeared in recent years in *College English, College Composition and Communication, Writing Program Administration, Teaching English in the Two-Year College, English Education, The Journal of Developmental and Remedial Education,* and *Focuses,* a journal in which writing centers are one of the areas of emphasis. A survey of recent writing center scholarship is published annually in the fall/winter issue of *The Writing Center Journal.* The tenth anniversary issue of *WCJ*—the fall/winter 1990 volume—includes a helpful index to the first ten volumes (distributed by NCTE).

Without these resources, each writing center program would exist in a vacuum bereft of a supportive inter-institutional context.

Overview of Themes

This essay is organized according to the themes that have emerged from the scholarship on writing centers. One of these themes is what we call "the big picture," an approach in which the authors touch on a variety of writing center issues. A second theme is history, one infrequently used but nonetheless necessary for knowing from where we came. A much larger body of work focuses on collaborative learning. Yet another concentration is the tutor: training, writing anxiety, and ethics. Writing centers and writing across the curriculum share parallel histories and, thus, not surprisingly, writing across the curriculum comprises another theme. The clientele of writing centers often includes basic writers, ESL students, and learning-disabled students; hence, the relationship of writing centers to these special-interest groups is another theme. The kinds of materials students use—computers, handouts, audiotapes—form still another theme. Finally, a few scholars examine the role of the writing center in teacher training.

The Big Picture

The concept of writing centers and tutoring dates back to classical times; for our purposes though, we will concentrate on publications issued during the last twenty or so years, a period that has seen an explosion of writing center publishing. Most books published on writing centers focus on a comprehensive picture— management, organization, funding, tutor training. One of the earliest of these is *New Directions for College Learning Assistance: Improving Writing Skills*, edited by Thom Hawkins and Phyllis Brooks (1981); the term *skills* in the title highlights the fact that writing centers at that time were struggling to deal with open admissions and an influx of nontraditional students. These eleven essays by writing center directors and tutors define the issues discussed in later collections: instructional approaches, ESL students, politics, evaluation, and research. At this point in their development, writing centers were on unsure footing and their future uncertain, as the editors speculate:

> extra-classroom efforts and remedial classes have too long a history for us to suggest that the next ten years will bring us the insight and skill to do away with our need for all the help we can get in teaching students to write. (99)

The emphasis on individualized instruction in the 1970s and early 1980s grew out of work such as Mina P. Shaughnessy's (1977) *Errors and Expectations: A Guide for the Teacher of Basic Writing* as well as Carol Laque and Phyllis Sherwood's (1977) *A Laboratory Approach to Writing* as teachers struggled to work with basic writers. Published in 1981, Harvey Wiener's *The Writing Room* directs its attention to basic writers and "support services" such as writing centers (196–203). As we shall see, the writing center perceived as a *service* to the institution is a concept that is slow to fade.

In 1982, Scott, Foresman and Company brought out two major resources for writing center directors: Muriel Harris's collection *Tutoring Writing: A Sourcebook for Writing Labs* and Steward and Croft's *The Writing Laboratory: Organization, Management, and Methods*. The latter provides a coherent study of one writing center while Harris and twenty-eight other authors offer views on diagnosis, structure, tutor training, and self-paced instruction.

Two years later, *Writing Centers: Theory and Administration,* edited by Gary A. Olson, signaled a movement away from skills enhancement toward a more theoretical perspective on writing centers as its contributors examined "the concepts underlying their work" and their application to both writing center and writing classroom. Indicative of the increasing theoretical foundations are essays that draw on Freire (Warnock and Warnock), Derrida (Thomas Nash), and Kohlberg and Perry (Karen Spear). However, there continued to be much practical advice even in this volume as other writers offered their advice on financial responsibility and records management.

Published in 1991, Wallace and Simpson's *The Writing Center: New Directions* uses a growth metaphor for the history of writing centers. The book explores theoretical as well as practical issues. A bibliographic essay at the end of the book contains some twenty-three entries, which readers of the present essay may want to consult.

The High School Writing Center: Establishing and Maintaining One, edited by Pamela B. Farrell (1989), harkens back to the early resource books, providing secondary school teachers with practical advice for getting started and developing wider horizons. As Farrell points out, while secondary school writing centers share purposes with their college counterparts, the high school writing center operates in a completely different institutional context.

Although approximately seventy to eighty articles focusing on writing centers are published annually, few examine the concept of the writing center, but those that have are significant. Stephen North's (1984) germinal article, "The Idea of a Writing Center," seeks to move writing centers from the "obscure backwater" of English departments by offering a declaration of independence. Tired of colleagues' perceptions that writing centers are only for remediation, North maintains that "dialogue about writing . . . is central to higher education" (440). Responding to North, Muriel Harris (1985), in an article entitled "Theory and Reality: The Ideal Writing Center(s)," argues that no *one* definition of a writing center is appropriate; instead, she insists there exist several "ideal" centers, each fitting its context.

Both of the previous articles "preach to the choir," so to speak. Richard Leahy's (1990) essay, "What a College Writing Center Is—and Isn't," addresses a larger audience and provides guidelines for what faculty should look for in a campus writing center. Leahy (1991) also offers one of the few overviews of writing centers at various institutions in "On Being There: Reflections on Visits to Other Writing Centers," a report from his sabbatical journey to other sites. This kind of metanalysis is rare in writing center scholarship and is, in fact, a gap which this volume seeks to fill.

Historical Approaches

Other writers define writing centers from a historical perspective. Lou Kelly (1980) reviews a half century of writing labs in "One on One, Iowa City Style: Fifty Years of Individualized Instruction in Writing." Muriel Harris (1982a) examines the rapid increase of writing centers in "Growing Pains: The Coming of Age of Writing Centers." Judith Summerfield (1988) offers a personal history in "Writing Centers: A Long View" and warns against so-called "progress" in writing centers that incorporate testing and computers.

Tutors and Collaborative Learning

Talk

Recent book-length manuscripts do not focus on fiscal management or other administrative concerns; rather, the big picture is being replaced

by scrutiny of specific writing center issues and concerns. Most focus
on talk, not surprisingly, since "talk is everything" in writing centers
(North 1984, 444). As writing centers increasingly discard instructional
methods except one-to-one tutoring, there is a developing body of
literature on how to talk, specifically Reigstad and McAndrew's (1984)
Training Tutors for Writing Conferences, Beverly Clark's (1985) *Talking
about Writing: A Guide for Tutor and Teacher Conferences,* Muriel Harris's
(1986) *Teaching One-to-One: The Writing Conference,* and Meyer and
Smith's (1987) *The Practical Tutor.*

Talk, collaborative learning, social construction—these terms form
the core theme for the majority of recent scholarship on writing centers. Davis, Hayward, Hunter, and Wallace (1988) investigate "The
Function of Talk in the Writing Conference: A Study of Tutorial Conversation" in one of the few research studies done in a writing center
setting. A second examination is Wolcott's (1989) "Talking It Over: A
Qualitative Study of Writing Center Conferencing." Both studies indicate the importance of individualizing talk for each student who seeks
help in the writing center.

These studies also show the tendency of tutors to take control of a
conference, a concern mirrored in Trimbur's (1987) "Peer Tutoring: A
Contradiction in Terms?" and Kail's (1983) "Collaborative Learning in
Context: The Problem with Peer Tutoring." How much collaboration
can be expected in a tutorial setting? According to Lisa Ede (1989), in
"Writing as a Social Process: A Theoretical Foundation for Writing
Centers": "Those of us who work in writing centers need to be part of
this conversation" on writing as social process. Drawing on the works
of Bruffee, Freire, and Bakhtin, today's writing center directors are
exploring the notion of authority and ownership of text in writing
center talk.

Training

Obviously, tutor training follows closely on the heels of any discussion
about talk. Beck, Hawkins, and Silver (1978) offer an early, general look
at training in their article "Training and Using Peer Tutors." Irene
Clark (1982) offers role-playing as a method in "Dialogue in the Lab
Conference: Script Writing and the Training of Writing Lab Tutors," a
technique developed more fully in her (1985) *Writing in the Center:
Teaching in a Writing Center Setting.* Evelyn Ashton-Jones (1988) explores talk and tutor training in her "Asking the Right Questions: A
Heuristic for Tutors," while Adams, Child, Harris, and Henriott (1987)

offer individual personal experience on training in their "Training Teachers for the Writing Lab: A Multidimensional Perspective." A second, earlier multiauthor perspective is Cynthia Onore's (1982) "In Their Own 'Write': A Portrait of the Peer Tutor as a Young Professional," which offers essays in which peer tutors argue that they "make the best tutors." The desire to tell tutoring stories is strong, and a monograph by Goldsby (1981), *Peer Tutoring in Basic Writing: A Tutor's Journal*, offers a longer personal essay by an undergraduate tutor. Maxwell's (1990) *When Tutor Meets Student: Experiences in Collaborative Learning*, offers tutoring experiences by nineteen undergraduate writing tutors at Berkeley. This anthology provides a model for other writing center programs that wish to publish tutor writing.

Finally, drawing on ten years of proceedings from the East Central Writing Centers Association conferences, Flynn and King's (1993) *Dynamics of the Writing Center: Social and Cognitive Interaction* shows "how structured interaction between the novice and expert in the writing conference can supplement classroom instruction in writing."

Writing Anxiety

One of the reasons peers make effective tutors is that they share some anxieties about writing with those whom they tutor. Bizzaro and Toler (1986) explore this paradox in "The Effects of Writing Apprehension on the Teaching Behaviors of Writing Center Tutors," a topic examined again three years later in Bishop's (1989) "We're All Basic Writers: Tutors Talking about Writing Apprehension."

Ethics

The collaborative learning model has a dark side for some teachers; for them, collaboration is simply another term for cheating. Few address this issue even though it is one of the main reasons why our colleagues are suspect of writing center pedagogy. However, Clark (1988a) focuses on this moral dilemma in "Collaboration and Ethics in Writing Center Pedagogy," as does Behm (1989) in "Ethical Issues in Peer Tutoring: A Defense of Collaborative Learning." Herek and Niquette (1990), in "Ethics in the Writing Lab: Tutoring under the Honor Code," question the appropriate limits of a tutor's input. See also Freed's (1989) "Subjectivity in the Tutorial Session: How Far Can We Go?" on subjectivity and objectivity in tutorials. An early article entitled "Ethics of Peer Tutoring in Writing" by Lichenstein (1983), an undergraduate tutor, offers six principles for tutors that define the ethical limits of collaboration.

Writing Across the Curriculum

Increasingly, writing centers are becoming the loci of writing-across-the-curriculum (WAC) programs. This collaboration between writing centers and WAC programs raises issues of where a center should be housed. Louise Smith (1986) argues for placing a center outside the English department in "Independence and Collaboration: Why We Should Decentralize Writing Centers." Taking a less separationist approach, the following scholars explore the connections between writing centers and writing across the curriculum: Dinitz and Howe's (1989) "Writing Centers and Writing-Across-the-Curriculum: An Evolving Partnership?"; Haviland's (1985) "Writing Centers and Writing-Across-the-Curriculum: An Important Connection"; Leahy's (1989) very sensible "Writing Centers and Writing-for-Learning"; and Wallace's (1988) "The Writing Center's Role in the Writing-Across-the-Curriculum Program." An article by Scanlon (1986), "Recruiting and Training Tutors for Cross-Disciplinary Writing Programs," focuses on a related issue.

Writing Centers and Special-Interest Groups

ESL Students

Although basic writing issues often dominated early writing center scholarship, this topic has become less prominent in recent writing center scholarship. Working with ESL students, however, represents a continuing challenge, one that has not yet been fully addressed. Thaiss and Kurylo (1981) offer suggestions in "Working with the ESL Student: Learning Patience, Making Progress," as does Hoffman (1982) in "Working with ESL Students." See also Phyllis Brooks's "Peer Tutoring and the ESL Student" (in Hawkins and Brooks 1981) and Alexander Friedlander's "Meeting the Needs of Foreign Students in the Writing Center" (in Olson 1984). Most tutor-training guides—such as those by Meyer and Smith (1987) and by Beverly Clark (1985)—offer a chapter on working with ESL students. Writing center staff must look to works such as Alice S. Horning's (1987) *Teaching Writing as a Second Language* for help. And, unquestionably, help will be needed as the nature of the U.S. student body continues to become ethnically diverse.

Computers and Materials

At one time, auto-tutorial programs and computer-assisted instruction (CAI) would have automatically been provided to ESL students to help them acquire writing skills. In fact, any student approaching the writing center might have been directed to a computer or tape recorder rather than a tutor for "individualized instruction." Most of that equipment has since been relegated to dark closets or college supply sales. Although much of the software—of the skill and drill variety—has gone the way of the buffalo, computers have survived. When used for word processing—not computer-assisted instruction— computers offer writers the opportunity for efficient manipulation of text. While some writing center directors still see computers as the evil "machine in the garden," many more embrace them. Farrell (1987) discusses the role of computers in "Writer, Peer Tutor, and Computer: A Unique Relationship," while Fred Kemp (1987) offers a thoughtful and cautious argument in his "Getting Smart with Computers: Computer-Aided Heuristics for Student Writers." (This article appears in a special-topics issue of the *The Writing Center Journal* that focuses on computers and the writing center, distributed by NCTE.) Several books and journal articles are published annually on computers and writing; for example, Selfe's (1989) *Creating a Computer-Supported Writing Facility: A Blueprint for Action* was recently published as a monograph and distributed by NCTE. Finally, we recommend the Rodrigues and Kiefer chapter in the present volume for a detailed discussion of the potential for computers and writing centers. An earlier discussion of electronic tutoring can be found in Kinkead's (1987) "Computer Conversations: E-mail and Writing Instruction," which describes an approach that is receiving increased attention as local-area and wide-area networks become commonplace.

Computers are also being used to connect writing center staff on different campuses by means of an intercampus network. Begun by Lady Falls Brown and Fred Kemp of Texas Tech University, the Writing Center Network (known as "Centaurs") is a national BITNET distribution list devoted to discussions of writing center practice and theory. To subscribe, send the message SUBSCRIBE WCENTER YOUR FULL NAME to LISTSERV@TTUVM1. Similarly, the WPA discussion list offers dialogue on all areas of composition programs: part-time faculty, textbooks, budget, assessment, computers, writing centers. This list was created by David Schwalm at Arizona State University and can be joined by sending the following message to LISTSERV@ASUACAD: Subscribe WPA-L YOUR FULL NAME. These discussion groups provide rapid responses from peers, a boon to the writing center director who operates in isolation.

Teacher Education

The link between teacher education and the writing center is the subject of a few articles, including Peggy Broder's (1990) "Writing Centers and Teacher Training," Irene Clark's (1988b) "Preparing Future Composition Teachers in the Writing Center," William L. Smith's (1984) "Using a College Writing Workshop in Training Future English Teachers," and Robert Child's (1991) "Tutor-Teachers: An Examination of How Writing Center and Classroom Environments Inform Each Other." Undergraduate peer tutors speak out in "An Argument for Peer Tutoring as Teaching Training" (Anderson et al. in Hawkins and Brooks 1981). Each of these essays argues that writing centers serve the future teaching profession by giving tutors extensive practice and useful theory.

Politics and the Profession

To date, little has been written about the politics of writing centers. However, as the profession has become more politicized, scholars have gone on the offensive to protest the marginalization of writing centers. (See Olson and Ashton-Jones 1988 for the results of their survey on the status of directors.)

Conclusion

Undeniably, this is not an exhaustive list of writing center scholarship, but we have tried to look selectively at the major themes. We suspect that we will continue to see more articles on social construction theory as well as an interest in cognitive studies and their application to writing center pedagogy. The current editors of *The Writing Center Journal* are sensitive to issues, and this awareness will most likely extend to the journal's table of contents. In fact, the spring 1992 issue does just that with its focus on the question of subjectivity and the "challenge of making contemporary theory meet our daily work" (123). On this issue, Kail and Trimbur (1987) note in "The Politics of

Peer Tutoring" that the question now is "how tutoring can best contribute to the development of writing abilities and the intellectual life of undergraduates."

Surely current literary theory will also find its way into writing center scholarship as we debate the definition of *text*. The poststructuralist orthodoxy that all texts should receive equal attention, plus Susan Miller's (1989) contention (see *Rescuing the Subject: A Critical Introduction to Rhetoric and the Writer*) that we should adopt a textual rhetoric, no doubt will be two theories debated in future writing center scholarship. (See also Joyner 1991 on power and conferences.)

Although the preceding discussion suggests a wide-ranging volume of writing center scholarship, there are gaps. Little has been written about cultural and linguistic diversity (see Gail Okawa's essay in this collection); likewise, gender as it relates to communication studies receives insufficient attention (see Kinkead 1987). Another topic that needs to be addressed is the direction a writing center should take as a research center. Should research in the writing center be restricted to qualitative and quantitative studies or should it include the "stories" of tutoring?

Books that focus on writing programs—such as Connolly and Vilardi's (1986) *New Methods in College Writing Programs: Theories in Practice* and Ed White's (1989) *Developing Successful Writing Programs*—mention writing centers only tangentially, leading some to believe that writing centers still exist on the margins. (Certainly Lindemann's classification of writing centers as "support services" in the *CCCC Annual Bibliography* lends credence to this belief; how will the new editors, Selfe and Hawisher, treat writing centers?)

Pedagogical conflicts also often exist between writing center philosophy and English department pedagogy. How can these be resolved? What are the physical boundaries of the writing center? What is the professional status of writing center personnel? Do different tenure and promotion policies exist for them? How does the composition community view writing centers? How do graduate programs prepare students to become writing center directors?

When Connors examined composition journals in 1984, he called *The Writing Center Journal* "a periodical [that] has run ahead of genuine disciplinary needs" (361). The questions a decade ago were much simpler: How do we train tutors? How do we find space? What records do we keep? The increasing number and complexity of questions indicate the growth and maturity of the writing center community and the continuing need for research and scholarship.

Bibliography of Writing Center Scholarship

Adams, Ronald, Robert Child, Muriel Harris, and Kathleen Henriott. 1987. "Training Teachers for the Writing Lab: A Multidimensional Perspective." *The Writing Center Journal* 7(2): 3–20.

Anderson, James E., Ellen M. Bommarito, and Laura Seijas. 1981. "An Argument for Peer Tutoring as Teacher Training." In Hawkins and Brooks, 35–37.

Ashton-Jones, Evelyn. 1988. "Asking the Right Questions: A Heuristic for Tutors." *The Writing Center Journal* 9(1): 29–36.

Beck, Paula, Thom Hawkins, and Marcia Silver. 1978. "Training and Using Peer Tutors." *College English* 40: 432–49.

Behm, Richard. 1989. "Ethical Issues in Peer Tutoring: A Defense of Collaborative Learning." *The Writing Center Journal* 10(1): 3–12.

Bishop, Wendy. 1989. "We're All Basic Writers: Tutors Talking about Writing Apprehension." *The Writing Center Journal* 9(2): 31–42.

Bizzaro, Patrick, and Hope Toler. 1986. "The Effects of Writing Apprehension on the Teaching Behaviors of Writing Center Tutors." *The Writing Center Journal* 7(1): 37–44.

Brannon, Lil, Stephen North, Joyce Kinkead, and Jeanette Harris. 1990. "An Interview with the Founding Editors." *The Writing Center Journal* 11(1): 3–14.

Broder, Peggy. 1990. "Writing Centers and Teacher Training." *WPA: Writing Program Administration* 13(3): 37–45.

Brooks, Phyllis. 1981. "Peer Tutoring and the ESL Student." In Hawkins and Brooks, 45–52.

Child, Robert. 1991. "Tutor-Teachers: An Examination of How Writing Center and Classroom Environments Inform Each Other." In Wallace and Simpson, 169–83.

Clark, Beverly L. 1985. *Talking about Writing: A Guide for Tutor and Teacher Conferences*. Ann Arbor: University of Michigan Press.

Clark, Irene Lurkis. 1988a. "Collaboration and Ethics in Writing Center Pedagogy." *The Writing Center Journal* 9(1): 3–12.

———. 1982. "Dialogue in the Lab Conference: Script Writing and the Training of Writing Lab Tutors." *The Writing Center Journal* 2(1): 21–33.

———. 1988b. "Preparing Future Composition Teachers in the Writing Center." *College Composition and Communication* 39: 347–50.

———. 1985. *Writing in the Center: Teaching in a Writing Center Setting*. Dubuque: Kendall/Hunt.

Connolly, Paul, and Teresa Vilardi, eds. 1986. *New Methods in College Writing Programs: Theories in Practice*. New York: MLA.

Connors, Robert. 1984. "Journals in Composition Studies." *College English* 46: 359.

Davis, Kevin, Nancy Hayward, Kathleen R. Hunter, and David L. Wallace. 1988. "The Function of Talk in the Writing Conference: A Study of Tutorial Conversation." *The Writing Center Journal* 9(1): 45–52.

Dinitz, Susan, and Diane Howe. 1989. "Writing Centers and Writing-Across-the-Curriculum: An Evolving Partnership?" *The Writing Center Journal* 10(1): 45–51.

Ede, Lisa. 1989. "Writing as a Social Process: A Theoretical Foundation for Writing Centers?" *The Writing Center Journal* 9(2): 3–14.

Farrell, Pamela B. 1989. *The High School Writing Center: Establishing and Maintaining One.* Urbana: NCTE.

———. 1987. "Writer, Peer Tutor, and Computer: A Unique Relationship." *The Writing Center Journal* 8(1): 29–34.

Flynn, Thomas, and Mary King, eds. 1993. *Dynamics of the Writing Center: Social and Cognitive Interaction.* Urbana: NCTE.   *Inappropriate*

Freed, Stacey. 1989. "Subjectivity in the Tutorial Session: How Far Can We Go?" *The Writing Center Journal* 10(1): 39–43.

Friedlander, Alexander. 1984. "Meeting the Needs of Foreign Students in the Writing Center." In Olson, 206–14.

George, Diana, Nancy Grimm, and Ed Lotto. 1992. "From the Editors." *The Writing Center Journal* 12: 123–24.

Goldsby, Jackie. 1981. *Peer Tutoring in Basic Writing: A Tutor's Journal.* Berkeley: University of California–Berkeley and Bay Area Writing Project.

Harris, Muriel. 1982a. "Growing Pains: The Coming of Age of Writing Centers." *The Writing Center Journal* 2(1): 1–8.

———. 1992. Rev. of *The Writing Center: New Directions* edited by Ray Wallace and Jeanne Simpson. *College Composition and Communication* 43: 98–101.

———. 1991. "Solutions and Trade-Offs in Writing Center Administration." *The Writing Center Journal* 12: 63–79.

———. 1986. *Teaching One-to-One: The Writing Conference.* Urbana: NCTE.

———. 1985. "Theory and Reality: The Ideal Writing Center(s)." *The Writing Center Journal* 5(2)/6(1): 4–9.

———. ed. 1982b. *Tutoring Writing: A Sourcebook for Writing Labs.* Glenview, IL: Scott, Foresman.

Haviland, Carol Peterson. 1985. "Writing Centers and Writing-Across-the-Curriculum: An Important Connection." *The Writing Center Journal* 5(2)/6(1): 25–30.

Hawkins, Thom, and Phyllis Brooks, guest eds. 1981. *New Directions for College Learning Assistance, No. 3: Improving Writing Skills.* San Francisco: Jossey-Bass.

Herek, Jennifer, and Mark Niquette. 1990. "Ethics in the Writing Lab: Tutoring under the Honor Code." *Writing Lab Newsletter* 14(5): 12–15.

Hoffman, Randi. 1982. "Working with ESL Students." *The Writing Center Journal* 3(1): 27–28.

Holbrook, Hilary Taylor. 1988. "Issues in the Writing Lab: An ERIC/RCS Report." *English Education* 20: 116–21. Rpt. in *The Writing Center Journal* 9.2 (1989): 67–72.

Horning, Alice S. 1987. *Teaching Writing as a Second Language.* Carbondale: Southern Illinois University Press.

Hughes, Judy A. 1991. "It Really Works: Encourging Revision Using Peer Writing Tutors." *English Journal* 80(5): 41–42.

Joyner, Michael A. 1991. "The Writing Center Conference and the Textuality of Power." *The Writing Center Journal* 12: 80–89.

Kail, Harvey. 1983. "Collaborative Learning in Context: The Problem with Peer Tutoring." *College English* 45: 594–99.

Kail, Harvey, and John Trimbur. 1987. "The Politics of Peer Tutoring." *WPA: Writing Program Administration* 11(1/2): 5–12.

Kelly, Lou. 1980. "One on One, Iowa City Style: Fifty Years of Individualized Instruction in Writing." *The Writing Center Journal* 1(1): 4–19.

Kemp, Fred. 1987. "Getting Smart with Computers: Computer-Aided Heuristics for Student Writers." *The Writing Center Journal* 8(1): 3–10.

Kinkead, Joyce. 1987a. "Authority, Gender, and Tutors." Paper presented at the 77th Annual Convention of the National Council of Teachers of English. Los Angeles, California. November 21.

———. 1987b. "Computer Conversations: E-mail and Writing Instruction." *College Composition and Communication* 38: 337–41.

———. 1985. "Tutors in the Writing Center." Paper presented at the 36th Annual Convention of the Conference on College Composition and Communication. Minneapolis, Minnesota. March 21–23. ERIC ED 258-173.

Laque, Carol F., and Phyllis A. Sherwood. 1977. *A Laboratory Approach to Writing.* Urbana: NCTE.

Leahy, Richard. 1991. "On Being There: Reflections on Visits to Other Writing Centers." *Writing Lab Newsletter* 15(8): 1–5.

———. 1990. "What the College Writing Center Is—and Isn't." *College Teaching* 38: 43–48.

———. 1989. "Writing Centers and Writing-for-Learning." *The Writing Center Journal* 10(1): 31–37.

Lichenstein, Gary. 1983. "Ethics of Peer Tutoring in Writing." *The Writing Center Journal* 4(1): 29–34.

Lindemann, Erika, ed. 1988. *Longman Bibliography of Composition and Rhetoric, 1986.* New York: Longman.

Maxwell, Martha, ed. 1990. *When Tutor Meets Students: Experiences in Collaborative Learning.* Kensington, Maryland: MM Associates. (Reviewed by Bradley T. Hughes in *WCJ*, Fall 1991, including ordering information.)

Meyer, Emily, and Louise Z. Smith. 1987. *The Practical Tutor.* New York: Oxford University Press.

Miller, Susan. 1989. *Rescuing the Subject: A Critical Introduction to Rhetoric and the Writer.* Carbondale: Southern Illinois University Press.

North, Stephen. 1984. "The Idea of a Writing Center." *College English* 46: 433–46.

Okawa, Gail, Thomas Fox, Lucy J. Y. Chang, Shana R. Windsor, Fran Bella Chavez, Jr., and LaGuan Hayes. 1991. "Multi-Cultural Voices: Peer Tutoring and Critical Reflection in the Writing Center." *The Writing Center Journal* 12: 11–33.

Olson, Gary, ed. 1984. *Writing Centers: Theory and Administration*. Urbana: NCTE.

Olson, Gary, and Evelyn Ashton-Jones. 1988. "Writing Center Directors: The Search for Professional Status." *WPA: Writing Program Administration* 12(1–2): 19–28.

Onore, Cynthia. 1982. "In Their Own 'Write': A Portrait of the Peer Tutor as a Young Professional." *The Writing Center Journal* 3(2): 20–31.

Reigstad, Thomas J., and Donald A. McAndrew. 1984. *Training Tutors for Writing Conferences*. Urbana: ERIC and NCTE.   n|a

Scanlon, Leone C. 1986. "Recruiting and Training Tutors for Cross-Disciplinary Writing Programs." *The Writing Center Journal* 6(2): 37–41.

Selfe, Cynthia. 1989. *Creating a Computer-Support Writing Facility: A Blueprint for Action*. Houghton, MI: *Computers and Composition*.

Shaughnessy, Mina P. 1977. *Errors and Expectations: A Guide for the Teacher of Basic Writing*. New York: Oxford University Press.

Smith, Louise Z. 1986. "Independence and Collaboration: Why We Should Decentralize Writing Centers." *The Writing Center Journal* 7(1): 3–10.

Smith, William L. 1984. "Using a College Writing Workshop in Training Future English Teachers." *English Education* 16: 76–82.

Steward, Joyce, and Mary Croft. 1982. *The Writing Laboratory: Organization, Management, and Methods*. Glenview, IL: Scott, Foresman.

Summerfield, Judith. 1988. "Writing Centers: A Long View." *The Writing Center Journal* 8(2): 3–10.

Thaiss, Christopher J., and Carolyn Kurylo. 1981. "Working with the ESL Student: Learning Patience, Making Progress." *The Writing Center Journal* 1(2): 41–46.

Trimbur, John. 1987. "Peer Tutoring: A Contradiction in Terms?" *The Writing Center Journal* 7(2): 21–28.

Wallace, Ray, and Jeanne Simpson, eds. 1991. *The Writing Center: New Directions*. New York: Garland.

Wallace, Ray. 1988. "The Writing Center's Role in the Writing-Across-the-Curriculum Program." *The Writing Center Journal* 8(2): 43–48.

Wiener, Harvey S. 1981. *The Writing Room*. New York: Oxford University Press.

White, Edward M. 1989. *Developing Successful College Writing Programs*. San Francisco: Jossey-Bass.

Wolcott, Willa. 1989. "Talking It Over: A Qualitative Study of Writing Center Conferencing." *The Writing Center Journal* 9(2): 15–30.

Index

and English department, 206
ESL services of, 209
evaluation of, 194, 208
future of, 208–209
history of, 193–194
outreach services of, 206
personnel of, 194, 206–207
physical design of, 194–198, 233
records kept by, 207–208
research at, 208
resource materials at, 205
services of, 202–206
testing at, 204–205
tutor selection and training at,
    201–202, 234
tutoring services of, 202
typical day at, 198–200
university setting of, 192–193, 232,
    233
word processing at, 202, 203
workshops offered by, 202, 205
and writing across the curriculum,
    205–206, 208

Vilardi, Teresa, 247

WAC. *See* Writing across the
    curriculum programs (WAC)
Wallace, David L., 242
Wallace, Ray, 240, 244
Warnock, John, 40, 240
Warnock, Tilly, 40, 240
WCJ (The Writing Center Journal), 94,
    238–239, 246, 247
"We're All Basic Writers: Tutors
    Talking about Writing
    Apprehension" (Bishop), 243
"What a College Writing Center
    Is—and Isn't" (Leahy), 241
*When Tutor Meets Student: Experiences
    in Collaborative Learning*, 243
White, Edward M., 247
Wiener, Harvey, 240
Windsor, Shana, 176, 177
Witham, Karen, 178–179
WLN (Writing Lab Newsletter), 238
Wolcott, Willa, 242
Word processing in writing centers,
    245

at Johnson County Community
    College, 159, 165
at Lehigh University, 90
at Medgar Evers College, 32, 36,
    41
at Purdue University, 17, 22
at University of Washington,
    185–186
at Utah State University, 202, 203
"Working with ESL Students"
    (Hoffman), 244
"Working with the ESL Student:
    Learning Patience, Making
    Progress" (Thaiss & Kurylo),
    244
Workshops offered by writing centers
    at Harvard University, 116, 123
    at University of Puget Sound,
        133–134
    at University of Washington, 186
    at Utah State University, 202, 205
WPA discussion list, 245
"Writer, Peer Tutor, and Computer: A
    Unique Relationship" (Farrell),
    245
Writer Teaches Writing, A (Murray),
    212
"Writer's Subject Is Sometimes a
    Fiction, The" (Lotto), 94
"Writing-Across-the-Curriculum: An
    Evolving Partnership" (Dinitz
    & Howe), 244
Writing across the curriculum
    programs (WAC)
    bibliography on, 244
    at Colorado State University,
        222–223
    at Harvard University, 123–124
    in high schools, outreach for, 42
    at Johnson County Community
        College, 159–160, 165
    at Lehigh University, 91
    at University of Puget Sound, 129,
        130, 134
    at University of Southern
        California, 109–110
    at University of Toledo, 48, 60, 65,
        68, 76
    at Utah State University, 205–206,
        208

Editors

Joyce A. Kinkead is professor of English and associate dean for Academic Affairs in the College of Humanities, Arts, and Social Sciences at Utah State University. For some thirteen years she has administered writing programs and writing centers. Current programs she administers include the Rhetoric Associates—a decentralized tutoring service for writing across the curriculum—and the Undergraduate Teaching Fellows in which outstanding students within a discipline are paired with faculty mentors. A founding member of the National Writing Centers Association, she served as executive secretary of the NWCA for eight years and co-editor of *The Writing Center Journal* for six years. She is the author of several articles and books, including *Houghton-Mifflin English,* a four-volume series for high school students. She serves on the NCTE Editorial Board as well as being a reviewer for *College Composition and Communication, College English, The Writing Center Journal,* and the *Journal of Advanced Composition.*

Jeanette G. Harris is professor of English and director of the composition program at the University of Southern Mississippi. From 1985 to 1990 she directed the composition program at Texas Tech University, and from 1982 to 1985 she directed the Writing Center at that school. Prior to that time, from 1977 to 1982, she directed the Writing Center at East Texas State University. She served as president of the National Writing Centers Association in 1984–85 and as co-editor of *The Writing Center Journal,* with Joyce Kinkead, from 1985 to 1990. Her publications include three composition textbooks, a study of expressive discourse, and numerous articles. At present, she is working on a long-term case study of three college students as writers.

Contributors

Irene L. Clark is director of the Writing Center at the University of Southern California, where she is also in charge of a computer lab. Her publications include articles in *The Journal of Basic Writing, Teaching English in the Two-Year College, College Composition and Communication,* and the *Writing Lab Newsletter,* and a recent textbook, *Taking a Stand* (HarperCollins). Her book, *Writing in the Center: Teaching in a Writing Center Setting,* recently published in a second edition, received an award from the National Writing Centers Association (1987), as did her article "Collaboration and Ethics in Writing Center Pedagogy" (1989). She makes presentations regularly at NCTE conventions, writing center conferences, and EDUCOM.

Brenda M. Greene is associate professor of English at Medgar Evers College, CUNY, where she chairs the Department of Language, Literature, Communication Skills, and Philosophy and teaches basic writing, composition, and literature. She has also directed the college's basic language skills program and received several research grants in the areas of basic writing and writing across the curriculum. She has conducted workshops, presented papers and written essays in these areas, and has published in *English Journal* and *Community Review.* Her forthcoming articles will be published in *Programs and Practices: Writing Across the Curriculum* (Boynton/Cook) and the *Journal of Basic Writing.* She is also a member of the NCTE College Section Steering Committee and has served on several committees in NCTE and CCCC.

Muriel Harris is professor of English at Purdue University and director of the Writing Lab. She founded and continues to edit the *Writing Lab Newsletter* and has authored a brief grammar handbook, the *Prentice-Hall Reference Guide to Grammar and Usage* and *Teaching One-to-One: The Writing Conference.* In addition to journal articles in publications such as *College English, College Composition and Communication, English Journal, Journal of Basic Writing, Written Communication,* and *The Writing Center Journal,* she has contributed book chapters, written a SLATE Starter Sheet on writing centers, edited *Tutoring Writing: A Sourcebook for Writing Labs,* and made presentations at the Conference on College Composition and Communication as well as keynote speeches and other presentations at regional writing center conferences and the National Peer Tutoring in Writing Conference. She has won awards from the National Writing Centers Association for her publications and service, and her research interests focus on writing center theory and pedagogy as well as individual differences in writing processes.

Kathleen Kiefer is professor of English and director of composition at Colorado State University. She has written widely about computers and writing as well as more general issues related to writing pedagogy. She is the author of two basic writing texts and co-author of *Writing Brief* (3rd ed.).

Edward Lotto is associate professor of English at Lehigh University, where he directs both the Writing Center and the writing program. He speaks regularly at the Conference on College Composition and Communication and the Wyoming Conference, and has published articles on the social context of reading and writing and the relationship between writing and literary theory. He is currently a co-editor of *The Writing Center Journal*; in addition, he is deeply involved in the intrigue and politics necessary to maintain the Writing Center at Lehigh University while working to develop the writing program there.

Ellen Mohr's teaching experience began almost thirty years ago in public education as a high school English teacher. For the past twelve years, she has taught freshman composition courses and coordinated the Writing Center at Johnson County Community College in Overland Park, Kansas. Under her direction, the JCCC Writing Center has been recognized as an exemplary program by the Kansas Board of Education and the National Council of Instructional Administrators. She has also been awarded JCCC Distinguished Service status, been nominated three times for the Burlington Northern Award, been given the Community College Consortium Recognition Award, and been named a League Fellow by the League for Innovation in the Community College. At JCCC she is the writing-across-the-curriculum consultant for the Center for Teaching and Learning and a leader in the Master Teacher Staff Development Workshops. Her recently published study of peer tutor programs, a sabbatical leave project, has been recognized nationally and can be found in ERIC, a clearinghouse for educational research. A former National Writing Centers Association board member, she is at present the consultant for the association's peer tutor special-interest group. A frequent presenter at writing center conferences, she has been an active member of the Midwest Writing Centers Association, serving as its chairperson and hosting several of its annual conferences.

Luanne Momenee is assistant director of developmental education and manager of the Learning Assistance Center at the University of Toledo, Scott Park Campus. She has taught English and writing at the secondary and postsecondary levels. She is actively involved in the Ohio and National Associations for Developmental Education and has presented papers at state, regional, and national conferences.

Joan A. Mullin is director of the Writing Center and the Writing-Across-the-Curriculum-Program at the University of Toledo. Since beginning both programs in 1988, she has presented papers on writing center theory and practice, classroom pedagogy, critical hermeneutic theory, and educational philosophy at such conferences as MLA, CCCC, ECWCA, Midwest Philosophy of Education, Bergamo, and NCTE. She has published in various journals such as the *American Journal of Pharmaceutical Education, The Sociology Teacher,* and the *Writing Lab Newsletter,* and is co-editing, with Ray Wallace, a collection on writing center theory. She has recently completed a guide to writing across the curriculum for the American Association of Colleges of Pharmacy and is working on a cross-disciplinary text for WAC instructors. She co-established the annual Ohio Conference on Learning Enhancement and serves as a board member for the East Central Writing Centers Association.

Julie Neff is director of the Center for Writing and Learning at the University of Puget Sound. She was president of the National Writing Centers Association and served for six years on the executive board. She has also been editor of the *Washington English Journal* and has presented papers at the Pacific Coast Writing Centers Association Conference, the Conference on College Composition and Communication, and NCTE regional and national conferences.

Gail Y. Okawa is former coordinator of the Multicultural Tutoring in Writing Program and of the Educational Opportunity Program Writing Center, University of Washington, and was active in the Pacific Coast Writing Centers Association from 1986–1990. She has also served as a writing specialist in the Student Support Services Program at the University of Washington and as assistant professor of English at Longwood College. Currently, she is a Ph.D. candidate in English (rhetoric and linguistics) at Indiana University of Pennsylvania, where her scholarly interests focus on the convergence of language, literacy, and cultural issues. She co-authored a *Writing Center Journal* article with Tom Fox and their writing center tutors, has made presentations at CCCC, NCTE, PCWCA, NWCA, National Peer Tutoring in Writing Conference, SAMLA, and others, and now serves on the CCCC Language Policy Committee and the NCTE Committee on Racism and Bias in the Teaching of English.

Dawn Rodrigues is associate professor of English at Colorado State University. Previously, she was director of the Computer-Assisted Writing Center at Colorado State University and Writing Center director at New Mexico State University. Her interest in computers and writing includes applications of technology in K–12, college, and professional settings. Her publications include textbooks, journal articles, and book chapters; in addition, she collaborated with Cynthia Selfe and William Oates on *Computers in English and Language Arts: The Challenge of Teacher Education* and with Raymond Rodrigues on *Teaching Writing with a Word Processor: K–13.* Recently, she was involved in a study of interface design for computer-training materials in business and industry. She has presented papers at CCCC, NCTE, and Computers and Writing conventions, and has conducted in-service workshops at schools and colleges across the country.

Linda Simon is director of the Writing Center at Harvard University. She is the author of several textbooks on writing: *Good Writing: A Guide and Source-*

book *Across the Curriculum, Contexts: A Thematic Reader,* and, with Nancy Sommers, *The HarperCollins Guide to Writing.* She has also written biographies of Alice B. Toklas, Thornton Wilder, and Lady Margaret Beaufort. Her articles and reviews have appeared in such journals as *The New York Times Book Review, American Scholar, The Nation, Smithsonian,* and *Michigan Quarterly Review.* She is at work on a life of William James.